{ CRIMINAL INJUSTICE

CARTER G. WOODSON INSTITUTE SERIES

Deborah E. McDowell, Editor

criminal INJUSTICE

{ SLAVES AND FREE BLACKS IN GEORGIA'S CRIMINAL JUSTICE SYSTEM · GLENN MCNAIR

UNIVERSITY OF VIRGINIA PRESS *Charlottesville & London*

University of Virginia Press

© 2009 by the Rector and Visitors

of the University of Virginia

All rights reserved

Printed in the United States of America

on acid-free paper

First published 2009

9 8 7 6 5 4 3 2 1

Library of Congress

Cataloging-in-Publication Data

McNair, Glenn, 1962–

    Criminal injustice : slaves and free Blacks in

Georgia's criminal justice system / Glenn McNair.

       p. cm. — (Carter G. Woodson Institute series)

    Includes bibliographical references and index.

    ISBN 978-0-8139-2793-0 (alk. paper)

    1. Criminal justice, Administration of—Georgia—

History—18th century. 2. Criminal justice, Administration

of—Georgia—19th century. 3. Discrimination in criminal

justice administration—Georgia—History. 4. African

Americans—Legal status, laws, etc.—Georgia—History—

18th century. 5. African Americans—Legal status, laws,

etc.—Georgia—History—19th century. 6. Slaves—Legal

status, laws, etc.—Georgia—History. 7. Free African

Americans—Legal status, laws, etc.—Georgia—History.

8. Crime and race—Georgia—History. 9. Georgia—Race

relations—History—18th century. 10. Georgia—Race

relations—History—19th century. I. Title.

    HV9955.G4M36 2009

    364.9758089'96073—dc22

                           2008043131

For my mother, Lauretta McNair

CONTENTS

ACKNOWLEDGMENTS

This book has been a work in progress for more than ten years. In those years, I have found myself in the debt of a number of individuals, without whose assistance the successful completion of this project would not have been possible. I received the initial inspiration for the project through the efforts of Dr. Martha Keber, who led a course in historical research methods during studies for my master's degree at Georgia College and State University. The research paper for that course evolved into my master's thesis under the direction of Dr. Robert Wilson III. Drs. Keber and Wilson supported me at every stage of the process; indeed, they convinced me that I had the makings of a historian. For that, I owe them a debt I can never repay. Work on my thesis, on the trials of slaves in Baldwin County, produced more questions than answers, and those questions led me to Emory University and James L. Roark. Dr. Roark was, and is, my adviser, mentor, and friend. His enthusiasm for Southern history, his keen intellectual eye, and his thoughtful—yet gentle—criticism helped me to shape the mass of data and the tangled ideas in my head into a dissertation. Dr. Dan T. Carter and Dr. Leslie Harris completed my dissertation committee, and their observations improved the dissertation immeasurably. The final guides on this intellectual odyssey were my editors, Richard Holway and Jeannette Hopkins. Mr. Holway was interested in this project before I ever put pen—well, word processor—to paper and has offered his guidance and enthusiastic support during the years it took for this book to become a reality. His professionalism and sensitivity have made the publication process straightforward and painless, something—from my limited knowledge of such matters—few authors are able to say. Ms. Hopkins worked with me on every page of the manuscript and along the way made me a better editor of my own work and that of my students. Her exacting standards and commitment to history and history books turned an encyclopedic dissertation into a book of which I am proud. My final obligations are personal and they are owed to my wife, Sylvie Coulibaly. She is a fine historian in her own right, and her thoughts, emotional support, and patience led me through those dark times of self-doubt that all first-time authors experience. I hope that this book, and my lasting respect and admiration, will serve as partial recompense for what she has given me.

NOTE ON METHODOLOGY

The 417 cases that form the core of analysis in chapters 3-6 are drawn from the minute books of Georgia's inferior and superior courts, housed at the Georgia Department of Archives and History (GDAH) in Atlanta. During the 1960s, archivists traveled to each of Georgia's county courthouses to photograph for microfilming all surviving colonial and antebellum court records. According to GDAH personnel, the records I have used are all that remain extant. Although these records do not constitute a majority of the capital trials that occurred, they are comparable to similar documents in other states and are consistent enough across time and jurisdiction to warrant confidence in their statistical sufficiency.

The minute books generally provide the title of each case, the names of the victim(s) and defendant(s), the name of the owner if the defendant was a slave, the result of the grand jury or other preliminary proceeding, and the final disposition of the case and any court-ordered punishment. Many case records provide a brief summary of the evidence, but in most cases the court clerk provided no such summary. In the majority of cases in which the defendant was sentenced to death, the clerk prepared a more detailed summary than usual of testimonial evidence.

I have supplemented the inferior and superior court minutes with court proceedings found in the *Colonial Records of the State of Georgia,* with newspaper accounts, with records of several late-eighteenth-century cases from the Telamon-Cuyler collection at the University of Georgia, and with appellate decisions from the *Georgia Reports* (see the appendix for a list of these cases.) The cases that constitute the data set for analysis of black and white defendants in the appellate process discussed in chapter 5 are drawn from the *Georgia Reports* and *Georgia Decisions.*

I used information from these sources to create a database, employing relevant variables that the sources allow: defendant/convict sex and status (slave or free), crime, crime type, victim status, victim's relationship to the defendant/convict, presence of co-defendants, types of goods stolen, weapons used in assaults, result of indictment or accusation, presence or absence of defense counsel, final case disposition, punishment mandated by the court, appellate filings, and the results of any appeal. Crimes are divided into three types: crimes against persons, crimes against property, and crimes against public order. I used the SPSS statistical program to calculate the frequency with which the criminal justice system prosecuted certain crimes to determine who was charged with those crimes and how often, who their victims were, the frequency of conviction and appellate success for the various crimes and classes of defendants, and the frequency and severity of punishment for the types of crimes and classes of defendants and victims.

CRIMINAL INJUSTICE

INTRODUCTION

RACE AND CRIMINAL JUSTICE

In the fall of 1995 I was a graduate student in history at Georgia College and State University in Milledgeville, Georgia. When a course in research methods required a seminar paper and I had no idea on what to write, my professor, Martha Keber, provided a list of primary sources stored at the nearby Baldwin County courthouse. She hoped that something I found there would inspire me to begin to write. Going down the list of tax and probate records, I was convinced that Professor Keber's well-intentioned effort would come to nothing, when I came upon a bound volume of county slave trial records. I had not studied slavery, but was amazed to learn that states put slaves on trial for capital crimes, those that carried the death penalty. After all, had not whites considered slaves animals, and nothing more?

While the trials of slaves intrigued me, I was somewhat ambivalent about researching the topic. On the one hand, it could be a great fit: I am black, a descendant of Georgia slaves, and I was a special agent with the U.S. Treasury Department's Bureau of Alcohol, Tobacco, and Firearms—and had been for six years. Before that, I had been a police officer in Savannah for nearly five years. My undergraduate degree was in criminal justice, and I had even attended law school for a time. Investigating slaves in the criminal justice system would give me the opportunity to write on a subject with which I had more than passing familiarity. But that was the problem. I was in the Master of Arts program in history because I wanted to leave law enforcement to begin a new career as a historian and teacher. Writing about slaves and crime would seem like falling back on the old, rather than venturing out into new intellectual waters. But nothing else on the source list caught or held my interest. I decided to write on slaves and the criminal law in Baldwin County, Georgia, from 1812 to 1838.

I did not expect to find much more than kangaroo courts that convicted blacks whenever it suited them. So I was once again caught off guard when I discovered that slaves had been tried before twelve-man juries, represented by attorneys, protected from double jeopardy, and acquitted in instances where—given the nature of the charges and the victims—I was sure they would have been convicted. Slavery was, apparently, far more complicated than I had imagined.

In my secondary research, I found that mature scholars were similarly attracted by the apparent evenhandedness of slave trial courts. They commented on the relative fairness of the proceedings, and on the similarity between the due process rights of slaves and those of white citizens, all the more amazing because the postbellum history of blacks and capital punishment was a story of naked racism and disparate treatment.

I wrote the assigned paper, but nagging questions remained, questions that were the product of the law enforcement past I was preparing to leave behind. Were these trials really fair? Did having the same trial rights as whites guarantee justice for black defendants? Could trials in which blacks were not judges or jurors really have produced consistently equitable results? Also, under what circumstances did blacks commit crimes? Were blacks and whites convicted at similar rates? Were men and women? Did race and status matter at sentencing? When slaves won cases on appeal, what happened when courts retried them? What role did community standards and expectations play for defendants considered racially inferior outsiders? The questions led to a search for answers—first to a master's thesis, then to a doctoral dissertation, and now to this book.

As a law enforcement officer, I knew from experience that answers to the questions in my mind lay in the interconnected parts of the criminal justice system and their relationship to public opinion on race, crime, and justice—what the historian Christopher Waldrep calls a community's legal culture: "the choices ordinary people make between formal law and vigilante justice," based on "concepts and habits of justice as well as understandings of the role and potency of formal and informal rules, rights, and authority." These attitudes come from a variety of sources and develop and persist over long periods of time.[1] In other words, how people interact with the legal system depends on what they believe the law should accomplish, whom it should serve and why, and how well it does its work compared with other institutions.

Today, blacks possess the same trial and due process rights as other citizens, yet study after study reveals they are subject to a wide variety of disparate treatments, from racial profiling to disproportionate representation on death rows. Underlying attitudes about race and crime—aspects of a community's legal culture—are critically important to understanding how, despite fair rules, courts end up dispensing unequal justice. The white majority in America has historically considered blacks a threatening criminal population, a conviction that has insinuated itself into the nation's legal culture from nearly every imaginable source—from minstrel shows and folklore to songs, from news broadcasts to televisions shows, from novels to music videos, from movies to websites, and from personal encounters with the criminal justice system.

Police officers, judges, juries, and lawyers carry this prejudice into courtrooms. Without consciously deciding to arrive at racially disparate results, these legal actors do so with great regularity. Police officers decide who to stop, question, and arrest. Prosecutors decide which cases to recommend for trial. Defense lawyers decide whether to urge their clients to accept guilty pleas or go to trial, whether to take the witness stand or not, and what to say once on it. Judges decide whether to accept guilty pleas offered, which rules of law will apply, and what sentences will be handed down. Juries decide whether or not to believe the testimony of defendants and witnesses. Appellate court judges come to decisions influenced by their views of the good society and the role of law in it and establish the rules that govern the system. Despite laws and regulations to control inappropriate discretion, the process is too complex to keep prejudice out. A single improper decision at any stage can result in injustice based on race. I have seen this happen on numerous occasions; I have also been a victim of it. Police have stopped me at gunpoint three times—twice while I was driving unmarked police vehicles. (I assure you, I was doing nothing illegal or dangerous and I do not appear threatening.) I could say that I couldn't imagine what might have happened had I not quickly identified myself on these occasions as a law enforcement officer—but I could. I might have been arrested—or shot dead. All one has to do is consider the tragic death of Amadou Diallo to know that I am not exaggerating.

On February 4, 1999, Diallo, a Guinean immigrant, was standing on the front steps of his Bronx apartment at approximately two o'clock in the morning when he saw a car with four white men slowly drive past. They were plainclothes detectives of the New York City Police Department. As Diallo stepped back into the vestibule of his apartment, the detectives stopped their car and got out to question the black man they had seen on the steps. When they identified themselves, Diallo reached into a jacket pocket. The officers shot Diallo nineteen times. He died slumped against the front door of his apartment. He had been reaching for his wallet so he could identify himself.

The case was, and still is, an international cause célèbre. To the world, it was an example of American racism and xenophobia at its worst. The State of New York put these four officers on trial for murder. I knew from the start they would be acquitted, because they had not, in fact, committed murder. Much of the media portrayed these white detectives as racists who decided to kill a black immigrant. What they had done was worse. According to their testimony, when they saw Amadou Diallo they saw a potentially dangerous criminal, not a resident standing on his own front steps. As they were driving past the building, what they saw was a black man slink furtively into the shadows, and they stopped to investigate. Perhaps he was a lookout for a drug dealer or a gang of burglars, or, as they testified, perhaps he was a serial rapist on the prowl in the neighborhood. When Diallo reached into his jacket pocket, perhaps he was not reaching for his wallet but for a knife or a gun. When they shot Diallo, the officers honestly believed that they were defending their own lives. Murder is the premeditated, unjustified killing of a human being. The law allows police officers to use deadly force to defend themselves from the imminent threat of death or serious bodily injury. The officers testified that they had been in just such a life-threatening situation. The jury believed them, just as I knew they would—not because the jurors were virulent racists, but because they believed the officers thought they were in mortal danger. But why did the officers feel this way? What had Diallo done to make them feel so threatened? He had simply stepped into his apartment house and reached to his pocket when they identified themselves as police officers. If Diallo had been white, would the detectives have seen a criminal, or a resident perhaps returning to his apartment after getting some air because he could not sleep, or perhaps a concerned citizen investigating the car creeping suspiciously down his block? Amadou Diallo died because these detectives proceeded from the assumption that he was a criminal. They based their assumption on the fact that his skin was black.

These officers were products of a social and legal culture that labels black men as inherently dangerous. They may have brought this attitude with them to the NYPD, or they may have developed it on the job. Police officers in inner-city neighborhoods have most of their violent confrontations with minority men; it is but one short step from viewing certain minority men as threatening to viewing them *all* in this way. This attitude pervades law enforcement agencies; in some respects it is an occupational hazard, because the attitude is not confined to white officers. One of the policemen who held me in his gun sights during a traffic stop was Hispanic. (The officers in the other two stops were white.) Defense lawyers, prosecutors, judges, and jurors are all influenced to some degree by this legal culture.

Given what I knew from my own experience about the ways in which subjective factors enter into an ostensibly objective legal process, when I began the research that would form the core of this book I wanted to know whether these factors were operative in Georgia during the era of slavery, and at which stages of the criminal justice process. Secondary sources on the subject tended to focus on one aspect of the system, such as appellate decisions, slave codes, slaves patrols, or punishment on plantations. No studies had analyzed all components of the criminal justice system together in comprehensive fashion.[2] To examine a piece of the system obscures the true nature of what slave and free black defendants faced and how prejudice might have worked against them.

I was especially interested in the relationship between the formal justice system and the informal justice handed down on plantations. The legal system, or formal authority, is never enough to control the antisocial behaviors that constitute criminality in any society; informal institutions, like families, churches, and neighborhoods, are often more powerful forces. Other forms of extralegal authority, like rioting, dueling, and vigilantism, compete directly with the formal criminal justice system. There is no normative mix of formal and informal authority; the proportion of each depends on local conditions. In societies where one is weak, the other tends to be strong, and vice versa.[3]

In the antebellum South, legislators and law enforcement officials deliberately kept formal authority weak—when compared with Northern states—because it competed with the private ideal of mastery that was the sine qua non of slave society. I wanted to know how the formal and informal systems of criminal justice related to each other. Were they in constant conflict, or did they complement each other? The nature of the relationship between the two systems is vital to understanding a legal culture, certainly Georgia's.

This book, then, is an attempt to paint as complete a portrait as possible of what the capital criminal justice system meant for blacks and whites in colonial and antebellum Georgia, and how that system operated. It is an effort to answer the rather large and perennial question, Is the law an autonomous or semi-autonomous force capable of producing results that can be consistently distinct from the interests of those who create and implement it, or is it a tool of those interests? In the context of slavery-era Georgia, could the criminal law produce justice for blacks, despite the imperatives of slavery and white supremacy? Georgia is an ideal site for this inquiry because its colonial founders explicitly rejected slavery as an economic and social system—the only colony to do so—yet Georgia became one of the most powerful antebellum Southern slave societies.

This book is organized around the stages of the formal and informal criminal justice processes, beginning with the crafting of laws and ending with punishment. Chapter 1 chronicles the beginnings of slavery in Georgia and the development of a legal culture that privileged slavery and white racial domination. Chapter 2 is an examination of the evolution of the criminal law for blacks. Georgia's first slave code concerned itself with the humane treatment of slaves and the misbehavior of whites, not blacks. As the colonial period gave way to the antebellum, lawmakers repealed most of the humane provisions of the law, and it became more restrictive and designed to protect white lives and property interests. Plantation codes mirrored the formal law in its goals and provisions. In chapter 3, I explore blacks' attitudes toward the criminal law and the circumstances under which they violated it, as well as the status of its victims and perpetrators. Not surprisingly, the criminal law lacked legitimacy in the eyes of blacks to a significant degree, especially laws that protected white property; as a result, theft was rampant among slaves. Black violence was the central preoccupation of the criminal justice system, and most of the cases adjudicated in courts resulted from violent confrontations between whites and blacks, most the products of white attempts at labor and racial control.

Chapter 4 outlines the trial process, its key actors, and its results. During the colonial period, black defendants had few procedural rights. By the start of the Civil War, they had most of the same rights as whites. This similarity in procedural rights did not, however, produce racially equitable results. Courts charged and convicted blacks at much higher rates than whites accused of the same crimes. Trials took place on plantations and farms, as well. There, slaves generally had only the procedural protection their masters' consciences provided. Appeals and pardons were the next stage of the criminal justice process, and I discuss these procedures in chapter 5. Masters of convicted slaves could appeal their sentences, and twenty-eight did so. Many of these appeals turned on issues of slavery and race. Nearly half of these appeals were successful; however, they did black defendants very little good: courts re-convicted most of them. During the antebellum period, more slaves were successful in having governors ameliorate their sentences, but only two dozen masters ever applied. Punishment was the final act in the criminal justice process, and is the subject of chapter 6. During the colonial period, the formal criminal justice system generally punished blacks and whites in the same ways for the same crimes, and for the same reasons. By the early nineteenth century, Georgia had begun to move decidedly away from corporal and capital punishments for whites while retaining them for blacks. The reason for this disparate treatment was the state's devotion to slavery. On plantations and farms, masters meted out whatever punishments they saw fit, with their consciences, the law's prohibition against slave murder, and neighborhood disapprobation as the only limiting factors.

In this book I ask whether the law had the power to produce justice for blacks despite the twin corrupting forces of slavery and racism. In Georgia, the answer was no.

———————

Historians cannot divorce themselves completely from the world in which they live, but this work is not a "presentist" enterprise. I am not reading current racial attitudes and practices into the past. I have let the historical record provide the answers to my questions.

I use the terms "black" and "Negro," rather than "African American," because in the context of colonial and antebellum Georgia, "African American" seems anachronistic. Speakers and writers of both races during the period covered used "black" and "Negro" regularly. I decided to do so as well.

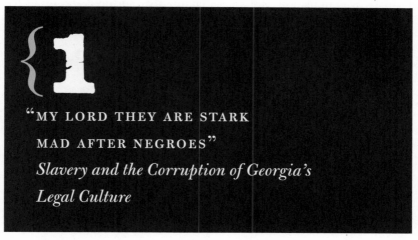

{ 1

"MY LORD THEY ARE STARK MAD AFTER NEGROES"

Slavery and the Corruption of Georgia's Legal Culture

Their constant Toast is the one thing needful by which is meant Negroes.
—Alexander Heron, 1748

Georgia's founders intended the colony to be unlike any other in British North America. It would be a colony where those denied opportunity in England could make new lives for themselves. Georgia would be an egalitarian society where thrift, hard work, and Christian brotherhood would be the guiding societal values. There would be minimal social conflict, because all would be able to provide a decent subsistence for themselves. Accordingly, there would be no need for an elaborate legal system or powerful, intrusive government. Parties would amicably resolve the few conflicts that might arise because everyone would share the same goals and values and be relatively equal in their material condition. A few wise leaders or a small town court made up of citizens would settle disputes that could not be rectified in this fashion.

Central to this utopian vision was a ban on slavery. Human bondage created conditions that undermined all the values the founders hoped the settlers would embrace. It created material inequality and made men lazy, greedy, and immoral. Moreover, slaves were internal enemies who perpetually threatened the stability and security—perhaps even the very existence—of societies who held them.

The colony's founders did all they could to keep slavery out, but in the end they failed. Georgia became all that they had feared: a slave-society with an avaricious white populace, significant inequalities in wealth, a growing, hostile slave population, and a legal culture that nurtured and protected slavery and white supremacy at the expense of justice and the rule of law—at least for black Georgians.

The Founding of Georgia

"No disagreeable sight to those who for seven weeks have seen nothing but Sea and Sky."[1] It was January 13, 1733, and James Edward Oglethorpe, a member of the British Parliament, was relieved to see the trees of the South Carolina coastline just outside Charlestown (Charleston). The ship *Anne* had brought Oglethorpe, the chosen representative of the "Trustees for Establishing the Colony of Georgia in America," and 112 English settlers—men, women, and children—to this spot. The trustees were a group of English lawyers, politicians, and businessmen with experience in philanthropic causes, from converting blacks in the colonies to Christianity to providing books to provincial libraries. Oglethorpe himself had been active in prison reform.[2] He headed up this expedition to realize a unique humanitarian vision.

The Colony of Georgia was a venture to help the destitute and dislocated of England. The trustees knew that many of the island nation's "poor subjects," through "misfortune and want of employment," found themselves "reduced to great necessity." But "if they had means to defray their charges of passage, and other expenses incident to new settlements, they would be glad to settle in any of our provinces in America." Once there, "by cultivating the lands at present waste and desolate, they might not only gain a comfortable subsistence for themselves and their families, but also strengthen our colonies and increase the trade, navigation, and wealth of these our realms."[3]

The trustees' motivations for founding Georgia were not entirely philanthropic. The colony would also foster economic prosperity for the metropole. Yeoman emigrants could produce silk and wine, luxury goods England imported at great expense. The revenue settlers obtained from exports could, in turn, purchase English manufactured goods, benefiting England and at the same time sustaining the new colony. Britons believed the silk industry alone could support twenty thousand settlers.[4]

The new colony would also strengthen the British territorial position along the southeast coast of America. The English thought that a settlement there would buttress their claims against the Spaniards, who made a legal claim to the same land. <u>Georgia would serve, too, as a military buffer between the English in South Carolina and the Spanish in Florida and protect</u> English provinces that had "been frequently ravaged by Indian enemies." More armed English settlers would prevent "like calamities."[5]

The trustees had shipped everything they thought the new settlers would need to succeed: "sufficient shipping, armor, weapons, powder, shot, ordnance, munition, victuals, merchandise and wares, as are esteemed by the wild people, clothing, implements, furniture, cattle, horses, mares, and all other things necessary for the said colony, and for the use and defence, and trade with the people there."[6] The maximum land grant for a charity settler, one who emigrated at the expense of the trust, was fifty acres. <u>Georgia was not intended for the poor alone</u>; a man who came to the province, at his own expense, with between four and ten servants received a grant of five hundred acres. (Persons with this level of wealth were obviously intended to form a leadership class for the charity settlers.)

The grant required every landholder, poor or affluent, to clear, fence, and cultivate his land and to plant one thousand <u>mulberry trees (for silk cultivation</u>) per one hundred acres. If the landholder did not complete such cultivation within ten years of the grant, the land reverted to the trust. The trustees granted all land in tail male—that is, if a landholder died without a male heir, the trust took possession of the land. Daughters could not inherit; nor could land be alienated (transferred) without permission of the trustees.[7]

There was a coherent logic behind the trustees' land policy. It made sense to restrict landownership in a population made up of many people who had proved they could not manage their lives in England. Also, modest land grants guaranteed effective defense of the province, since fifty-acre land grants would ensure enough men to serve in the militia by making land available to more men than fewer, larger grants would. Allowing daughters and widows to inherit would also have meant fewer men for military service when single women married, or widows remarried, because less land would then be available for men. The prohibition against female inheritance guaranteed a man on each plot of land. In addition, the land policy denied unskilled farmers access to land they might misuse, and made it available to others who might more profitably cultivate it. Keeping most landholdings small and in the hands of men could create a stable, self-sustaining, and prosperous military garrison. So ran the rationale of the trustees.[8]

The trustees hoped private donations would fund the project in its entirety. In the early years, the East India Company, the Bank of England, and nearly every town in England sent gifts to the colony. Thomas Penn, son of Pennsylvania's founder, William Penn, and proprietor of that Quaker colony, made donations. The renowned evangelist George Whitefield preached a special sermon to raise funds. Still, such gifts were never enough, and need forced the trustees to turn to Parliament for annual appropriations that would become the source of heated debate in the House of Commons over the next decade.[9]

The members of the trust themselves had no doubt that the colony would succeed. The location was perfect. Oglethorpe saw it as nothing short of paradise: "The Air is Healthy, being always serene, pleasant and temperate, never subject to Excessive Heat or Cold, nor to sudden Changes; the Winter is regular and short, and the Summer cool'd with refreshing Breezes." Clearing away the wilderness would happen with relative ease. "The Woods . . . are not hard to be clear'd, many of them have no Underwood, and the Trees do not stand generally thick on the Ground, but at considerable Distances asunder. When you fell the Timber . . . the Root will rot in Four or Five Years, and in the mean Time you may pasture the Ground." "A half a Dozen strokes of an Ax" were sufficient to kill a tree. A "year or two" of rain would soak the trees, so that "a brisk Gust of Wind fells many acres for you in an Hour, of which you may then make one bright Bonfire." The cleared land, in turn, would enable settlers to farm abundantly. The soil was "impregnated with such a fertile Mixture that they use no Manure. . . . It will produce almost every Thing in wonderful Quantities with very little Culture." All the farmer had to do was "scratch the earth and . . . cover the Seed."[10]

On February 12, 1733, a month after Oglethorpe's first glimpse of the South Carolina coast, his party landed at Yamacraw Bluff, on the outskirts of what would become Savannah. Within days, a settler, Peter Gordon, wrote in his journal that Oglethorpe "imployed" the new settlers "in cutting down trees, and clearing the place which was intended for the town." They "advanced in their work," and "cleared a pretty large space of ground." The settlers accomplished their tasks with "as much success and dispatch as could possibly be expected." The men dug trenches for the emplacement of palisades against attacks by Indians or the Spanish. They split rails for clapboards and built houses. The settlers did not do this work alone; the trustees had hired a group of slaves from South Carolina to help in the heavy labor of clearing the land and building the town. Oglethorpe had issued every able-bodied settler a musket and bayonet. The militia began to drill.[11]

In the early months everything went so well that, in May, Oglethorpe traveled to South Carolina to secure additional backing for the colony from its established and wealthy neighbor. Some would-be speculators envisioned another booming South Carolina and wanted to invest in that promising project early on. In Charlestown, several men who hoped to set up rice plantations in Georgia tried to bribe Oglethorpe to induce the trustees to reverse their restrictive land policies, and also to permit slaves into the colony. They believed Georgia could not fulfill its economic potential without slaves and unrestricted land ownership. Oglethorpe rejected their proposal summarily. He had agreed to slaves' assisting in the preparatory work of the new colony as a temporary expedient. A permanent slave population and fee-simple land tenure (unconditional ownership with unrestricted power of disposition) would work against everything he and the trustees hoped to accomplish. The presence of slaves made whites indolent and greedy.[12] NO SHIT!

When Oglethorpe returned to Savannah, he found that the earlier hard-working settlers had "grown very mutinous and impatient of Labour and Discipline." Without his strong guiding hand, the settlers had come to resent laboring in Georgia's tropical heat, especially when slaves could be forced to do the work instead. This was exactly what the trustees had feared. To ward off such problems, inherent in slavery, before they got out of hand, Oglethorpe ordered that all slaves hired for the early work of the colony be promptly returned to their owners in South Carolina.[13]

Much of the growing discontent Oglethorpe witnessed among the settlers might be attributed to their lack of agricultural expertise and their demographics. Of the first forty-four male settlers whose occupations are known, only three had agricultural experience. Ten had experience in carpentry, joinery, and related skills, and also included were a miller, a baker, a surgeon, an apothecary, and a cordwainer—a man who makes shoes from soft leather. Between 1732 and 1742, eighteen hundred settlers sailed to Georgia at the trust's expense. The historians E. Merton Coulter and Albert B. Saye, who compiled occupational data on eight hundred of them, found that only fifty-five had experience in agriculture. Three hundred sixty-three had been laborers or servants, though some of these may have worked in agriculture. A similar study of settlers who came over at their own expense reveals that only twenty-nine were farmers. Further, among the first group of settlers who arrived aboard the *Anne*, 25 percent were under ten years old, and twenty-one were over forty. Such a high percentage of settlers outside the prime working years of fifteen to thirty could also have been a disadvantage in the first years.[14]

{ The Ineffectiveness of Colonial Law and Government

In the first few months of settlement, Oglethorpe was the sole government of the Colony of Georgia. The trustees expected him to act as executive. Because the Georgia charter barred any trustee from holding office or owning land in the colony, Oglethorpe could not actually be named governor, but he did have the power to administer oaths, distribute land, and grant licenses to those who wished to emigrate after their arrival in the province.[15]

The trustees retained the power to "form and prepare laws, statutes and ordinances, fit and necessary for and concerning the government of the said colony, and not repugnant to the laws and statutes of England." They had the authority to "nominate, make, constitute, commission, ordain and appoint" all "governors, judges, magistrates, ministers and officers, civil and military, both by sea and land." They were to "erect and constitute judicatories and courts of record, or other courts . . . for the hearing and determining of all manner of crimes, offenses, pleas, processes, plaints, actions, matters, causes, and things whatsoever, arising or happening within the said province of Georgia or between persons of Georgia."[16] The Crown had to approve legislation the trustees crafted.

A town court consisting of three bailiffs, the recorder, and the registrar of the county, in consultation with twelve-man juries, was to adjudicate all civil and criminal matters. The colony would use the English system of grand and petit juries. The town court would meet at six-week intervals. Lawyers would play no role in proceedings before the court and were forbidden to "plead for Hire." The hope was that a man who appeared before the court would argue "his own Cause," as "in old times in *England.*"[17] As a result, there would not be a single lawyer in the colony for four years.

Since the colonists themselves had no training in law and no experience in self-government, the Crown and the trustees denied them the legislative powers of self-rule for eighteen years, at which time the province was to become a royal colony. There was no provincial assembly, no representative system, and no elections for local administrative offices. In effect, Georgia was a colony governed at the top by a group of men an ocean away who, with few exceptions, would never set foot on its soil.[18]

Oglethorpe instituted the trustees' plan of governance in July 1733, six months after he had planted the colony. The first civil government consisted of first bailiff Peter Gordon, second bailiff William Waterland, third bailiff Thomas Causton, recorder Thomas Christie, and registrar Joseph Hughes. None had experience in law or government, and several could not read or write; they were not qualified to carry out the duties of their offices, and at least one of them knew it. In his journal, Peter Gordon wrote, "The government of our new settlement being thus modell'd, wee were now to act in a sphere different from any thing wee hade ever appear'd in before, the nature of which wee were but too little aquainted with; and I cannot help saying not sufficiently qualified for offices of so great power and trust, and the disposal of such number of peoples libertyes." The settlers were willing to accept the judgment of these men in minor matters, "but when they considered them as a sett of men, in whose hands and powers their lives and fortunes were intrusted and that tho they should be ever so much oppress'd or aggrieved, there was no redress to be expected except but by application to the trustees in England. . . . They therefore by no means looked upon them as people of consequence enough or sufficiently qualified for so great a trust as was reposed in them. This produced a disregard both for them and their proceedings."[19]

As the only person in the province with any significant parliamentary or legal experience, Oglethorpe might have trained those who would serve in the various governmental capacities, but he did not.[20] He could not be everywhere at once, and problems arose that required immediate attention. The lack of legal training, combined with a governing elite several thousand miles away, set the stage for an ineffective and largely unresponsive government and weak legal institutions. Operating through the trustees and the Crown took months, and there was no guarantee that a solution proposed would be adequate for conditions and dynamics that had possibly changed. Oglethorpe's handpicked local officials were ill prepared to handle the myriad responsibilities settling a hostile frontier land entailed. The stage was set for civil disorder.

The Prohibition of Slavery

In the second year, a group of settlers began to meet regularly at the Savannah home of settler John West. The subject of these meetings was the trustees' flawed design and the de facto prohibition of slavery. Early in the third year, 1735, several settlers approached Elisha Dobree, a transplanted South Carolinian, and requested that he draft a petition to the trustees imploring them to allow slavery in the province. Dobree refused this commission but reported it to the trustees. In November, the Earl of Egmont, one of the principal trustees, received a letter from a South Carolina merchant who had settled in Georgia in hopes of making his fortune. In his letter to Egmont, Samuel Everleigh made clear that he was convinced that such dreams would come to nothing in Georgia; he was going back to South Carolina because the trustees did not "allow the use of negro slaves," without which the colony would "never prove considerable by reason the heat of the climate will not permit white men to labour as the negroes do, especially in raising rice, nor can they endure the wet season when rice is to be gathered in." He also opposed the trustees' system of land tenure because women could not inherit.[21]

Peter Gordon noted also in his journal a coalescing negative public opinion about the land and inheritance policies. Settlers lived "in continuall fear of forfeiting their lands, knowing it is impossible for them to comply with the conditions upon which they hold them." Land restrictions certainly discouraged settlers and hindered economic growth, but they were not nearly as harmful to the fortunes of the colony as "the settling of inheritance upon the male issue only" and, failing that, the land's reversion to the trust. This practice deprived "daughters, brothers, and all other relations from enjoying what has been ever looked upon as a naturall right." The inheritance policy alone was "suffitient to destroy" the colony.[22]

Proslavery sentiment and opposition to the trustees expanded and congealed around four Lowland Scots, Patrick Talifer, Davis Douglas, Patrick Houstoun, and Andrew Grant, and an Englishman, Robert Williams. These men had, after their arrival in 1734, almost immediately begun to complain about the trustees' policies and the colonial administrators. Their most significant complaint was against the prohibition of slavery. In a letter that reached the trustees in August 1735, Talifer outlined in brief the standard arguments in favor of slavery that advocates would use for the next fifteen years: Europeans were constitutionally unable to work in the tropical climate; servants were more expensive to maintain than slaves; and white indentured servants were degenerate and lazy. African slaves made a more reliable labor force because their color made it more difficult for them to escape. Using slaves was perfectly safe, provided the colony limited their numbers and confined them to unskilled manual labor, so they would not pose an economic threat to white workers.[23] Those who supported the Talifer group came to be known as the Malcontents.

The trustees, having seen the danger inherent in this growing proslavery sentiment, decided to counter the opposition before it corrupted and destroyed their entire scheme. In April, they had issued "An Act for Rendering the Colony of Georgia more Defencible by Prohibiting the Importation and use of black Slaves or Negroes into the Same." Oglethorpe's de facto ban on slavery was now de jure. In crafting the Georgia charter, the trustees, as noted earlier, had sought to accomplish three major goals: (1) to provide a safe and prosperous haven for persecuted European Protestants and the poor and dispossessed of England; (2) to create a military buffer between the English settlement in South Carolina and the Spanish one in Florida; and (3) to establish an area for the production of high-priced commodities like wine and silk. Chattel slavery was antithetical to all these aims. Silk and wine "would not require such Labour as to make Negroes necessary for carrying them on." Emigrant families could do the needed work. Further, a large population of slaves created the ever present danger of insurrection. Widely dispersed settlements characterized plantation societies, which made impossible the compact military province the trustees envisioned. Moreover, purchasing a slave rather than buying a servant would take one white man away from the defense of the colony and replace him with a black man who might pose a threat to the colony. White men would spend their time not in labor but "employed in keeping the Negro to Work, and in watching against any Danger he or his Family might apprehend from the Slave; and that the Planter's Wife and Children would by the Death, or even Absence of the Planter, be in a manner at the Mercy of the Negro." In addition, the Spanish would continually entice slaves to run away or rise up against their masters.[24]

The trustees envisioned a society of sober, egalitarian, and industrious Christians; the experience of slavery in British North America had shown them that slavery produced in whites inequality and indolence instead. A white man with a "Negro Slave, would be less disposed to labour himself." The purchase price of a single slave was equivalent to the subsistence of a white servant for an entire year. Most settlers could not afford to buy and maintain slaves. To do so would force them to indebt themselves; not to do so would force them to leave the colony. Allowing those who could afford slaves to buy them would breed jealousy and envy among those who could not.[25]

Responses to the trustees' act barring slavery varied by settlement. The charity of the trustees and private donors sustained Savannah, the least thrifty settlement. Savannians blamed their own failures on a lack of labor and the trustees' land policy. Augusta, on the Savannah River at its border with South Carolina, resembled the eastern slaveholding colony; Indian traders and a number of migrants from South Carolina had settled the area. Augusta settlers clamored for slaves and imported them illegally. But in two self-sufficient settlements in the southeastern part of the colony—Ebenezer, established by Salzburgers, industrious German Protestants who had fled religious persecution in their native land, and Darien, settled by equally industrious Highland Scots—there was minimal agitation for slaves. Still, there might have been a greater desire for slaves than the public pronouncements of Ebenezer and Darien leaders suggested. The settlement least involved in the labor and slave controversies was Fredericka, a fort on the Florida border occupied by a military garrison under Oglethorpe, whose leadership set the antislavery tone.[26]

While slavery and land tenure provoked the most dissension among settlers, dissatisfaction with government was not far behind. The colonists singled out one provincial official for public condemnation, the storekeeper Thomas Causton, who temporarily replaced Peter Gordon as first bailiff in 1734 and quickly developed a reputation for cruelty and tyranny. In the most infamous example of Causton's despotic behavior, he classified the Indian trader James Watson a lunatic and jailed him after an Indian companion drank himself to death and Watson admitted a role in the tragedy. Rumors began to circulate around Savannah that Watson had poisoned the Indian and Causton had acted to prevent difficulties with the trustees' Native allies. Public anger rose against his handling of the case and his administration of justice. The trustees sided with Causton, considering any criticism of him as criticism of them. Favoring firm administration, the trustees removed Gordon as first bailiff and replaced him permanently with Causton.[27] It was a decision that demonstrated the trustees' tin ear for the sound of colonial discontent and intransigence when it came to settlers' concerns.

A Savannah grand jury lodged a protest in 1737: "Thomas Causton, by his arbitrary Proceedings, hath endeavoured to render the Power and Proceedings of Grand Juries ineffectual, especially this Grand Jury, by intruding upon it when inclosed and about Business, and using Members thereof with great Haughtiness and Ill-nature, and threatening to dissolve them." Causton also used his political power to help friends. In 1737, one colonist,

William Alionby, filed a felony complaint against another, John White. The town court bound White over for trial at its next term. Magistrate Thomas Christie issued a warrant ordering jailers to release White, at Causton's behest. White promptly disappeared from the province. The Savannah grand jury went on to lament "the great Encouragement of enormous Offenders, contrary, as we conceive, to the Law of our Country, the Peace of our Sovereign Lord the King, his crown and dignity, and particularly to the Welfare of this your Colony." It complained that as "the Inhabitants of this Town and County have been and are still subject to many Inconveniences, for Want of a Body of Laws and Constitutions of this Province; it being exceedingly difficult in many Cases, both for Grand and Petit juries, to discharge in a proper manner the great Duties that are incumbent on them by their Oaths."[28]

The growing divisions and rancor in Georgia was generally between those who wanted slavery and those who did not. This discord was unfolding in a province that lacked the qualified personnel and the legal and governmental institutions to ensure that this internecine strife did not undermine the trustees' entire colonial design.

The Parliamentary Debate on Slavery

Back in London, the trustees, largely unaware of the magnitude of the unrest brewing in Georgia, relied on Oglethorpe to report on affairs in the province. Oglethorpe was an irregular correspondent, and when he did write, his reports to the trust were often incomplete. The trust corporation began to get two contradictory accounts of the state of the colony and the reasons for its difficulties: Oglethorpe's reassurances, and the Malcontents' insistence that the colony was failing—and failing because of the unhealthy environment, poor soils, and the trustees' land and labor policies. Pro-trustee settlers blamed any difficulties on the settlers' indolence and desire to pursue non-agricultural vocations.[29]

To assure themselves of what the situation really was, the trustees appointed a resident secretary, William Stephens, a longtime Member of Parliament who had impressed one trustee with a survey of South Carolina he had prepared. Stephens began to send reports back to London, but it became clear to him that the trustees did not want to know the true conditions but sought written confirmation of the success of their endeavor. They reprimanded him for telling them otherwise, whereupon he dispatched the kinds of reports they wanted to see.[30]

The trustees were convinced that the labor needs of Georgia could be met by settlers and their servants, but during the period of settlement, as it turned out, securing and maintaining white servants was a difficult task. In the other colonies, indentured servants who completed their terms of service, usually from four to seven years, received "freedom dues" in the form of clothing, tools, seed, and, occasionally, arms. The big attraction for would-be servants was land; an ex-servant earned up to fifty acres to start a new life. Georgians, however, were far less generous with their white servants. The largest possible land grant for those completing a term of service was twenty acres. The trust came to realize that its frugality created the labor shortage; it gradually increased "freedom dues," so that by 1743 a servant ending his indenture could expect to receive, at the trustees' expense, fifty acres of land, a cow and a sow, tools, and a year's subsistence.[31]

A significant portion of the white indentured servants in the colony were under contract with the trust. They were responsible for a wide range of tasks, from tending cows to building roads and bridges, to operating mills. Although between 1733 and 1752 more than two thousand white servants came to the province, there was a constant labor shortage. A great many ran away before completing their terms of service, and the legal apparatus was wholly incapable of pursuing and capturing them.[32]

Masters did not consider even servants who honored their contracts capable and industrious workers. William Stephens's 1738 troubles with his servants are illustrative. His "two first Women Serv[an]ts . . . proved errant whores." His "Men Servants have never yet been all well together; . . . Y[e]t the Doctor has scarcely one day missed." As a group, he considered his servants "a vile Crew (as you can easily imagine who knew from whence they spring)" and wondered "whether Laziness be what their Masters find the worst fault they are guilty of," though laziness was sufficiently detrimental when their work would not "pay for their food and their Cloathing." Like Stephens, Savannah doctor Noble Jones said that servants were "always sick, in trouble, or robbing him and running away." Paul Amatis, gardener for the trustees, considered white servants' principal concerns hunting, fishing, and "other pleasures."[33]

Peter Gordon's journal provides perhaps the most thorough discussion of the failings and problems of servants during the settlement period. "I am perswaded that of all the miserable objects on earth there is non make a worss figure thane the generall run of white servants abroad, owing intirely to their drunkenness and other vitious habits they hade contracted at home."

Yet white servants expected better treatment than did slaves in other colonies. Masters elsewhere provided slaves with small plots of land they were to use to raise some part of their own subsistence. The same could not be done with servants, since "white servants must be treated in a quite different manner, for as they have from their infancy been accustomed to live in a different manner to what the negroes doe, so they must be fed and cloathed much better and concequently at a much greater expence; otherwise you cannot expect to receive any satisfaction or advantage from their servitude." Gordon reasoned that providing more for white servants over the course of their terms of service more than offset the initial higher cost of a Negro slave. Moreover, slaves appreciated in value at a much higher rate than did white servants because of slaves' lifetime servitude. After white servants' terms of service, they were of no more value to their former masters.

Gordon himself believed black slaves were a much better source of labor than white servants. Slaves were "unacquainted with the many vices that are but too common amongst owr white servants." Masters could train slaves up "in a manner" that would best serve their purposes, "either to the field or to the house (which would not answear any end with a white servant because his time is so short)." With "good usage," a Negro slave would "turne out a trusty and faithfull servant as long he lives."[34]

A petition addressed to the trustees, in December 1738, made the growing opposition to their social and economic design more formal. The petitioners protested that, after years of their sincere toil and faith in the trustees, "it must be obvious that People cannot subsist by their Land according to the present Establishment; and this being a Truth resulting from Trial, Practice and Experience." The economy of the province would never advance, because "it is well known that Carolina can raise everything that this Colony can, and they having their Labour so much cheaper, will always ruin our Market, unless we were in some measure on a Footing with them." It was possible to produce silk and wine in the colony, but white men could not do it: "The Cultivation of Land with white Servants only cannot raise Provisions for our families, as before mentioned, therefore it is likewise impossible to carry on these Manufactures according to the present Constitution." Two reforms would alleviate the settlers' suffering, the petitioners said, and place the colony on the road to prosperity. These were land tenure in fee simple and the introduction of Negro slavery with "proper Limitations." Slavery "would occasion great numbers of white People to come" to the colony and render the settlers "capable to subsist." "By allowing these Two

Particulars," the trustees would fully satisfy everyone, prevent "impending ruin," and make Georgia "the most flourishing Colony possessed by his Majesty."[35]

Most of those who signed the petition were Savannians. While "adventurers" like Talifer and Williams—settlers who had paid their own way into the colony—had provoked the petition, approximately the same number of charity settlers and servants had signed it. The petition did not reflect the ethnic and regional diversity of the colony; all of the signers but twelve were English or Lowland Scots, and none were Salzburgers or Highland Scots. Within weeks, members of this latter group would submit their own petition opposing the introduction of slaves.[36] Since most of the signers had been in the colony since 1735, they had experience with the trustees' plan, and were now convinced that it would never produce what it promised and that change was necessary.

In response to the first petition, the trustees said they were "not surprized to find unwary People drawn in by Crafty Men, to join in a Design of extorting by Clamour from the trustees an Alteration of the Fundamental Laws, framed for the Preservation of the People, from those very Designs." The board had no intention of changing its plans on land and slaves, because if it did, "It would destroy all industry among the white Inhabitants; and . . . by giving them a Power to alien [alienate] their Lands, the Colony would soon be too much like its Neighbours, void of white Inhabitants, filled with blacks, and reduced to the precarious Property of a few, equally exposed to domestick Treachery and foreign Invasion."

For several members of local government who had signed the petition, the trustees reserved special ire: "The trustees cannot but express their Astonishment, that You the Magistrates, appointed by them be the Guardians of the People by putting those Laws in Execution, should so far forget your Duty, as to put yourselves at the Head of this Attempt."[37] For the trustees, the petition was the handiwork of self-interested men and their misguided followers, not a reliable source of accurate information.

The trustees' concern about "domestick Treachery and foreign Invasion" was not unfounded, and proved prescient. In June 1738, they learned of a proclamation issued by the Spanish in Florida saying that "all negroes who did or should . . . run away from the English should be made free." The proclamation had the desired effect: "several negro slaves who ran away tither . . . were thereupon made free." To one trustee, the Earl of Egmont, this proclamation showed "the prudence of the trustees in not suffering the use of negroes in Georgia." Some settlers expressed a sense of the danger posed by slaves. In a June 1739 letter to the earl, John Hows said that he opposed the introduction of Negroes because "there would be danger from negroes rising and cutting their throats."[38]

A band of twenty Angolan slaves in South Carolina intent on seizing the opportunity for freedom the Spanish offered made real Hows's fear. On September 9, 1739, according to Oglethorpe's published account of the incident, the group "surprized a Warehouse belonging to Mr. Hutchenson at a place called Stonehow." The band killed several white men and burglarized and burned their homes, securing "a pretty many small Arms and Powder." The next day, they "marched Southward along Pons Pons, which is the Road through Georgia to Augustine, killing more Whites along the route." The rebel contingent "increased every minute by new Negroes coming to them," their number reaching "above Sixty, some say a hundred." Armed whites pursued the fugitives, and "the Negroes were soon routed." In the end, "about 40 Negroes and 20 whites were killed." This was the Stono Rebellion. The slave uprising hardened the trustees' resolve to ban Negro slaves from Georgia.[39]

While members of the trust were steadfast in their unwillingness to allow slavery, a number had come to realize—even before the Savannah petition was filed—that their land tenure policy was retarding the colony's economic growth. In March 1738 several trustees privately agreed to revise the land policy to allow women to inherit, provided "they marry a man who will reside in the country, and has no land of his own." The revision would ensure that land would remain in the hands of men capable of bearing arms, at the same time giving settlers "security that the lands they have cultivated must go where they would wish it."[40]

The members of the trust understood that this minor alteration of their land tenure policy would not satisfy the settlers, so in 1739 they decided to allow female inheritance without the marital restriction, and in 1740 they ruled that if a landowner had no children, the land would not devolve to the trust but could be left to a person the landowner had chosen. Landowners could also lease their land for up to seven years, "upon Condition of the Tenants residing upon and improving the same." The trustees raised the maximum amount of land anyone could inherit from five hundred to two thousand acres, and they loosened the requirements for the cultivation of mulberry trees. Land would still be forfeited if owners did not make mandated improvements. In March 1741 the trustees again reduced the cultivation requirements, and in 1742 they decided that if a married land-owner died, his wife would inherit the house, with the land itself divided between her and the eldest son. If there was no son, the land would fall to the eldest daughter or could be willed to someone else.[41] From the settlers' perspective, the trustees' willingness to amend their land policy meant that they had heard the complaints. The only remaining obstacle that stood between the settlers and prosperity, in the view of many, was the ban on slavery.

{ *Growing Opposition to the Trustees' Ban on Slavery*

The year 1740 began on a positive note for the trustees. Patrick Talifer and the core group of Malcontents, convinced that the trustees would never give up their foolhardy opposition to slavery, abandoned Georgia for South Carolina. With these troublemakers out of the way, the trustees sought to convince Parliament that the Malcontents had been wrong in their grim assessment of the colony, and thus enhance the trust's prospects for continued funding. They asked William Stephens to prepare an accurate report on the colony.[42]

In his report, *A State of the Province of Georgia,* Stephens painted a portrait of the colony that the trustees hoped to see. "The Town of Savannah was laid out, and began to be built, in which are now 142 Houses, and good habitable huts." There was "a Court-House, a Goal [*sic*], a Store-House" and "some other Publick Buildings." Rounding out this tableau was "a publick Garden of ten Acres cleared, fenced, and planted with Orange-Trees, Mulberry-Trees, Vines, some Olives which thrive very well, Peaches, Apples, &c." Other towns in the province were similarly thriving, and there was "a considerable Trade in the [Savannah] River." The soil "when cleared" was "productive of Indian Corn, Rice, Peas, Potatoes, Pumions, Melons and many other kinds of Gourds, in great Quantities"; and "Wheat, Oats, Barley, and other European Grains . . . may be propagated in many Parts . . . with Success." The cultivation of silk was progressing: "Notwithstanding the Quantity of Silk, hitherto made, has not been great, yet it increases, and will more and more considerably, as the Mulberry-Trees grow, whereof there are a great Numbers yearly planted."[43]

On the character of the settler population itself, Stephens was encouraging but ambiguous: "Indeed, good and bad which came from England, were mostly Inhabitants of Towns there"; "but such seldom turn out good Husbandmen with their own Hands; yet some of them proved very useful in the New Colony." In the end, "the Ability of the Inhabitants to support themselves must still in great Measure depend on the Industry and Frugality of each. Divers in the Province who understand Planting, and are already settled, provided they can attain to some Live-Stock, can and do support themselves." Stephens recognized that the colony's success depended on the quality of its settlers and their willingness to work. Only "some" had proved "very useful." If the trustees had read between the lines, they would have spotted clues to a labor problem. But Stephens chose not to mention Negro slaves or the need, or lack of need, for them at all.[44]

In response to what they considered Stephens's misrepresentations, John Fallowfield and Andrew Duche, two settlers who had signed the 1738 petition, drafted and circulated a counter-petition in November 1740 that included seventy-six signatures, including those of thirteen of the émigrés to South Carolina. Among the signers were twenty-one charity settlers, thirty-nine who had paid their own way to the colony, and nine who had come as indentured servants. (The status of seven others is not known.) The signers denied that agriculture in Georgia was as productive as Stephens claimed. If the colony was so successful, why had so many industrious settlers chosen to leave? Because they had come to realize the "impossibility, and Improbability of living in this place," the counter-petition claimed. Augusta was flourishing, but the petitioners maintained that this was because settlers employed one hundred slaves without permission, but with impunity.

A second petition to the king and Parliament backing the one of December included sixty-seven settlers' signatures and addressed the two objections the trustees had raised to the admittance of slaves—that is, the threat slaves posed to the physical safety of the colonists, and the protestations of fellow settlers. To the first, they argued that importing a limited number of agricultural slaves would prevent insurrections like the one at Stono. To the second objection, they maintained that opponents of slavery had bribed the Salzburgers and Highland Scots to express protest. The petitioners further argued that white men simply could not do the work required to make a success of the colony; compelling them to do so reduced them to virtual slavery. Twenty other settlers sent a third petition to the trustees later in the month, reiterating the arguments of the previous two.[45]

Shortly after deserting Georgia for Charlestown, the Malcontent Patrick Talifer delivered a parting shot at the trustees in the form of a tract, *A True and Historical Narrative of the Colony of Georgia*. Talifer challenged

Stephens's sanguine representation of Georgia and lambasted the trustees and their socioeconomic design. Stephens's *A State of the Province* had stated in passing that the soil was quite fecund once *cleared*. For Talifer, this was a nearly impossible task for white laborers: "The Felling of Timber was a Task very unequal to the Strength and Constitution of White Servants, and Hoeing the Ground, they being exposed to sultry Heat of the Sun, insupportable; and it is well known, that this Labour is one of the hardest upon the Negroes, even though their Constitutions are much stronger than white People, and the Heat no way disagreeable or hurtful to them." While Georgia's summer heat posed no problem for blacks, in whites it produced "inflammatory Fevers of various kinds both continued and intermittent, wasting and tormenting Fluxes, most excruciating Cholicks, and Dry-Belly-Achs; Tremors, Vertigoes, Palsies, and a long Train of painful and lingering nervous Distempers; which brought on to many a Cessation both from Work and Life." These malarial conditions, Talifer said, rendered half of the white working population useless from March to October.

As for the land, "No Regard was had to the *Quality* of the Ground in the Divisions, so that some were altogether Pine-Barren, and some swamp and Morass, far surpassing the Strength and Ability of the Planter." The tracts of land were "likewise shaped in long pointed Triangles, which considerably increased the Extent of Inclosure and rendered great Parts of each Lot entirely useless." Even if the land were of better quality and more beneficially situated, what, asked Talifer, "could be done at any Rate with such small Parcels of Land separate from one another?"

At the conclusion of his tract, Talifer summed up the causes of the province's failure under twelve rubrics, most of which involved land and slaves: "The representing of the Climate, Soil, &c. of Georgia in false and too flattering Colours. . . . The restricting the Tenure of Lands from a Fie-simple to a Tail Male, cutting off Daughters and other Relations. . . . The restraining the Proprietor from selling, disposing of, or leasing any Possession. . . . The restricting too much the Extent of Possessions, it being impossible that fifty Acres of Land, much less Pine-Barren, could maintain a white family." The trustees also hindered the colony's growth and prosperity, by "laying the Planter under a variety of Restraints in clearing, fencing, planting &c. which was impossible to be complied with," and by "assigning certain fixed Tracts of Land . . . without Regard to the Quality of the Ground, Occupation, Judgment, Ability or Inclination of the Settler, &c. &c. &c."

But the greatest single problem, in Talifer's view, was the prohibition on the introduction of slaves: "But chiefly denying the Use of Negroes, and persisting in such Denial, after by repeated Applications we had humbly remonstrated the Impossibility of making Improvements to any Advantage with white Servants." Oglethorpe himself knew success could not be had without slaves. Stephens noted, in July 1741, that Malcontents considered Oglethorpe a hypocrite because he kept "Negroes on his own Land, within forty Miles of this Place [Savannah], vis in Carolina."[46]

In attempting to shape political opinion in Parliament, the Malcontents had an unlikely ally, the son of the trustees' resident secretary William Stephens. Thomas Stephens had arrived in Georgia with his father in 1737, and within two years had become convinced that the colony was going to fail and that the social and economic design of the trustees would be responsible. When he began to clash with Oglethorpe over provincial administration, his father thought it best for him to take a brief leave from the colony. Thomas Stephens did sail back to England, in October 1739, but within days he had met with the Earl of Egmont and reported that those who had signed petitions against slavery had done so because Oglethorpe had coerced them. In November, he sent the trustees a tract entitled *Thoughts on the Colony of Georgia,* arguing that the colony was in a state of decline, with their policies at the root of the problem. He said the trustees' out-of-hand dismissal of the 1738 petition made matters worse. When neither Egmont nor the other trustees took his claims seriously, Thomas Stephens decided to go over their heads to Parliament to urge a cut in the annual appropriation for the Georgia colony.[47]

In 1742, the trustees submitted their annual petition to the House of Commons for financial support. The members rejected it. The Earl of Egmont was at a loss to explain, but MPs had become increasingly skeptical about the viability of the colony and the accuracy of the trustees' reports. Thomas Stephens, acting as agent of the Malcontents, seized this moment to deliver the coup de grace to the trustees' plan, and in April he published *The Hard Case of the Depressed People of Georgia* and submitted a petition to the Privy Council on the Malcontents' behalf. In *The Hard Case,* Stephens reiterated the Malcontents' key arguments—that the trustees' scheme was wholly impractical, and that the colony would be brought to ruin without slaves and a wholesale revision of the system of land tenure. He asked "whether the trustees, by their inflexible Adherence to these pernicious and impracticable Schemes and Maxims of Government, should not compensate for the Fortunes of so many Thousands of unhappy Adventurers, and account for the Publick Money and Donations consumed therein" and concluded, "The People have been legally ruined."[48]

Stephens's petition argued that all past petitions sent to England representing the dire straits of the colony were true. The protesting colonists, for seven years, had been suggesting alterations to improve the province and alleviate the suffering, all to no avail. The trustees' refusal even to entertain changes to their scheme had brought the colony to the brink of collapse.[49]

Stephens also listed what he regarded as myriad failings of Georgia's legal system. "The Magistracy has been filled with mean, illiterate and dishonest Men, whereby justice has been partially administered, and many Cruelties exercised on the People; that in some Towns Magistrates or Courts of Justice could not be obtain'd, tho' Application has been made for them." A variety of "Imprisonments and Corporal Punishments have been illegally and arbitrarily inflicted by Persons acting under the General [Oglethorpe] without legal process, any Commission or legal Qualification." Colonial officials had declared "the Laws of England, whether Common of Statute Laws" no "Laws in Georgia." Stephens concluded "that there are no Body of Laws prepared by the Trust for the Government of the Colony, nor Records duly kept; that the Verdicts of the Juries have been falsified by the Magistrates." From these injustices "no Appeal [was] allowed from Georgia to the trustees."[50]

The trustees, declaring Stephens's public pronouncements libelous, lodged a formal complaint with the House of Commons, with a hearing slated for May. The Commons ordered the trustees to produce all regulations relating to land tenure and all representations received from the province regarding its state. The Committee of the Whole House reviewed the evidence, heard testimony from Thomas Stephens, and issued six resolutions that highlighted Georgia's continuing economic and military value. The trustees were vindicated. A group of members led by Sir John Bernard attempted to introduce legislation legalizing slavery in Georgia; opponents defeated this resolution by a vote of 35 to 18. Bernard attempted to reintroduce the resolution, but MPs voted it down 43 to 34. Nonetheless, members who had voted in favor of the legislation indicated that unless the trustees reformed their land tenure policy, they would oppose future financial support. This was exactly what Thomas Stephens hoped to hear. He did not care for what the Privy Council had to say. The council ruled that Stephens's petition contained "false, scandalous and malicious charges tending to asperse the characters of the trustees" and ordered him to appear before the House of Commons for formal reprimand by the Speaker.[51]

In the months following the Stephens hearings in spring 1742, the trustees began to consider revising their antislavery position, despite their victory. They appointed a committee to study the advisability of allowing slaves into the province and asked William Stephens to assess the opinion of Georgians on the issue. These moves did not signal a firm desire to repeal the 1735 law prohibiting slavery, but they were an acknowledgment of the possibility. The trustees also made another significant change in their land tenure policy: land grants to persons who brought servants to Georgia with them, and were recipients of the larger land grants of up to five hundred acres, would be made in fee simple rather than tail male. This land could not be alienated for ten years, and the owner had to cultivate at least one-eighth of it. No one could possess more than two thousand acres, except through inheritance, in which case such persons could sell or alienate the excess land. In January 1743, the House of Commons appropriated up to £12,000 for Georgia.[52]

While the trustees considered what to do about slavery, they continued their efforts to enforce the 1735 antislavery law, seizing and auctioning off illegally imported slaves for charity. But enforcing the ban did not improve the economic prospects of the colony, and during the next decade Parliament decided to refuse funding for its support, and private contributions to the enterprise dwindled to almost nothing. It became increasingly clear that more settlers and a more vigorous economy were needed if the province was to survive. It was unlikely that the required settlers would come from England. Georgia would have to look to the other English colonies in North America and to the West Indies, where slavery was woven into the fabric of society.[53]

{ *Legal Slavery Comes to Georgia*

In 1742 Oglethorpe and the provincial militia defeated the Spanish in the Battle of Bloody Marsh, effectively ending the Spanish threat to South Carolina. Oglethorpe returned to England, and with his departure the trustees lost their most powerful voice in local affairs. South Carolinians now began to migrate into the province, bringing their slaves with them. On July 7, 1742, the Earl of Egmont resigned as common councilor of Georgia, "by reason of . . . ill-health and partly from observing the ill behaviour of the

Ministry and Parliament with respect to the colony." Even Johann Martin Bolzius, leader of the antislavery Salzburgers at Ebenezer, could no longer withstand the personal and political attacks of the Malcontents and the renewed pressure from increasing numbers of settlers for slaves. In 1748 Bolzius wrote to the trustees, "It may be, that I am mistaken in my sentiments of Settling the Colony by the help of white Servants. . . . And be it far from me that I should be any ways accessary to the present method the People have taken already opposite to the tenour of the said Act [the 1735 act barring Negroes]. . . . Things being now here in such a melancholy situation that I most humbly beseech their Honors not to regard any more our or our Friend's Petition against Negroes."[54]

More and more settlers became openly contemptuous of the trustees and their plans, including many in government. A majority of the magistrates, for example, favored the introduction of slaves. In 1748 a settler named Alexander Heron wrote, "It's well-known to every one in the Colony that Negroes have been in and about Savannah for these several Years, that the Magistrates knew and wink'd at it and that their constant Toast is the one needful thing by which is meant Negroes." In June 1746 Savannian John Dobell wrote to a member of the trust, "My Lord they are stark Mad after Negroes, and this is the Cause that they endeavour to Poison and spoil all the trustees good Designs."[55]

Georgians began to rent slaves from South Carolinians, with the understanding that if authorities discovered the illegally hired slaves, the hirers would notify the owners so they could take the slaves back across the border into South Carolina before officials in Georgia could seize them. This plan worked, and colonists began to lease slaves for longer and longer terms, some for as long as one hundred years, paying full price in advance for them.[56] William Stephens wrote of the practice: "Notwithstanding our great Caution some People from Carolina soon after their Settling Lands on the Little Ogeechee, found Means of bringing and employing a few Negroes on the said Lands sometime before it was discovered to Us." When authorities discovered their slaves, masters "withdraw them for fear of their being seized and soon after withdrew themselves and their Families out of the Colony." Many Georgians engaged in this illegal slaveholding, "particularly the whole Inhabitants of Augusta who have had Negroes among them for many years past." If not allowed to own slaves, these Georgians were prepared to "remove to the Carolina Side, where they can carry on their Trade and Plantations with the same advantage as where they now are." This willingness to leave the colony in pursuit of slave-driven prosperity was growing, as "several others of late" expressed themselves "in the same Strain."[57]

In 1746, Oglethorpe, still monitoring colonial affairs from England, reported that a group of South Carolinians had crossed the Savannah River at Augusta with cattle and slaves and set up a plantation. Slave traders were openly plying their trade in Savannah, and before long Savannians were buying slaves directly from the decks of trans-Atlantic slave ships.[58]

The Georgia trustees, unable any longer to bear the weight of the growing actuality of slavery on the ground and a loss of support in nearly all quarters—and the reality of a stagnating and fractious colony—abandoned their humanitarian vision. On August 8, 1750, the trust issued an act that re- pealed the 1735 law barring slaves, conceding that there were no longer any substantive reasons for prohibiting slavery: "In its Infancy the Introduction of Black Slaves or Negroes would have been of dangerous Consequence but at present it may be a Benefit to the said Colony and a Convenience and Encouragement to the Inhabitants thereof to permit the Importation and Use of them into the said Colony."[59] The trustees confined themselves to the military implications of slavery and did not mention the institution's deleterious effect on whites. The moment for that had long passed.

There is no evidence in the surviving historical record that the act lifting the ban on slavery was ever approved by the Privy Council, the Board of Trade, or King George II. In fact, there is no evidence that they even saw it. Nevertheless, colonists acted as if it had the force of law, and on January 1, 1751, slavery became a "legal" institution in the colony of Georgia.[60]

Georgia became all that the Malcontents had hoped for and predicted. The white and black populations soared. In 1751 there were only nineteen hundred whites and four hundred blacks in the colony; by 1773 there were eighteen thousand whites and fifteen thousand blacks. Between 1761 and 1773, Georgia's exports increased from 1,600 tons valued at £15,870 to 11,300 tons valued at £121,677. Rice exports increased one thousand percent between 1755 and 1775; there were similar increases in exports of indigo, tobacco, timber, and skins. Georgia's slave population continued to grow exponentially: by 1860 it was 462,198, second only to Virginia's. Georgia would also become, and remain, a regional economic power. On the eve of the Civil War it was the largest cotton producer among the original slave states.[61]

Betty Wood persuasively argues, in *Slavery in Colonial Georgia,* that "unthinking decisions" did not produce slavery in Georgia as they had in most other North American colonies. Georgia had promised to be the only colony from which slavery was banned—a class-based, not race-based, colony committed to upward mobility of the poor and creation of a white yeoman class with no elite supported by a slave race. Over the course of fifteen years, white Georgians engaged in a vigorous debate over the advantages and disadvantages of a slave-based social and economic order, and after careful deliberation they chose to establish such a society.[62] Colonial Georgians entered the business of human bondage voluntarily and with their eyes wide open. In so doing, they created a unique culture of mastery. Georgia masters had to fight to get and keep their slaves; therefore, they were jealous and protective of them in ways perhaps that slaveowners in other colonies—where slavery had been introduced gradually and with comparatively little difficultly—were not. The consequences are apparent in the system of justice, or injustice, that evolved for slaves and free blacks in late colonial and antebellum Georgia.

The Georgia trustees' original frame of government and the battle for slavery weakened the colony's legal and governmental institutions. Trust members believed that their socioeconomic design produced happiness and prosperity for those poor of England whom they sent to Georgia and that, therefore, no need existed for strong government. Because they knew better than those they were trying to save, there was also no need for representative government; the trustees considered Oglethorpe and the administrators he chose sufficient for peaceful living in the pacific idyll they imagined Georgia to be. The reality, of course, was quite different. When divisions emerged in the colony, Oglethorpe could not hold it together single-handedly, and he would not be there forever. His ill-prepared agents could not maintain order, especially when certain of these men shared the sentiments of the opposition and switched allegiances. In this poorly governed milieu, a group of well-organized men and their sympathizers were able to subvert the law of its founders and bring slavery to Georgia.

Slave societies considered the ideal master–slave relationship to be one undisturbed by outside forces and relationships, where the slave was an extension of his master's will. For over a decade Georgia masters enjoyed such a relationship with their slaves. Slavery—at least as far as the trustees, Parliament, and the Crown knew—was against the law; therefore those who held slaves did so beyond the eyes and outside the control of the law. This, combined with Georgia's weak and ineffectual legal institutions, led to a legal culture among masters characterized by a high level of autonomy and suspicion of, and even disrespect for, the rule of law.

In 1733 a Colonel Scott, whom Oglethorpe had appointed to be in charge of the government while he was temporarily away, ordered a servant belonging to a Mr. Gray to attend to him and several visitors from South Carolina for a few hours. Gray, apparently believing that Scott intended to keep his servant, refused to send him and assembled a "larg faction," all of whom agreed that they would rather "lose their lives" in protecting the servant than surrender him. When Scott got wind of this attempt to usurp his authority, he sent bailiff Peter Gordon and an armed guard to commandeer the servant. When Gordon arrived at the house, Gray and his allies refused to open the door, and a tense standoff began. The women in the house "declared that there were twenty arm'd men without, ready to defend him [the servant] in case any attempt was made to take him away by force." Gordon explained that he had been ordered to take the servant and would not leave without him, but he did not intend to use force. The servant would only be gone a short while. If they still felt aggrieved, they could take up the matter with Oglethorpe when he returned in a few days.

Gordon wrote in his journal what happened next: "I could not prevaille, by all the fair means I could possibly use, so I resolved to carry it a little farther, and with some small little opposition I gott upstairs where the servant was, and ordered him to come down emediately, which with some reluctance he obey'd. But still the difficulty was to get him out of the house, for they begane to be very clamorous, and still resolved not to part with him." Gordon told them that their refusal constituted mutiny and would be punished as such, but he tried to reassure them that "if they let the servant goe peaceably, in obedience to command," he would be returned in a few hours and not punished for his refusal to cooperate. "This last they agreed to and the servant was returned in an hours time. So we happily gott over this affair which might have been attended with fatall consequences."[63]

In October 1741 William Stephens learned that two Augusta slaves, jailed in Savannah for "foul Crimes," had escaped from the gaol. Their master "had been allowed the Use" of two Dutch servant children, a boy and a girl, but treated them cruelly, did not properly feed and clothe them, and exiled them to his plantation, under the supervision of the two escaped slaves. The slaves were authorized to punish the servant children if they did not complete their assigned tasks. One slave attempted to rape the girl, who complained to her master, but rather than chastise the slave, "he . . . beat her [the girl] with his Cane, and then ordered her to be stript stark naked, haul'd up to a Beam by her arms tied, in the Presence of these two Negroes, and afterwards to be terribly whipped." The magistrates in Savannah, when told of the incident, ordered the servants taken from the master and the slaves jailed to await the next term of the town court. The master himself was arrested, although the court allowed him to post bond and he was released. The two slaves escaped. There is no record of the court punishing the master for any of his behavior.[64]

These two cases represent in microcosm the relationship between masters, slaves, servants, and the law. Before the trustees "legalized" slavery in 1751, as these cases demonstrate, masters did as they liked with both slaves and servants, outside the practical confines of the law. When the law was brought to bear, it was inadequate to the task. In the first case, a master believed that his rights in his servant trumped an official government order, and he was prepared to protect those rights by force, as were the servant and other members of the household. Peter Gordon, the representative of governmental authority, was forced to bargain with a master because he could not be sure his authority alone was sufficient to compel compliance with his dictates. The Gray household itself did not accept Gordon's authority, as might be expected in a jurisdiction where inhabitants respected law and government and viewed them as legitimate and competent.

In the second case, a master tortured a child servant without any regard for the law. He gave no thought to punishing the alleged rapist or turning him over to authorities; losing a slave was apparently more distasteful than losing a servant. Even if colonists put the accused slaves on trial, there was no body of law to determine their fates. We have no way of knowing what the town court might have done without common-law precedents or statutes to guide it. Legal authorities could not even retain custody of the accused slaves; they escaped, and the government did nothing to find them or to punish their owner.

The kind of legal impotence displayed in these two cases could work for or against slaves and servants, depending on the desires and dispositions of their masters. The slaves and one of the servants benefited from their masters' need to protect their own investments and prerogatives. The law was unable to keep masters from securing these interests, and it would have, in all likelihood, been equally unable to keep masters from harming their servants and slaves if they chose to do so, as was evident in the account of the child servants.

During the Georgia trusteeship masters learned that when it came to their slaves—and, to an extent, their servants—the law was best avoided, and when it could not be evaded, it should be co-opted or overpowered. This legal culture that privileged slavery and mastery would structure masters' and white Georgians' relationship with the law for the remainder of the time that human bondage existed in Georgia. For blacks, this meant they could not depend on the law to reliably protect them or provide them with justice.

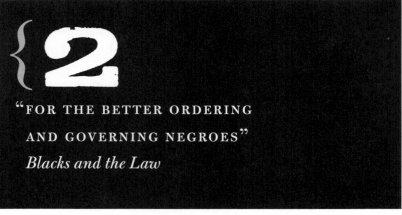

Slaves ought to be settled and Limited by positive Laws so
that Slaves may be kept in due Subjection and Obedience.
—Act for the better Ordering and Governing Negroes
and other Slaves, 1755

While slavery had been a reality in Georgia since the 1730s, it had existed without a supporting legal structure. The trustees wrote the colony's first slave code in 1750 and included it in the act that legalized African enslavement. This code reflected the trustees' own view of slavery: that it was an institution destructive of whites' morals and that it threatened the colony by creating a hostile African population. But they hoped it would ensure that human bondage would be conducted in a fashion that was both safe and productive for white Georgians and humane for their black slaves. Their benevolent influence prevailed only for a few years; within five years, proslavery legislators would take control of the law. The criminal law that emerged protected slavery, white racial domination, and white lives and property at blacks' expense.

{ *The Slave Codes*

To counter one of the trustees' greatest fears—that of a large and potentially dangerous slave population—the slave code of 1750 established a quota. Every person "inhabiting and holding and cultivating Lands" within the province could import no more than four male slaves per white male servant who was between sixteen and sixty-five years of age and capable of bearing arms. All slaves had to be registered. The code also strictly limited the skills bondspeople could acquire. It confined Georgia bondsmen to "manuring and cultivating" their masters' lands; no artisan could train a slave to his trade. Skilled slaves usually had a higher degree of mobility, greater influence with fellow bondsmen, and, no doubt, enough ego to be potentially ungovernable. The trustees believed slave artisans also drove down the wages of white mechanics by providing services at lower long-term cost; they worried that mechanics would have to accept lower wages to compete. Trust members, though unwilling to train slaves to the trades, did offer incentives to teach slaves how to cultivate silk to sustain their dream of producing exotic trade goods.

The slave code imposed penalties for any harm to slaves. Any master who inflicted "Chastisement endangering the Limb of a negro" was fined "five pounds Sterling Money" for a first offense; for a second offense, he was fined £10 or more. Anyone accused of killing a slave was to be tried "according to the Laws of Great Britain." The trustees were concerned with the souls as well as the bodies of bondsmen. Slaveowners who did not "permit or even oblige" their black servants to receive religious instruction on the Sabbath were fined £10 sterling, a higher sanction than that imposed for endangering a slave's limbs.

Unique in the Georgia slave code of 1750, compared to those of other colonies, was its concern with the misbehavior of whites, and not that of black bondsmen. The only such provision that applied to blacks' behavior—and it applied to whites as well—outlawed interracial sex and marriage. There were no prohibitions against slave criminality of any kind.

One possible explanation for this benign, and even benevolent, code was the trustees' view that proscriptive legislation might not be necessary if the slave population could be kept small and under rigorous white surveillance. Another was that slaves would also be less likely to engage in rebellious behavior if treated humanely. The logic of this rationale reflected the trustees' continuing naiveté and inexperience but also their commitment to humanitarianism. An influx into Georgia after 1750 of experienced slave masters from South Carolina and the West Indies transformed the rather innocent notions that had shaped the 1750 code, replacing them with the timeworn methods relied upon by those who had kept men and women in chains for several generations.[1]

Neither the Board of Trade nor the Privy Council had approved the 1750 code; masters therefore did not have the enforceable rights of the code, and if they acted as though the law were actually in force, one could mount legal challenges to their rights and prerogatives. In theory, blacks could have sued for their freedom. In 1755, Georgians passed an act "For the better Ordering and Governing Negroes and other Slaves in this Province," turning for advice to the more experienced South Carolinians. The new code was a nearly verbatim copy of South Carolina's 1740 slave code. Legislators designed this body of law to regulate every significant aspect of black life.

The 1755 code's first goal was to control movements and gatherings of blacks. No slave in the city of Savannah or any other Georgia town could travel outside the city or town limits without a master's written pass; no rural slave could leave the plantation without such a pass. Any slave caught abroad without a pass, or a white person responsible for the slave's proper conduct, could be whipped. If a black person refused to answer questions about travel any white person posed, that slave could be "moderately corrected" on the spot. If the slave assaulted or struck the inquisitor, the slave could be "Lawfully killed." Slaves could not travel the roads in groups of more than seven unless accompanied by a responsible white person; those who violated this provision were to receive twenty lashes. There were limits to the punishments that could be meted out. If anyone "Bruised, Maimed or Disabled" a bondsperson, the state fined the offender six shillings. If a beating resulted in the slave's being unfit to work, the law required the assailant to pay a per diem of twenty shillings.

Justices of the peace could recruit as many as necessary to break up any assembly of blacks that threatened the peace or security of the neighborhood. Masters who allowed their slaves to convene meetings or to "beat Drums blow Horns or other Loud Instruments" were to be fined, reflecting the fear that slaves might use these African forms of communication to convey their "wicked Designs and purposes."[2]

"Every Owner of Twenty Slaves" had to have one "white Servant upon his plantation Capable of bearing arms," and every owner of fifty slaves had to have "Two white servants as above and for every Twenty five Slaves above fifty one White Servant more capable of bearing arms." Any farm or plantation with one or more slaves had to have at least one white person in residence. Legislators who supported this paradoxical relaxation of the slave population quota may have believed that the closer surveillance contemplated would allow fewer white men to control a larger number of blacks. They may have also reasoned that since the immigration of whites was not keeping pace with the importation of African slaves, there was no need to hinder economic expansion for the sake of maintaining an impossible ideal.[3]

The law prohibited slaves from bearing firearms unless in possession of a license written by their masters permitting them to hunt, or unless hunting occurred under the direction of a white person at least sixteen years old. Bondsmen could convey arms to their masters unsupervised if they had a license to do so. Paradoxically, Georgia legislation authorized slaves to be armed and recruited into the militia. This bizarre, contrary state of affairs was an acknowledgment of the precarious situation of a province with a white population too small to defend itself alone. This was also a recognition of diverse modes of black behavior, that some slaves were dangerous and untrustworthy and others were loyal enough—or restrained and isolated enough—to be entrusted with white lives.[4]

The most important provisions of the code defined capital crimes. All felonies were punishable by death. Any "Slave free Negro Mulato Indian or Mestizo" who burned or destroyed any "Stack of Rice corn or other grain" produced in the colony was guilty of a felony. So was anyone who burned or destroyed "any Tar kiln Barrels of pitch Tar Turpentine or Rozin" or any other goods manufactured in the province, and anyone who stole a slave. Any slave convicted of homicide, except by "misadventure" or at the direction of his master, was to be executed. So was any slave or member of an "inferior" class who attempted to incite or participate in a slave insurrection. If a white person was wounded, maimed, or bruised, even during a first offense, the law required that the offender be executed. Any person of color who attempted to poison anyone was guilty of a capital felony.

The lives of lesser participants in such felonies could be spared if the example of the execution of fewer criminals would deter others. Those who committed non-lethal assaults on whites, for first and second offenses, were subject to whatever punishment the presiding justices of the peace saw fit to hand down, provided it did not extend to "Life or Limb." But for a third such offense the state took the life of a bondservant.[5]

Georgia legislators strengthened code provisions that protected slaves' lives and whites' property values. Anyone who murdered his slave, or that of another, was guilty of a felony, with the benefit of clergy, thus avoiding a death sentence. If the first-time killer was not the owner, the law simply required him to make restitution. The slave code deemed anyone who killed a second time a murderer subject to "the laws of England," yet required the murderer to forfeit "no more of his Lands and Tenements Goods and

Chattels than may be Sufficient to Satisfy the owner" of the slain slave. If the killing occurred while lawfully correcting the slave, the killer simply forfeited the sum of £50 sterling. Any person who willfully "cut the Tongue put out the eye castrate or Cruelly Scald burn or deprive any slave of any Limb or Member" was obliged to pay a fine of £10 sterling.[6]

The 1755 code signaled the end of the trustees' authority and confidence that slavery could be a humane institution. It demonstrated a view prevalent among whites that slaves and free blacks were dangerous to a white slaveholding society. From that moment forward, the law gave precedence to slavery and to white supremacy over due process and justice for blacks.

The 1755 slave code regulated behavior between blacks and whites in Georgia for ten years; then, in 1765, legislators made several revisions to the penalties for the unlawful injury or killing of a slave. No longer for a first offense of killing a slave was compensation to the murdered slave's owner enough. Now, a first-time murderer was "altogether and forever uncapable of holding any place of Trust, or exercising enjoying or receiving the profits of any Office, place of employment, civil or Military" within the colony. The code no longer required one who killed a slave in the "sudden heat of Passion and without an ill intent" to pay a fine of £50 sterling; now the fine was trebled to a maximum of £150. Anyone who intentionally maimed and mutilated a slave by removing a limb or body part no longer forfeited a mere £10; the new fine was £50 sterling. Georgia legislators were making it very clear that slaves' lives could not be taken cheaply, not because of their innate value, but because black labor was becoming the lifeblood of the colony.[7]

Lawmakers now also put in place several provisions to refine and enhance definitions and penalties for forms of black criminality. Whereas it had been unlawful as of 1755 for blacks to destroy or burn grains and naval stores manufactured in the colony, it was now a capital felony to destroy or set fire to such supplies, regardless of their point of origin. Legislators expanded the definition of poisoning and offered incentives to slaves to inform on those who had been involved in, or even contemplated, committing this crime. Any black person with knowledge of a poisoning who did not reveal it was to be put to death. As an inducement, the state would pay slave informants twenty shillings a year, as long as they resided in the colony. Any black who furnished, procured, or administered a poison was guilty of a felony and subject to a death sentence; the same was true for a person who instructed slaves in the use of any "Poisonous Root, Plant, Herb or other sort of poison whatever."[8] No slave could administer medicine to another except under the direction or supervision of a white person.

The elaborate anti-poisoning provisions of 1765 were a consequence of the colonists' frequent receipt of news from other colonies about slaves who had poisoned and struck out violently against their masters. One such account, from Jamaica, reported that a band of renegade slaves had broken into the home of their master and "cut off his hands, then his arms, then his feet, and legs, and then broke his thighs. They afterwards killed three of his children." The rapid increase in Georgia's slave population heightened white fears of black unrest. Between 1750 and 1766, the number of blacks in the colony increased from five hundred to approximately seventy-eight hundred. Probably of even greater concern was the relative increase in the black population. In the early 1750s, blacks accounted for 20 percent of the total population; by 1765, they were 40 percent. The 1765 revision of the code raised the penalty for assault on a white person. Before 1765, courts could sentence blacks who struck whites to corporal punishment for the first two instances of such attacks; on the third instance, they would be sentenced to the gallows. After the 1765 revision, even a second assault resulted in the death penalty.

Most of the trustees' humanitarian provisions from previous slave codes were now gone. Gone were those provisions for slave maintenance and spiritual instruction. The only salutary remnants of the earlier codes were the list of unacceptable punishments and the prohibition against slaves working on the Sabbath.[9]

In 1767, the Georgia colonists were shocked to learn that British authorities had disallowed their slave code because of an unacceptable definition of slaves as chattel rather than real property, a definition that had great potential consequences. Some contemporary legal authorities believed that if the law defined slaves as real property, they were bound to the land and could not be sold or disposed of away from it—that owners had the right to the labor of their slaves but not to their bodies. This legal definition of slave property would be disastrous for a market-oriented slave economy, especially one in its infancy. If, however, the code defined slaves as chattel, they could be disposed of like other items of personal property. The harmful effect on slaves of defining them as chattel was not the issue; the issue was that this definition clashed with existing property law. The British disallowance of the slave code caused considerable distress in the colony. In the words of Governor James Wright: "The Negro Law is so absolutely Essential to our

Local Circumstances, that without a Law to keep our Slaves in Order, no Man's life or Property would be safe a Moment. In Short our very existence depends upon it." Wright disregarded the instructions of his superiors and kept the invalid code in effect for another year, just as Georgians had done with the slave code of 1750 that the Crown and Board of Trade had failed to approve. This disregard of the law is evidence of a legal culture that prioritized slavery over legality. After further consultation with the Board of Trade, Georgians crafted a new slave code that the board approved, and that went into effect in 1770.[10]

Among the loopholes closed by the 1770 code were those that omitted any prohibition against black Georgians' stealing anything, killing each other (except by poisoning), breaking into or burning any dwelling or other building, or raping a woman. Had this been a legislative oversight, or did it reflect an absence of black criminal behavior? According to the testimony of slaveholders from across the colonial South, slaves certainly did steal, kill each other, break into buildings, and rape women, both white and black. Or did such crimes occur so infrequently that no intervention by the court system was necessary? Or perhaps masters had been handling such matters themselves on the plantation, privately, as they had done during the years of the trusteeship? After 1770, it became a capital felony to "commit or attempt to commit a rape on any white person whomsoever" (black women remained unprotected), to "maliciously kill any slave or other person," to "steal any goods or chattels whatsoever," or to "break open, burn or destroy any dwelling house or other building whatsoever."

The 1770 code had loopholes of its own. It mandated death for maiming or wounding a white person or for striking one a second time. A Negro who attempted to strike a blow or cause serious injury, but failed, escaped punishment because there had been no injury or actual physical contact. A slave who had lawful possession of a firearm and shot at his master with intent to kill, but missed, was guilty of no crime. Nor was a slave who attempted to strike an overseer with an ax but failed to strike him. No slave society could allow such behavior to fall outside the boundaries of the law. In 1816, the general assembly made it a crime to assault a free white person with intent to kill or with a weapon likely to produce death.

Concern about black rebellion was responsible for the second new provision. In 1829, authorities in Georgia discovered copies of the fiery polemic, *An Appeal to the Coloured Citizens of the World,* by David Walker, the black abolitionist from Boston, in which Walker prophesied the violent overthrow of Southern slavery at the hands of slaves. In the same year, legislators made it a capital crime for a black Georgian, slave or free, to "circulate, bring, or cause to be circulated or brought into this state . . . any written pamphlet, paper or circular for the purpose of exciting to insurrection, conspiracy or resistance among slaves, negroes or free persons of color of this state."[11]

The code of 1770 retained provisions that provided minimal protection for slaves' lives, and hence for white property interests. Any individual who killed a second slave was guilty of murder and subject to execution. (First-time slave murderers still received the benefit of clergy.) The code required one who killed a slave in a moment of passion to pay the slave's appraised value, not the £150 of 1765.[12] The code of 1770, with periodic revision, served as the backbone of the formal criminal justice system until the end of the Civil War.

If the letter of Georgia's colonial slave law was severe, in practice it was not nearly so, in large part because masters failed to enforce some parts of it. Many permitted slaves to gather in illegal assemblies, travel without passes, trade without licenses, purchase liquor, hire out their own time, and hunt with firearms. Indeed, newspaper editors repeatedly complained about lax code enforcement. The reason for this laxity was not generosity or a lack of concern; rather, it was that masters resisted any outside force that might impinge upon their prerogatives as supreme arbiters of all matters occurring on their farms and plantations. The result was an uneasy tension between slaveowners and the criminal law. So, too, administering entire slave codes as written would have required immense bureaucracies, something that a South suspicious of centralized government power would never countenance. Authorities in Georgia and elsewhere did not strictly enforce slave codes because no one expected them to do so. The codes were expansive enough to be pressed into service in the event of serious black unrest, but they did not need to be as rigidly adhered to in times of quietude.[13]

In 1811, the Georgia legislature proposed overhauling the state's criminal code for whites, to bring it more in line with the changes in Western criminal justice theory that had taken place over the preceding quarter-century. At the same time, the general assembly agreed to certain changes in the criminal law for blacks. A measure to reform the system for whites was stalled for several years, but lawmakers created a new tribunal for the trials of black defendants. In 1816, legislators reformed the state's criminal law for whites. Georgia became the first state to have a modern penal code, one that combined common and statute law. In the watershed year of 1816, and in the decade and a half that followed it, Georgia's representatives and senators altered the criminal code for slaves and free blacks as well.[14]

In 1816, burglary and arson replaced the earlier crimes of burning goods or buildings and breaking into dwelling houses. The new law defined burglary as "breaking and entering into the dwelling or mansion of another, with intent to commit a felony." The requirement of intent was a much narrower standard than that of 1770; a black defendant had not only to break into a dwelling, but to enter it with the intent to commit a serious crime. Under the old law, at least in theory, merely breaking down a door was sufficient to mandate a trip to the gallows. Similarly, under colonial law, setting fire to any building, or to any among a significant range of commodities, warranted a death sentence, while under the revised code, arson was defined as the "malicious and wilful burning of the house, or outhouse of another." Again, "willful and malicious" imposed a more restrictive definition—one that had the potential of saving black lives. In 1820, lawmakers further narrowed the definition of arson. Slaves and free persons of color could be convicted of arson only if they burned a house in a town, or, if in a rural area, an *occupied* house *at night*. The structure of this arson law reflected the reality that it was far more threatening to life and property to set a fire in a town, where the danger of a fire spreading was great, than in a rural area, where distance separated structures. This law, too, had the effect of raising the bar for convicting black defendants of arson—a salutary definition that remained on the statute books until 1861, when legislators returned to the definition of 1816, undoubtedly because Georgians worried about possible damage by insurgent black arsonists during a civil war.

In 1816, lawmakers reduced the number of crimes that mandated a death sentence, removing all theft crimes from the list of capital felonies. In 1821, assault with intent to kill, maiming a free white person, burglary, arson, and attempted poisoning were still death penalty offenses, but based on a change in the penal code that year, presiding inferior court justices could administer other punishments, "proportionate to the offence, and that best promote the object of the law, and operate as a preventive for like offences in the future." By 1850, the only crimes that demanded a death sentence were insurrection or attempted insurrection, murder and poisoning, and rape or attempted rape of a white female.

In 1861, some black lives were in all likelihood spared when the legislature defined "insurrection." Prior to that year, statutes did not delineate which acts constituted the crime; the state could—and did—charge blacks who committed a variety of acts, from verbally defying masters to shooting at them, with insurrection. After 1861, to be convicted, a defendant had to have "combined resistance to the lawful authority of the master or the State, with intent to the permanent denial thereof, when the same is manifested or intended to be manifested by acts of violence"—the "mere resistance of a slave, or his attempt to escape, or actual escape, from the master, shall not constitute insurrection."[15] To charge and convict slave defendants had become more difficult through this rather narrow definition.

OF COURSE ~~Reform~~ *WAS* Reform of the criminal law may have been principally motivated by the need to protect an increasingly valuable source of labor. With the closing of the international slave trade to America in 1808, and the cotton boom that began shortly before, slaves prices rose dramatically, and they continued to rise for the rest of the antebellum period. Killing slaves became an increasingly expensive proposition—especially after 1793, when Georgia stopped compensating the owners of executed slaves for loss of their property.

Increased legal protection for slaves' lives also enabled Georgians and other Southerners to deflect criticism from abolotionists. Georgia's governor George Towns, in his 1849 message to the state legislature, addressed the "fell spirit of blind and infuriated fanaticism displayed," in "most, if not all, of the non-slaveholding States of the Union" on the issue of anti-slavery. "In the present excited state of the public mind upon the subject of slavery throughout the Union, it is believed to be the duty of the Legislature to review previous legislation upon the subject and so modify and change the same as to demonstrate to the world that . . . we are actuated by a humane and Christian policy in protecting this portion of our population by wholesome laws." In response to Towns's message, lawmakers revised the slave code to extend to bondspeople all of the trial rights enjoyed by whites. Towns went on to say that even though legislators had designed these policy changes to reflect the humane spirit of his slaveholding society, Georgia would continue to "enforce perfect subordination with the slave," and to "inflict exemplary punishment upon those who seek within our jurisdiction to interfere with our domestic policy."[16] It seems evident that humanitarian concern for slaves ranked somewhere near the bottom of the list of motives for the amelioration of the slave codes.

All Southern slave states had codes, similar to Georgia's revised codes, that established the property rights of owners, supported the disciplinary prerogatives of masters, provided safeguards for the white community against slave insurrection and other black violence, and held slaves and free blacks legally responsible and punishable for actions that violated the codes. The newer slave states were adopting the codes of their predecessors in human bondage. Just as Georgia had initially adopted South Carolina's code, Tennessee adopted North Carolina's, and Kentucky and Mississippi borrowed heavily from Virginia's. The Gulf states modeled their codes after those of South Carolina and Georgia. As a former French colony, Louisiana was the only state not to acquire its slave law from others; its slave code was based on the Code Noir that Louis XIV had decreed in 1724. The growing similarity in the codes generally was the product, in part, of the universal regulatory structures necessitated by chattel slavery; the institution itself required certain kinds of laws.[17]

Masters and legislators did not want the slave codes to be strictly administered, and erratically enforced public laws alone could not control black criminal conduct. Had Georgians relied exclusively on state mechanisms of control, as they saw it, they would have found themselves awash in a sea of criminality. Southern law enforcement could not curb offenders, black or white. Regarding black behavior, therefore, a clear division of responsibility arose between masters and the state for controlling slave criminality. Masters maintained law and order within the boundaries of their farms or plantation estates, and the state maintained control outside these boundaries. In Georgia, masters preferred to dispense justice themselves. The state intervened only as a last resort, or when interests outside the plantation/farm were at stake.

The best evidence of Georgia's dual system was the courts' and the masters' handling of intra-plantation slave murder. There is not a single case in the trial records of a prosecution of a slave for murdering another slave on the same farm or plantation. Masters did not take their slaves into court when it was their private interests alone that were at stake. Either that, or slaves simply did not kill each other on the plantation—but trial records from around the South and slave narratives from Georgia suggest that this was not the case. Masters generally turned to the courts only when their slaves harmed the interests of others, or when the slaves of others harmed their interests. There are also only a few cases of intra-plantation arson.

The most frequently prosecuted intra-plantation crimes were the slave murders of masters, mistresses, or overseers, and serious slave assaults against overseers. In these cases, the state judged and punished slaves because their owners were not available to do so, or because an overseer was not the property of those who had hired him and thus was an outside interest.[18] The reluctance of the state to infringe on the prerogatives of masters reflected its desire to protect private authority from any outside encroachment, even its own, and was a logical continuation of a colonial legal culture that placed mastery above legal authority.

Masters never convened to determine the rules that would govern black behavior on their lands. They read many of the same agricultural and plantation management journals, and a certain consistency of rules existed, but a considerable range in plantation "law" from one place to another was possible, and probably the norm. Ex-slaves recalled a number of different rules. Taken together, however, these rules, with variations or not, were nearly as all-encompassing as the slave codes themselves. Masters prohibited Georgia bondsmen from leaving their plantations without passes; from "talking back" to whites; from hitting other slaves; from "fussing, fighting and ruckussing"; lying and stealing; owning or possessing firearms; selling or buying anything without the master's consent; attending any secret meeting; harboring or assisting any runaway; abusing any farm animal; and from mistreating any member of one's family.[19] This striking similarity between public law and plantation law meant that white Georgians expected slaves to conduct themselves in a proper fashion whether on or off their plantations, and that they were subject to both public and private chastisement for violation of this complementary set of laws. They were under the watchful eyes of the entire white population, acting as informers or as surrogate masters.

Slave Patrols

A legislative act of 1757 established the state's patrol system as the public enforcement arm of the criminal justice system. The act's preamble explains its rationale: "It is absolutely necessary for the Security of his Majesty's Subjects of this Province, that Patrols be established under proper Regulations, in the settled parts thereof, for the better keeping of Negroes and other Slaves in Order and prevention of any Cabals Insurrections or other Irregularities amongst them." The captain or commanding officer of each militia company was to summon his junior officers and divide the militia districts into as many smaller subdivisions as could be effectively patrolled, as long as these subdivisions did not exceed "twelve miles in extent." The patrol law commanded all plantation owners, as well as all "other Inhabitants," "Alarm Men," and "Foot and Horse" members of the militia, to make themselves available for service on the patrols, though they could hire substitutes. Slave-owning women and white male servants, too, had to participate in patrols. Masters had to provide their servants with "a Horse and furniture for service." Georgia was not alone in requiring women to serve on slave patrols; South Carolina did so as well, though there is no evidence that women actually did ride the roads. Apparently, women made use of the provision in the patrol act that permitted the hiring of substitutes.[20] Since Georgia had a similar provision, it may well be that the state's slave-owning women also hired substitutes. In Georgia, each militia captain's list contained the names of all persons eligible for patrol service, and at each muster the captain chose from that list up to seven persons for duty. Each person chosen provided "one good Gun or Pistol in Order, with six cartridges suitable for such gun or pistol and one good cutlass."[21]

Patrols might visit plantations in their districts whenever they chose, but they had to do so at least once a month. Slaves caught outside "the Fences or cleared Ground of their Owners Plantations" without a pass or not in the company of a responsible white person could be whipped. Patrollers could search any white person's house, as well as "any disorderly tipling-House or other House suspected of harbouring, trafficking or dealing with Negroes," if they reasonably believed a runaway slave was hidden there.[22]

Legislators revised the act of 1757, which served as the foundation for the patrol system, several times through the end of the antebellum period. In 1765, they increased the number in a patrol from seven to ten and required patrollers to visit each plantation at least once every two weeks; after 1845, plantation visits had to occur at intervals of no more than fifteen days. Lawmakers restricted service on patrol, in 1765, to those between the ages of sixteen and sixty. An 1824 amendment forbade women to ride on patrols.[23]

Patrol laws very similar to Georgia's existed in every slave state. In some states, the law mandated patrols; in others, local communities authorized patrols but did not require them. Patrols generally consisted of a captain and three others, appointed for a period of a few months, and the laws required them to ride the roads to inspect farms and plantations every few weeks or so. For example, in Virginia, county courts appointed patrols for terms not to exceed three months, their purpose being to visit "all negro quarters and other places suspected of having therein unlawful assemblies" and to "arrest such slaves as may stroll from one plantation to another without permission." Alabama demanded that every slaveholder under the age of sixty, and every non-slaveholder under forty-five, serve on patrols that were required to visit plantations at least once a week during their members' terms of service.[24]

Patrols in areas with large slave populations and greater public concern about slave unrest were more active and more efficient; elsewhere, patrols were sporadic, and service considered an unwelcome chore. Slaveholders who balked at the responsibility often paid substitutes to stand in for them; elite members of society routinely avoided riding with patrols. So, for example, Georgia senator Robert Toombs paid fines annually over the course of a number of years, assessed because he refused to serve as a patroller. In Wilkes County, the names of a number of the area's most prominent citizens appeared in court documents as defaulters.[25]

With masters and the upper classes intent on avoiding patrol duty, much of the responsibility fell on non-slaveholders, principally young men for whom patrolling seemed a sport. But avoidance of patrol service by many, and the youthful inexperience of those who did serve, led to extremely low levels of efficiency. One Georgia planter lamented, "Our patrol laws are seldom enforced, and even where there is a mock observance of them, it is by a parcel of boys or idle men, the height of whose ambition is to 'ketch a nigger.'" Even Georgia grand juries echoed this sentiment. What might be described as "fraternization with the enemy" also hampered effectiveness. Whites on patrols often helped slaves break many of the laws they were supposed to enforce. Slaves sold goods they had stolen from their masters to poor whites; slaves and yeomen drank, gambled, and stayed out together past curfew. Nor was patrol inefficiency unique to Georgia; in Florida, for example, grand juries complained about the problem as well.[26]

For all such reasons, according to the historians John Hope Franklin and Loren Schweninger, "it was virtually impossible to maintain surveillance over the black population day and night in all parts of a county. There were too many places to hide and too many hours at night for runaways to move across the countryside, visiting, drinking and stealing." The same might be said of non-runaways. In Greene County, slaves moved about nearly at will. Since three-fourths of the county's slaves lived on farms with fewer than twenty slaves and there was little opportunity to develop an independent community on a master's property, slaves on one farm or plantation established significant relationships with slaves on other farms or plantations.

Necessity-born mobility of slaves and the failure of patrols to control it was the subject of much local consternation. In November 1853, the Greene County grand jury "deplored the laxity and supineness evidenced in our regulations . . . so as to render our patrol laws a dead letter." Even after John Brown's unsuccessful insurrection attempt in Harper's Ferry, Virginia, in 1859, Greene County citizens failed to shoulder the responsibility of patrol duty. In 1860, a grand jury once again remarked on the poor performance of the patrols, observing, "The patrol law is very loosely enforced in our county."[27]

Non-slaveholders, many of whom often disliked masters as much as slaves, took out their frustrations on both. Masters repeatedly took such patrollers to court for trespassing on their plantations or physically abusing their bondspeople. Ex-slaves recalled the efforts of masters to keep patrollers away from their plantations. Lewis Ogletree, of Spaulding County, said, "It wasn't any use for the 'patty-role' to come to Marse Crowder's 'cause he would not permit him to tech one of his darkies." Anna Parkes remembered a patrol pursuing a slave of one J. D. Ingram onto the Ingram plantation, whereupon Ingram commanded a patroller to "turn around and leave his premises." When the patroller refused and continued his pursuit, Ingram picked up a rifle and shot the patroller dead, remarking to his wife, "Well Lucy, I guess the next time I speak to that scoundrel he will take heed." Even prominent Georgians, like congressman and Confederate vice-president Alexander Stephens, and supreme court chief justice Joseph Henry Lumpkin, refused to allow patrols onto their plantations. Masters even denied sworn peace officers access to their slaves. Former bondswoman Minnie Davis remembered the town marshal coming to her plantation to whip her mother because she had written notes stating that she had whiskey for sale. The master would not allow her to be touched.[28] Once again, the demands of mastery trumped those of law.

Tension between masters and patrols reflected the greater tension between a social and economic system based on notions of individual autonomy and a criminal justice system that encroached on this authority in order to function. To the extent that masters kept brutal patrollers away, slaves benefited. But if the master or mistress were the source of the brutality, barring the patrols potentially denied slaves legal protection from abuses that might go undetected.

But usually masters wanted runaways captured, and when patrols failed to turn up runaways, many masters hired professional slave catchers—men who specialized in tracking fugitives. Trackers charged by the day and mile for expeditions that might last for weeks. For the poor whites who were usually the trackers, the $10 to $50 earned from a successful capture was a princely sum. One such man, Oliver P. Findley of Greene County, in 1847 captured three runaways belonging to a county planter. He charged the master $35, which included a $5 fee for whipping one fugitive. Slave catchers of greater experience and reputation commanded higher compensation. John Upp of Middleburg, Virginia, earned $150 for returning a runaway after a two-week pursuit.[29]

Slave catchers used specially trained bloodhounds they kept caged and never allowed near blacks except during training exercises. The trainers would give the dogs a black person's clothing and teach them to follow its scent; indeed, trainers often compelled slaves to stage escapes to provide practice for the dogs. Slave catchers and trainers hired dogs out for tracking at $5 per day, and $10 to $25 per day for catching fugitives. Former slave Hannah Murphy recalled, "I seen many mens runnin' away from de bloodhouns'. Sometimes we chillins be in the quarter playin' and a man would come runnin' along fast, breathin' hard, so skeared! De hounds be behind him." Slave hounds were fierce, and if not restrained, at the end of a pursuit they might tear a fugitive to pieces. An ex-bondsman remembered seeing a slave caught by the "nigger hounds." His "skin was cut and torn in any number of places and he looked like one big mass of blood."[30]

In 1855, the Georgia Supreme Court addressed the use of slave-catching dogs and the damage caused to slave property. Gardner Davis had hired Stephen, a slave owned by Mariana Moran, for one year. Stephen escaped, and Davis hired a slave catcher to pursue him with dogs. During the chase, Stephen fell into a river and drowned, whereupon Moran sued Davis for Stephen's value. At trial, the presiding judge had instructed the jury that, "under ordinary circumstances the owner, the hirer, or overseer of a slave, has the right to pursue the slave if he runs away, with such dogs as may track him to his place of concealment . . . provided it be done with such dogs as cannot lacerate or wound or materially injure the slave; and if in doing so, harm should befall the slave, the hirer or overseer will not be responsible for the injury."[31] In the view of the court, the only way liability would attach was if a slave catcher had not properly trained the dogs. The jury found in Davis's favor, and Moran appealed the case to the Georgia Supreme Court.

In upholding the verdict of the lower court, Chief Justice Lumpkin relied on the slave code of 1770 and related legislation that made it lawful for "every person" to apprehend fugitive slaves. Based on this general principle, and an absence of relevant legislation, Lumpkin ruled that it was certainly allowable to use properly trained dogs to capture runaways. The reason for this discretion was financial. Lumpkin noted that the South had "lost, already, upwards of 60,000 slaves worth between 25 and 30 millions of dollars." So instead of "relaxing the means allowed by law for the security and enjoyment of this species of property, the facilities afforded for its escape . . . constrains . . . us to redouble our vigilance and to tighten the chords that bind the negro to his condition of servitude—a condition which is to last, if the Apocalypse be inspired, until the end of time."[32] Slave-catching dogs could be employed because masters needed the widest possible latitude to prevent the loss of slave property. An injured slave was better than a successful runaway.

Patrollers and slave catchers routinely beat bondsmen who were discovered off their plantations without passes. Often patrols came onto the plantations to beat bondsmen for the sheer amusement of it; others whipped slaves on the flimsiest of justifications. Many slaves feared to report such abuses to their masters, lest the patrollers seek retribution. Numerous of Georgia's ex-slaves likened the patrols to the actions of the Ku Klux Klan, as did blacks in Virginia and the Carolinas. One former slave said the same men who had manned the patrols before the Civil War donned the white robes of the KKK after it.[33]

But despite their fear, many slaves resisted the patrols, developing early-warning systems to sound the alarm when they approached, building trapdoors in their cabins to allow slaves without passes to escape, and tying vines across the roads to trip the horses of advancing patrollers. Captured slaves might fight violently to escape their pursuers. One Georgia slave, Adam, was caught off his plantation at the cabin of his girlfriend; he turned over a pot of boiling lard onto the patrollers and made good his escape. Another slave was attending a secret prayer meeting when patrollers broke into the house; a quick-thinking slave hurled cinders and ash from the fireplace into the faces of the patrol members. In the ensuing confusion, all of the slaves escaped. In some jurisdictions, slave resistance alarmed the white citizenry and fostered a desire for additional security measures.[34]

The Slave Legal Personality

Georgia law defined the slave legal personality as different from that of the white citizen; according to the imperatives of slavery, the law treated bondsmen both as persons and as property. The essence of chattel slavery was the buying and selling of human beings as articles of property, like horses or wagons, but this logic could not extend to the criminal law, because slaves were volitional human beings. Failure to recognize slaves' will, and the ability to act in accordance with that will, would have meant that a slave could not be held accountable for his actions. Slaves might kill or destroy property and their masters would be held culpable. <u>The will of bondspeople had to be recognized, if only to a limited degree, for them to be subject to criminal law.</u>

CATCH-22

However, a full recognition of black humanity and will would have undermined the central tenet of American slavery: that slaves were simply extensions of their masters' wills. So the law created an elaborate fiction, one in which <u>slaves were simultaneously persons and property.</u> This fiction of <u>"animate chattel"</u> is captured in a conversation between T. R. Gray and Nat Turner in William Styron's novel *The Confessions of Nat Turner:* "'The point is that *you* are *animate* chattel and animate chattel is capable of craft and connivery and wily stealth. You ain't a wagon, Reverend, but chattel that possesses moral choice and spiritual volition. Remember that well. Because that's how come the law provides that animate chattel like you can be tried for a felony, and that's how come you're gonna be tried next Sattidy.' He paused and then said softy without emotion, 'And hung by the neck until dead.'" The chief justice of Georgia's Supreme Court expressed this sentiment more formally in 1855, when, in *Cleland v. Waters,* Joseph Henry Lumpkin wrote, "Slaves are property—*chattels* if you please; still they are rational and intelligent beings. Christianity considers them as such and our municipal law, in many of its wise and humane provisions, has elevated them far above the level of brutes."[35]

America's courts are based on the common law, on "those principles and rules of action . . . which derive their authority solely from usages and customs of immemorial antiquity, or from the judgments and decrees of the courts recognizing, affirming, and enforcing such usages and customs, and in this sense particularly the ancient unwritten law of England."[36] In the context of colonial and antebellum criminal justice, the common law defined the relationship between the accused and the legal system, determining the definition of crimes, the rights defendants enjoyed before the courts, and the punishments meted out to those convicted. However, the common law was inapplicable in the cases of early slave offenders because <u>slavery did not exist under English common law.</u> As a consequence, whites had a relatively free hand in drafting legislation to meet the needs of their slaveholding societies, and the separate body of law that took the form of the slave codes was developed to govern the actions and define the rights of blacks in white communities. To Georgia's leading antebellum legal authority, Thomas R. R. Cobb, a separate slave code was necessary because the penal statutes applied only to those who could be deprived of freedom. Slaves, by definition, were not free people, hence not subject to the laws of free people.[37]

While all Southern states developed separate penal statutes for blacks, by the end of the antebellum period most had allowed the common law to inform those codes, to provide the most basic protection for the slave lives and white property values that the two equated. The North Carolina Supreme Court, for example, engaged in a full-fledged debate over several decades to arrive at a proper relationship between the slave code and the common law. The reasoning in these cases and the principles articulated in the decisions generally proved representative of those in other states. In *State v. Boon*, the defendant Boon, a white man, had appealed his conviction for the murder of a slave. In his opinion Justice John Hall argued that the position of slave was not analogous to that of villeins (medieval English serfs), whom the common law protected. Instead, slaves' status in law was the result of positive legislation; the murder of a slave was not a crime unless a specific statute prohibited it. Chief Justice John Louis Taylor took an opposite tack. Calling on natural-law theory, Taylor argued that no man had the right to take the life of another except in self-defense, even the life of a slave. He insisted that such total dominion over the life of another was not necessary for the proper functioning of slavery, and that to allow it would be an affront to "reason, religion, humanity and policy."[38]

Defense lawyers argued variations of these two positions in the North Carolina Supreme Court in a number of other cases, with the Taylor position prevailing. Slaves thereafter received the protections of the common law. Tennessee adopted common law protection for slaves in the 1829 case *Fields v. State;* Alabama, in an appellate case in 1843; and Texas, in 1847. The Louisiana Supreme Court ruled in favor of common law protection four times during the 1840s and 1850s. Only South Carolina and Georgia rejected common law protection.[39]

Georgia took its minority stand in an 1851 case, *Neal v. Farmer.* Nancy Farmer had brought suit against William Neal in Greene County Superior Court to recover damages for loss of a slave whom Neal had killed. Farmer proved the killing, and Neal put up no defense. The jury found in Farmer's favor and awarded $825, whereupon Neal moved for a new trial, arguing

This does not surprise me.

that Farmer had failed to prosecute him in criminal court before initiating a proceeding in civil court, a prerequisite under the common law. The court denied his request on the ground that the murder of a slave was not a felony under the common law, and that therefore a prior criminal proceeding was not necessary. Neal's appeal to the Georgia Supreme Court argued that the murder of a slave was a felony under English common law; the "killing of any person in the peace of the King" was murder and a felony, and therefore, since slaves were persons, killing one was a felony. Neal's attorney claimed that slavery had existed in England before the Norman Conquest, and afterward in the form of villeinage, but Farmer's counsel reiterated the argument presented in the lower court, that slavery as practiced in Georgia never existed in England.

Justice Eugenius Nisbet, siding with Farmer, held that slavery under Saxon rule was certainly like chattel slavery in Georgia, but that it occurred before England came into existence in any relevant form and no purpose would be served by delving into the "mists and fog and darkness" of that bygone age to find answers to contemporary questions.[40] As to villeinage as a form of slavery, Nisbet ruled that it had ceased to exist more than 150 years before the founding of Georgia; therefore, the common law protections afforded to villeins could not apply to slaves, because these laws were long since obsolete. Nisbet went on to say that even under the laws of villeinage, the positions of slave and villein differed; villeins possessed certain civil and political rights and were subjects of the king. When it came to the "civil rights of the master," slaves had "none whatever."[41]

The supreme court also held that bringing slaves under the protective umbrella of the common law would destroy slavery itself. "It is theoretically everywhere, and in Georgia experimentally true, that two races of men living together, one in the character of masters and the other in the characters of slaves, cannot be governed by the same laws. Whatever rights humanity, or religion, or policy, may concede to the slave, they must, in the nature of the relation, be often different from those of the master." The personal rights of bondsmen, "if they might be so designated," were "essentially different from those of the master, and cannot therefore be the subject of a common system of laws." Such rights had to be *defined by positive enactments, which, whilst they protect the slave, guard rights of the master.* Common law protection of slaves' lives went against the very nature of human bondage: "If it protects the life of a slave, why not his liberty? And if it protects his liberty, then it breaks down, at once, the *status* of the slave." In Nisbet's view, it was "absurd to talk about the Common Law being applicable to an institution which it would destroy."[42] In Georgia, the common law protected the lives and interests of masters, not slaves, and only the masters' interests shielded slaves from the punitive aspects of the criminal law.

The Legal Status of Free Blacks

In 1790, the free black population of Georgia stood at 398; by 1860, the free black population had grown to 3,500, still less than one percent of the state's total black population of 465,698.[43] In addition to being included in the slave codes, free blacks were also subject to a number of other legal restrictions that did not apply to free whites. The codes barred them from possessing firearms and from serving on juries or in the militia.[44] (It is a matter of extreme irony that slaves could possess firearms under certain conditions and free blacks could not.) The law denied free persons of African descent the right of citizenship, just as it was denied to slaves. According to the Georgia Supreme Court, "Free persons of color have never been recognized here as citizens; they are not entitled to bear arms, vote for members of the legislature, or to hold any civil office. They have always been considered in a state of pupilage, and have been regarded as our wards. . . . They have no *political* rights." Free black men and women were children incapable of exercising the rights of citizenship or of protecting themselves.

[Handwritten margin note: Even true TODAY!]

In Georgia's race-based slave society, free blacks were a threat because they had the potential to blur hard-and-fast color lines between slave and free, black and white. Free blacks were living, breathing reminders to Georgia's slaves of the possibility of freedom. Those seen to be intelligent undermined the theories of Africans' intellectual inferiority upon which slavery relied. If they were industrious and civil, their behavior challenged whites' notions of blacks' indolence and innate savagery. For all such reasons, they had to be controlled and kept in a condition as much like that of the slaves as possible. White Georgians brought both law and custom to bear to accomplish this task.[45] By placing free blacks within a legal structure crafted to ensure the smooth functioning of slavery, white Georgia legislators were committing their state not only to slavery, but to white supremacy as well.

[Handwritten margin note: PEOPLE BETTER TAKE HEED TO THE UNDERTONE OF GEORGIAN HISTORY TOWARDS BLACKS!]

The trustees who drafted the first slave code did so in the conviction that slaves had to be protected from whites, and not the other way around. But that humanitarian influence was, in less than five years, replaced by a system

that favored slavery and white racial domination, one that continued until
the end of slavery. The only legal protections slaves enjoyed came to them
through their masters' legal personality and self-interest. But the overwhelming majority of slaves never came into contact with the criminal justice system, and their master's plantation law was the law that mattered most. The
formal law of the state and the informal law of the plantation combined to
produce a criminal justice system intended to keep slaves in "due Subjection and Obedience." Harold Davis, a historian of Georgia, sums up the
legal and social position of slaves well: "A slave had rights under law barely
sufficient to preserve his life, and he had no rights to preserve his humanity
except against such extreme abuses as maiming and castration. Legally as
well as actually, slaves were at the bottom of society." Free blacks fared little
better. Like slaves, they had only the rights the state gave them, and those
rights were few. They could marry, hold property, and sue in civil court,
but while slaves had the protection of masters' self-interest, free blacks did
not; hence, they were more vulnerable in many respects. In the criminal
law, they occupied the same place as slaves. In Georgia and the rest of the
Slave South, the criminal law served to build and reinforce race and status
hierarchies.[46]

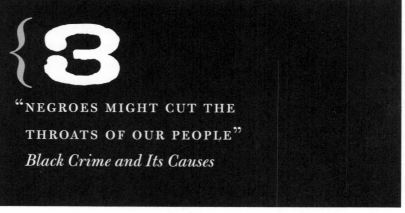

"NEGROES MIGHT CUT THE THROATS OF OUR PEOPLE"
Black Crime and Its Causes

> *When arguing for ourselves, we lay it down as fundamental, that laws, to be just, must give reciprocation of right: that without this, they are merely arbitrary rules of conduct, founded in force, and not in conscience.*
> —*Thomas Jefferson*

> *As many enemies as you have slaves. They are not enemies when we acquire them; we make them enemies.*
> —*Seneca*

For the law to be respected, all must be protected by it and subject to it. If it operates equitably, a legal system has legitimacy; as long as the people believe—correctly or incorrectly—that their life chances are maintained, improved, or left largely unaffected, challenges to the system will be few.[1] But if, as Jefferson warned, law is maintained not by "reciprocation of right" but by "force," the system loses legitimacy and there is no moral obligation to obey. Crime is often the result.

In Georgia, from the dawn of the American Revolution through the end of the Civil War, blacks had no part in crafting or enforcing the criminal law, formal or informal. The law controlled them, but it protected them only when their interests seemed to coincide with the interests of whites. A perceived beneficial confluence of interests generally only applied to slaves; free blacks had a certain value to society broadly, but rarely to particular whites. For slaves and free blacks, the criminal justice system in Georgia had no legitimacy.

Many slaves responded to their asymmetrical and involuntary relationship with the law by adopting a compensatory perspective about the sanctity of white property. Since whites had stolen them or their ancestors from their homelands and thereafter had denied them rights, including rights of property ownership, white chattels were not sacrosanct either. Jefferson understood that depriving slaves of property rights could lead them to disregard the property rights of others. "That disposition to theft with which they have been branded, must be ascribed to their situation, and not any depravity of the moral sense. The man, in whose favor no laws of property exist, probably feels himself less bound to respect those made in favor of others."

To slaves, there was a moral distinction between "stealing" and "taking." "Stealing" involved depriving other slaves of their property. (While slaves could not own property legally, masters allowed them to possess property and consider it their own.) Slaves could not "steal" from their owners because the property never really changed hands. Such acts constituted "taking" and were just desserts. Frederick Douglass put it this way: "Considering that my labor and person were the property of Master Thomas, and that I was by him deprived of the necessities of life . . . it was easy to deduce the right to supply myself with what was my own." For Douglass, stealing from his master was "only a question of *removal*—the taking of his meat out of one tub, and putting it into another; the ownership of the meat was not affected by the transaction." Douglass went on to assert, "I hold that the slave is fully justified in helping himself to the *gold and silver, and the best apparel of his master, or that of any other slaveholder; and that such taking is not stealing in any just sense of that word.*" Douglass extended his disregard of whites' property rights to the greater society because it was complicit with masters in denying slaves their rights to property. "Society at large has bound itself, in form and in fact, to assist Master Thomas in robbing me of my rightful liberty; therefore, whatever rights I have against Master Thomas, I have, equally against those confederated with him in robbing me of liberty. As society has marked me out as privileged plunder, on principle of self-preservation, I am justified in plundering in turn. Since each slave belongs to all; all must therefore, belong to each."[2]

Armed with this logic, slaves deprived their masters and other whites of their goods with distressing regularity. For some slaves, their understanding of white property rights and the immorality of slavery quelled any feelings of guilt, but for others, they never did. Some slaves understood that the property crimes they felt obligated to commit were wrong in both white and black value systems. The law allowed free blacks at least some property rights, hence they may well have been more willing to honor white property rights, although since white commitment to slavery and white supremacy kept most in poverty, they were not likely to be fully committed to respecting white property interests.[3]

While whites were certainly concerned about property crime, it was black violence that worried them most and black violence that was the central preoccupation of the criminal justice system. No matter how benign and benevolent the paternalism of slave masters, the fist, the whip, the revolver, and the shotgun maintained the "peculiar institution." Some slaves believed that this reality justified not simply theft but violence against their owners and other whites as a legitimate means of defense, or to secure their freedom. Douglass insisted that if a slave "kills his master, he imitates only the heroes of the [American] revolution." The need among whites to maintain economic and racial order through force, and the willingness of some slaves to resist that force with force, led to violent confrontations. The overwhelming majority of cases brought before Georgia courts during the colonial and antebellum periods, nearly 70 percent, were crimes against persons, such as murder, attempted murder, rape, attempted rape, manslaughter, and poisoning.[4] Many such crimes were outgrowths of clashes between blacks and whites produced by conditions endemic to Georgia's race-based slave society.

In *Notes on the State of Virginia,* Thomas Jefferson observed, "The whole commerce between master and slave is a perpetual exercise of the most boisterous passions, the most unremitting despotism on the one part, and degrading submissions on the other." This exercise in mastery affected not only slaveowners, but their children as well. "Our children see this, and they learn to imitate it. . . . The parent storms, the child looks on, catches the lineaments of wrath, puts on the same airs in the circle of smaller slaves, gives a loose to his worst of passions, and thus nursed, educated and daily exercised in tyranny, cannot but be stamped by it with odious peculiarities." For Jefferson, slavery turned whites into "despots" and slaves into "enemies," and it created a culture of violence that imperiled both.[5]

Assault with Intent to Kill

Not until the early nineteenth century did the offense of assault with intent to kill appear in Old South criminal codes. It replaced earlier statutes that prohibited various kinds of serious physical attacks on whites. In 1816,

Georgia was one of the first states to pass a law on assault with intent to kill. Although the statute was now on the books, prosecutors rarely used it in states outside Georgia; there was not a single case in the antebellum records of Texas, North Carolina, Louisiana, or Delaware.[6] In Georgia, nearly 19 percent of cases prosecuted in the colonial and antebellum periods were for assault.[7] As with other crimes, assault was almost wholly a male affair. Prosecutors indicted or charged slave men in 92.7 percent of the cases; just over a quarter of all bondsmen faced charges for this crime. The state indicted only one free black woman for assault with intent to kill. Counties accused free black men in 3.8 percent of the assault cases, followed by slave women, who appeared in court in 2.5 percent of the cases.[8] Whites considered slave men to be the most threatening members of the black populace, and the prosecution statistics reflected this.

The vast majority of the victims of homicidal assault were whites. Twelve percent of the victims in these cases were masters, mistresses, and overseers. The relationship of the rest to their assailants could not be determined.[9] A higher number of master-class victims is likely because many assaults occurred in circumstances in which whites attempted to punish bondspeople. In September 1864, A. J. Bryan was called to a Macon County plantation to help discipline Elias, a slave who was said to have beaten a woman earlier in the day. When Bryan arrived, several other white men told him Elias was in his cabin. They found Elias standing in a corner. Despite his fear that Elias might be armed, Bryan grabbed the slave by the collar, whereupon Elias called for help. Slaves Ben, Sam, and Redmond entered the cabin, armed with axes. A tense standoff began. Sam and Redmond swung their axes, forcing the white men to retreat; Elias brandished a knife. One of the white men had a gun and raised it to shoot; Bryan commanded him not to. The white men got out, but not before the slaves had slashed two of them.[10] Elias had refused to be whipped and was willing to kill or die to prevent it, and several other slaves were equally willing. Slaves had compelled white men charged with enforcing black subordination to retreat.

In the winter of 1852, James Stripling hired a slave named Wade from his master to cut and split fence rails. After three days, he concluded that Wade had done only one day's work, and that he had stolen some small items from around the farm. Stripling decided to whip Wade, approached him in a field, and commanded him to remove his shirt and submit to a whipping. Wade refused, picked up his ax, and began to walk away. When ordered to stop, Wade advised Stripling "not to push on him," whereupon Stripling asked a white boy to bring his unloaded gun; the boy brought an ax instead. Wade began to climb over a fence, but Stripling pulled him off. When the boy arrived, Stripling told him to throw the ax he had brought over the fence where Wade's ax had fallen so that neither would have a weapon. He told the boy to help him grab Wade, but Wade pulled out a knife and warned he would stab if they came any closer. Stripling grabbed Wade and demanded that he submit to the whipping. Wade said he would yield, but only if Stripling allowed him to keep his shirt on. No, said Stripling—Wade had been too abusive. Wade jerked loose and walked away. The pair came to a farm, and when Stripling tried to grab him again, Wade brandished his ax. Stripling asked the farm wife for an ax, which she provided. Stripling approached Wade with the ax, and Wade drew his ax back in self-defense. Stripling swung his own ax but missed. When Wade began to swing, Stripling retreated behind a tree, then pursued Wade to the next farm, where he asked the lady of the house for a gun. Ignoring the double-barreled shotgun in Stripling's hand, Wade moved toward Stripling and Stripling pulled the shotgun's trigger, but the gun misfired. Wade charged with his ax. While the two struggled, Mrs. Lane, the resident of the house, struck Wade with an ax, ending this fight to the death.[11]

This case is instructive on the attitudes of both whites and blacks about violence, and about the boundaries between obedience and assault. Wade had refused to be whipped at all, but then agreed, provided he could keep his shirt on. He accepted Stripling's unconditional *right* to discipline him, but only agreed to be punished under terms of his own choosing. Stripling accepted his own rights but none of Wade's. The boy and the farm women operated under Stripling's authority to bring Wade under control, since insubordinate slaves were a danger to all whites. All parties were willing to use deadly violence. This speaks volumes about the violent nature of the entire culture, and it is particularly noteworthy that a white woman—though one from the non-elite classes—was willing to confront a slave in a violent encounter.

Whites around the South feared poisoning as an especially heinous form of assault with intent to kill; many masters and mistresses lived in constant dread of being poisoned by their black servants. Yet poisoning accounted for only 1.7 percent of all criminal prosecutions. Like all prosecutions for slave violence—especially that directed at owners—actual acts were fewer than the level of fear implied. The situation was quite different in colonial

Virginia, where between 1740 and 1785 the state tried more slaves for poisoning than for any crime other than theft.

In a reversal of the patterns of other criminal offenses, the majority of black Georgians charged with poisoning were women; 57 percent were slave women. This is entirely logical. Poisoning required no physical strength or weapons, just a sufficient quantity of poison and ready access to food. Since most cooks were slave women, they had the greatest access to the Big House larder and cook stove. These women were a genuine threat to those who owned them. Almost 67 percent of victims in Georgia from 1755 to 1865 were masters, mistresses, or overseers; none were slaves, which was in marked contrast to a number of other Old South states.[12] For Georgia, poisoning was a potentially easy way for slaves to kill a hated master or mistress.

On October 15, 1863, James Steele sat down to a breakfast of fried ham, bread, and coffee on his Cherokee County plantation, joined by his wife Sarah and son Robert. After eating some of the meal, Steele felt weak and disoriented, as did his family. He remained "insensible" until almost dusk, when he passed out, having no memory of the rest of the day. When he came to, a neighbor, Samuel McConnell, and a Dr. Young were in his home. He did not recall wandering with his family around the yard in a delirium, laughing and picking up sticks, followed by a dutiful slave. An investigation into the poisoning commenced immediately. A slave reported that he had seen Sam, a Steele slave, before breakfast putting his hand over the coffee pot. Sam also allegedly had said he would not live under Steele's dominion another year and that he would "have his day." Authorities arrested Sam. At the jail, Governor Joseph E. Brown questioned Sam, and he admitted to having the poisonous seeds, but insisted he had given them to the cook, Mariah. Law enforcement officials did not explore what might have been a conspiracy to murder a master during wartime. The county prosecutor did not charge the cook; a jury convicted Sam, and he hanged on April 1, 1864.[13]

On the morning of October 6, 1859, members of Benjamin Williams's family seated themselves for breakfast in their Harris County plantation home. John Williams ate a piece of ham and noticed it tasted bitter; he drank a bit of coffee and noticed that it, too, was bitter. Benjamin Williams speculated the family had been poisoned. To test the theory, Williams gave the family dog a large chunk of bread. Before he had eaten half the bread, the dog "dropped dead in his tracks." Benjamin Williams questioned Sarah, the cook, who admitted to preparing the food. Williams asked if she had drawn the water used in the preparation of the meal; she said she had not, but used water that was already in the well bucket. A doctor arrived and dispensed medicines to the family; he also questioned Sarah. She confessed to possessing "white powders" and took a neighbor to a hiding place beneath a fence rail. The powder was strychnine. Sarah said that William Howell, a local white man, had been to the house the night before. At trial, Howell admitted giving Sarah the poison but said that he had poisoned the well water without her knowledge; she had refused to do so. Despite Howell's confession, the jury convicted Sarah, and she hanged.[14]

This case is especially interesting because of its interracial nature: a free white man and a black slave woman had conspired to kill a white family. Such interracial cooperation in serious crime was rare. Was this a business arrangement of some sort? Did Howell hire Sarah to eliminate an enemy or a rival? Or was Howell's motivation even more personal? Were he and Sarah lovers? The latter alternative seems to me to be the most probable one. Howell was willing to risk his own life to save Sarah's. This hardly seems the behavior of a mercenary sort who would hire a slave to do his bidding. In all likelihood, Howell and Sarah planned to kill her owners because they imagined she could be free and they could be together.

{ Manslaughter

In antebellum Georgian law, manslaughter was the unlawful killing of another without malice. There were two types of manslaughter: voluntary and involuntary. Voluntary manslaughter occurred when a killing took place "upon a sudden heat of passion," without premeditation. When someone killed another in the course of a lawful activity undertaken without "due caution and circumspection," the crime was involuntary manslaughter.[15]

Manslaughter, of all the serious crimes, was the one most affected by slavery. Authorities accused only six blacks in colonial and antebellum Georgia with the crime, all of them slave men. The victims in these manslaughter cases were all black. One could conclude that blacks seldom killed each other, or whites at all, during the course of heated confrontations, which would certainly be unusual given the violent nature of Southern life. This unexpected statistical profile is explained by the imperatives of chattel slavery and white supremacy. Blacks killed each other during conflicts that met the criteria for manslaughter; they were ordinarily charged with murder and then convicted of the reduced charge of manslaughter. Convicting slaves of the lesser crime spared their lives and preserved their value as property and labor. No manslaughter victims were white, because the killing of a white person was either murder or justifiable homicide; there could be no middle ground.

Manslaughter cases turned on the issue of provocation—inflammatory acts that reduced the culpability of those who killed in response to them. To acknowledge that slaves could be provoked by whites' actions was to enable bondspeople to judge white behavior and to legitimize certain kinds of black violence, and no slave society could permit such legal loopholes. Whites, however, could commit manslaughter against slaves; many such incidents occurred during the course of whippings. Confrontations between slaves and whites during incidents of corporal discipline crystallized all of these issues. Masters, mistresses, and overseers could severely beat slaves and slaves could not strike back. Those who killed slaves during the course of beatings could avail themselves of the manslaughter statute to avoid the gallows. Thus, the manslaughter law protected white lives and slavery at the expense of slaves.

Randal Jordan was an overseer on the Dougherty County plantation of John H. Dawson; Mariah was a thirteen-year-old slave girl who lived there. On July 23, 1853, Jordan decided to whip Mariah, and so, a fellow overseer said, he began to beat her with a large leather lash, one designed to cause severe pain without breaking the skin. He struck the young girl again and again for perhaps half an hour, administering between four hundred and one thousand lashes. The witness-overseer shouted for Jordan to stop, but Jordan kept on beating the prostrate girl. The slave's father ran to her aid, only to be struck by the same lash that Jordan was using on his daughter. Nearby slaves screamed out that the overseer was killing Mariah; Jordan continued to apply the strap. When Mariah lay still on the ground, not breathing, white froth spilling from her lips, Jordan stopped his bloody chastisement, but only to say he thought she was "possuming." When Mariah failed to cease her "possuming," Jordan sent for a doctor and ordered slaves to take the unconscious girl to the master's house. When the doctor arrived, the young girl was, in his words, "perfectly dead." The doctor said it was the worst beating he had ever seen; a number of the lashes had cut to the bone. A Dougherty County jury convicted Jordan of voluntary manslaughter, not murder.

This lenient verdict outraged the Georgia Supreme Court. In the words of Justice Charles McDonald: "I have looked in vain through the evidence for a single mitigating circumstance in this case to reduce the crime below the grade of murder. The prisoner had power over the slave. He exercised it most cruelly, inflicting on her a beating, from four hundred to a thousand blows, which showed in the language of the law 'an abandoned and malignant heart.'" But despite their disgust with the jury's verdict, the justices were powerless to alter the result because jurors were the ultimate triers of facts; if they found mitigating circumstances, their judgment had to stand. They had, and it did.[16] They obviously concluded that the fatal beating had been done without "due caution and circumspection," but deduced no malice from Jordan's sadism.

While whites could avail themselves of the manslaughter statute during confrontations that grew out of corporal punishment, slaves could not. In 1854, a jury convicted Jim of killing his overseer during a fight precipitated by the overseer's attempt to punish him. At trial, Jim's lawyer asked that the jury be instructed to the effect that if the overseer had attacked Jim with a weapon likely to produce death, he was justified in killing his assailant, or if a master or overseer inflicts unmerciful or unreasonable punishment on a slave and the slave strikes back in a moment of passion, the resulting homicide is manslaughter and not murder. The Georgia Supreme Court rejected these arguments, Justice Ebenezer Starnes reasoning in his opinion: "Our laws refuse this indulgence to the passion of the slave, to his sense of provocation, and command him to restrain it, when chastised by his master; because, to allow it, would be to make him the judge, (and to suffer him to act upon his judgment,) as to the reasonableness or unreasonableness of the extent and degree of that patriarchal discipline which the master is permitted to exercise." Allowing a slave to judge the actions of his master would "place him continually in a state of insubordination, and to encourage servile insurrection and bloodshed. Our law thus wisely lessens the privileges of the comparatively few, for the greatest good of the whole."

The court went on to conclude that slaves need not take matters into their own hands, because Georgia law prohibited "immoderate chastisement"; therefore, slaves could turn to the courts for protection.[17] The justices did not explain how the courts would provide such protection against the wishes of the masters who had victimized the slaves. Of course, others could charge a master after he had killed a slave, but putting a master on trial after the fact was of no consequence to a dead slave.

With the exception of North Carolina, all of the supreme courts in slave states that addressed the issue in the antebellum period reasoned as Georgia had, refusing to hold that provocative acts committed by whites in authority over slaves could reduce murder to manslaughter. The North Carolina Supreme Court arrived at its minority position in *State v. Will (a slave),* in 1834. Will, involved in an argument with his overseer, "made off" in the middle of it and the overseer shot him in the back. Will was able to continue to run, but the overseer, Baxter, and several slaves overtook him. In the ensuing scuffle, Will pulled a knife and stabbed Baxter in the arm; Baxter died as a result. The jury found Will guilty of murder and sentenced him to hang. Judge Gaston of the supreme court first ruled the murder of the overseer was not a justifiable homicide because, in running away, Will was guilty of a "breach of duty," but his conduct fell short of "resistance" or "rebellion" and did not justify Baxter's brutal actions. To conclude that a slave could not be moved to murderous passion by an act of inhumanity by his master or one "clothed with the master's authority," said Justice Gaston, was not law befitting a "Christian land" of "civilized people." Since there was no statutory law on the issue of provocation or the mistreatment of slaves, Gaston turned instead to the common law, which declared "passion, not transcending all reasonable limits, to be distinct from malice. . . . The prisoner is a human being, degraded indeed by slavery, but yet having organs, dimensions, senses, affections [and] passions like our own." The supreme court found that Will had exhibited neither express nor implied malice and that his killing of Baxter was manslaughter, not murder. North Carolina probably accepted the concept of slave provocation because, unlike the other slave states, it did not have a law that protected slaves from cruel treatment and, therefore, slaves could not rely on the law to protect them in instances like those Justice Starnes had described in *Jim v. State*.[18]

To keep slaves in subjection, the law could not allow them to judge and act upon the violent actions of masters, mistresses, and overseers. But what of the violent provocation of whites who were not in authority over slaves? Could slaves meet violence with violence in confrontations with such whites where the aggressive force was less than deadly? In Georgia, the answer was no. In *John v. State*, in 1854, Chief Justice Joseph Henry Lumpkin ruled: "As to manslaughter; an offence, which, in the opinion of this Court, cannot exist under our law, as between a slave and a free white person, where the former is the slayer. That every such killing is murder or justifiable homicide." Lumpkin observed that there might be circumstances under which a slave would have to "take the life of a white man to save his own, who has no right to punish or control him in any manner whatever," in which case the killing might be "excusable," but he had "formed no very definite opinion upon this subject." But the "stern and unbending necessity" of slavery forbade "that any such allowance should be made for the infirmity of temper or passion on the part of a slave, as to reduce or mitigate his crime from murder to manslaughter."[19]

In other words, a slave could kill a white person to save his own life—and his master's property—but had to accept non-lethal attacks on himself. With this ruling, Georgia was in line with most of the other slave states. North Carolina and Tennessee were the only two states in the antebellum years to expressly rule that a homicide where whites not in authority over the slave defendant could be reduced from murder to manslaughter, if there had been sufficient provocation. But, even in these states, what constituted provocation differed from the standard applied in cases involving whites. Slaves occupied the lowest societal rung and therefore were already considerably degraded; hence, acts that would be considered provocation for whites, like assault or battery, were insufficient. Only if the physical attack was fairly serious in nature could it be considered mitigating provocation, a determination to be left to individual juries. In an examination of several thousand cases from around the South, the historian Thomas D. Morris could find not a single case in which a trial jury reduced a charge from murder to manslaughter.[20] Apparently, Southern juries did not believe that there was anything a white person could do—short of attempted murder—that justified deadly violence by a slave.

The legal rationale for not allowing slaves to be charged with manslaughter in the deaths of whites was that doing so would weaken slavery. If so, free blacks should have been able to avail themselves of the manslaughter statute, and in one Georgia county in 1857 one free black man did. Milledge Gay had a reputation in his Newton County neighborhood for being extremely cruel to Negroes. In March, Gay found a hole in the wall of his smokehouse and concluded that some of his meat had been stolen (although there was no conclusive evidence that anything had been taken) and that Michael Davis, a free person of color, had committed the theft. Gay said if he caught up with Davis, he would send him "to the other side of the Jordan." He did find Davis. He tied him to his horse and whipped him. He released Davis, but later he went back to find Davis to beat him again. As Gay led Davis along the road back to the scene of the first whipping, the pair saw a snake. Gay decided to kill it, and Davis picked up a lightwood stick and helped. Once the snake was dead, Gay turned his back on Davis, who seized the moment and struck Gay on the head with his club. Still conscious, Gay threatened to kill Davis, who struck him again and left him on the road to die. The prosecutor tried Davis in Newton County Superior Court, and the jury convicted him of manslaughter and sentenced him to the lash.

Davis's manslaughter conviction was based largely on Gay's reputation for cruelty and his mistreatment of the free man.[21] This ruling was not binding on other jurisdictions, and the issue of free blacks and manslaughter was never brought before the supreme court. While it is not possible to predict accurately how an appellate court would rule on an issue, considering the Georgia Supreme Court's commitment to slavery and its desire to deny free blacks the benefits of citizenship, it is hard to imagine the court siding with a free black like Davis. In most instances, the goal was to treat free blacks as if they were slaves under the criminal law. This case is informative not only on free blacks' relationship with the law, but also on their anomalous position in society as well. Gay treated Davis—a free man—like a slave; he could be bound and beaten with impunity. If Gay was confident enough to whip a free man like a slave, no doubt other men felt the same, and acted accordingly.

Murder

Murder was the most frequently prosecuted crime in the period from 1755 to 1865, accounting for more than 35 percent of all indictments and accusations, nearly twice that of the nearest crime, assault with intent to kill. This high percentage of prosecutions is not surprising, since murder was the most serious crime and the most difficult to conceal. Although 34 percent of Georgia's murder victims are not identified in the record, in all likelihood the greater part of these victims were white, because they were the majority in all other categories of violent crime except manslaughter. Of those whose identities are known, nearly 26 percent were white men, 23.8 percent were slave men, 5.4 percent were white women, and 2 percent were slave women. Seven and one-half percent of all victims were blacks whose sex and status are not known.[22] While it is not clear whether the majority of murder victims was white, it is telling that the largest groups of known victims were white men and slave men, the two groups most likely to find themselves in violent confrontation.

The true nature of homicide cases is revealed in the relationship between murderers and their victims. Of those whose relationship to the defendant could be determined, almost 42 percent were slaves' relatives or acquaintances, and 27.4 percent were masters, mistresses, or overseers. Nearly 29 percent were white people whose relationship to the defendant is not known; just over 2 percent of murder victims were free black kin or acquaintances.[23] The high percentage of murders of friend or relations is to be expected, because murder historically has been a crime that grows out of close personal interaction; stranger-on-stranger murder has been the exception rather than the rule. So, too, the relatively high proportion of master-class victims is also indicative of the deadly tensions intimacy and the conditions of slavery often produced. When the numbers of black and white victims within farm and plantation households and extended networks of kin and friends are combined (69.1 percent), it becomes clear that these private spaces were far more dangerous than public ones.

Most blacks accused of murder were slave men, accounting for 85 percent of homicide defendants. Slave women made up the next largest group, at nearly 13 percent, followed by free black men, at 2 percent. No free women ever faced murder charges.[24] And, of all crimes, murder was the one most likely to involve co-conspirators, with forty-three cases involving multiple offenders. Murder was also the only crime to involve more than four perpetrators (see table 1). Whites were generally the victims in multi-offender crimes; only four cases where blacks were the victims involved more than one perpetrator, compared to seventy-seven cases for white victims (see table 2). In all likelihood, the pattern of multi-assailant murder is explained by the fact that most murders occurred spontaneously during conflicts between two men. Slaves who conspired to kill were most likely acting on a collective grievance; occasions were probably rare when a single slave adversely affected a group of slaves to the point where murder seemed the most viable solution. The nature of slavery dictated that any number of whites might find themselves in this kind of deadly and adversarial relationship with slaves; all masters, mistresses, and overseers—in theory—were in this position.

The most common weapons used in murders and serious assaults in colonial and antebellum Georgia were clubs, knives, axes, and hands and feet—a distribution of weapons typical of antebellum America among whites and blacks, North and South.[25] In Philadelphia, the knife or razor was the weapon of choice among black murderers, accounting for the majority of deaths; only one defendant used a firearm. Firearms were much more

TABLE 1. PRESENCE OF CO-DEFENDANTS BY CRIME

Crime		Number of Co-defendants			
		1	2	3	4
Murder	Number of cases	21	13	4	5
	% within crime	14.3	8.8	2.7	3.4
	% within number of co-defendants	35.6	50.0	33.3	83.3
Attempted murder	Number of cases	4		4	
	% within crime	5.1		5.1	
	% within number of co-defendants	6.8		33.3	
Arson	Number of cases	2	3	4	
	% within crime	4.7	7.0	9.3	
	% within number of co-defendants	3.4	11.5	33.3	
Poisoning	Number of cases	1	1		
	% within crime	14.3	14.3		
	% within number of co-defendants	1.7	3.8		
Burglary	Number of Cases	17	4		
	% within crime	32.7	7.7		
	% within number of co-defendants	28.8	15.4		
Rape	Number of cases	2			
	% within crime	11.8			
	% within number of co-defendants	3.4			

Source: See appendix.

common items in the rural, frontier South than in the urban, developed North. In South Carolina, most murders by both whites and blacks were accomplished with knives or clubs, not guns. For example, in the Horry District, stabbing led shooting by a ratio of 5 to 3. In Edgefield, killers made use of weapons other than firearms in twenty-four of thirty-seven murders. South Carolinians who did not employ knives or clubs to kill each other chose rocks, axes, and an array of poisons.[26] In Georgia, assailants used firearms in twenty cases, 16.9 percent of the total. This use of firearms by even

TABLE 2. PRESENCE OF CO-DEFENDANTS BY VICTIM STATUS

Number of co-defendants		Victim Status						
		Slave male	Slave female	White male	White female	Free black male	White person[a]	Black person[b]
0	Number of cases	34	3	86	42	2	65	14
	% within number of co-defendants	10.9	1.0	27.6	13.5	0.6	20.8	4.5
	% within victim status	94.4	100.0	64.2	85.7	100.0	73.0	87.5
1	Number of cases	2		22	4		11	2
	% within number of co-defendants	3.4		37.3	6.8		18.6	3.4
	% within victim status	5.6		16.4	8.2		12.4	12.5
2	Number of cases			9	3		10	
	% within number of co-defendants			34.6	11.5		38.5	
	% within victim status			6.7	6.1		11.2	
3	Number of cases			9			3	
	% within number of co-defendants			75.0			25.0	
	% within victim status			6.7			3.4	
4	Number of cases			6				
	% within number of co-defendants			100.0				
	% within victim status			4.5				
Unknown	Number of cases			2				
	% within number of co-defendants			100.0				
	% within victim status			1.5				
Total	Number of cases	36	3	134	49	2	89	16
	% within number of co-defendants	8.6	0.7	32.1	11.8	0.5	21.3	3.8
	% within victim status	100.0	100.0	100.0	100.0	100.0	100.0	100.0

Source: See appendix.

[a] Gender unknown.

[b] Status and gender unknown.

that many black murderers strongly suggests that arms were more widely available to slaves and free blacks than is commonly thought, and that whites who passed legislation to limit blacks' access to them were acting on a real rather than imagined threat.

Whites considered slave murderers to be one of two types. The first was the "bad nigger"—a unique and enigmatic plantation character—a slave who broke with convention, disregarded the white man's law, and was not afraid to strike out against anyone, black or white, bold or stupid enough to cross him. Many masters owned at least one bondsman whom they feared would kill them if given the chance. A Georgia planter described Jack, his slave carpenter, as "the most notoriously bad character and worst Negro of the place." He was "the only Negro ever in our possession who I considered capable of Murdering me, or burning my dwelling at night, or capable of committing any act." "Bad niggers" refused to submit to discipline. Available sources on the plantation experience are replete with examples of slaves who would not allow masters and overseers to whip them. Such cases occurred in every part of the South. Every district, if not every plantation, had at least one or two. Such men and women had to be handled with extreme severity. As one overseer told the landscape architect and journalist Frederick Law Olmstead, "Some negroes are determined never to let a white man whip them and will resist you, when you attempt it; of course you must kill them in that case."[27]

The response to "bad niggers" in the slave quarters was contradictory. On the one hand, slaves applauded and revered those who were brave enough to stand up for themselves in a system that punished such defiance swiftly and severely. Ex-slaves from around the South spoke often of "bad niggers" they had known or heard about. Robert Falls proudly recalled that his father was "so bad to fight and so troublesome" that his masters had sold him no fewer than four times. His mother was equally incorrigible; her owner, too, had sold her, but the slave traders brought her back when they found that they could not handle her. Sarah Wilson recalled Uncle Nick, a slave who regularly fought whites and stole food to feed hungry slaves. On the other hand, these desperadoes did not necessarily distinguish between whites and blacks, and slaves, too, often found themselves the victims of the "bad nigger's" unpredictable rage. The ex-slave James Lucas remembered them as "mean slaves, de same as dey was mean marsters." One former slave woman neatly summed up the modus operandi of the breed: "He am big and 'cause he so, he think everybody do what him say." Slaves often found themselves in need of protection from such plantation bullies. The "bad nigger" was a tragic figure and a bad example. Many found themselves physically and emotionally broken or dead, a negative object lesson for all.[28]

While "bad niggers" were certainly terrifying, the ones whites should have feared most were those they considered to be "good" slaves—those who displayed no outward signs of animus or aggression. These seemingly trustworthy and innocuous slaves could lash out violently, often without warning, and usually in response to some provocation. The act that initiated the violent backlash might have been one committed many times before, but on this occasion it was more than the bondsperson could bear. The most common spark for this explosion was a whipping or other attempt at discipline.[29]

In February 1850, Thomas Heath, overseer on the plantation of Harry Harris in Meriwether County, approached Monroe, a slave, and ordered him to join several other slaves in milling logs on another part of the plantation. Monroe refused. He did not want to be "running all over the plantation." Heath pulled out his whip and lashed Monroe, who grabbed a large stick that was lying nearby and struck Heath on the head. The overseer attempted to get up from the ground and Monroe hit him again. Heath died from his wounds. Witnesses described Monroe as a good and peaceful slave; he and Heath had experienced no prior difficulties. Other Georgia overseers suffered Heath's fate. In 1829, three slaves murdered Malcolm Dickerson, an overseer on a Green Island plantation; the slaves struck Dickerson on the head with an ax and buried him in a marsh. The same end awaited the overseer on the Dougherty County plantation of William S. Holt. This overseer was planning to whip a slave when the slave fled into a swamp. The overseer directed two slaves to help him search for the runaway. The group caught up with the fugitive, but the three slaves then jumped the unsuspecting overseer, disemboweled him, and dumped his body in the swamp. A slave killed the overseer Patrick Carrol in 1860 when he instructed the slave to complete a task. The two argued, and the slave struck and killed Carrol with a fence rail.[30]

Like slave men, slave women struck out with homicidal violence to avoid physical abuse. Sarah was working on her master's Meriwether County plantation when the overseer, Jenkins, approached and demanded she put down the fence rail she was holding because he intended to whip her. She complied, and Jenkins struck her with a switch. It broke, and Jenkins tried to lash Sarah with a second switch. It also broke. He then jumped behind

Sarah and grabbed her. The bondswoman struck Jenkins in the shoulder, and he fell away. Bystanders did not immediately realize what had happened until they saw the blood pouring from Jenkins's shoulder and the knife in Sarah's hand. <u>She had severed Jenkins's carotid artery;</u> he bled to death in a matter of minutes. Witnesses later reported that they had seen Sarah "fingling with that knife" before. On that fateful day in 1858, it was put to much more serious use.[31]

Many slaves surely fantasized about killing their masters, waiting for the opportunity. Such an opportunity came for one group of Laurens County slaves in the summer of 1860. On the day before Independence Day, their master William Rogus lay asleep, the casualty of a drinking spree. His wife had left him to sleep it off. Dick, Nelly, Caroline, Josephine, and Bibb knew this might be their only chance to kill their owner; no other white people were around and their victim was drunk. Nelly stood guard outside the house while the others entered Rogus's bedroom. Dick went in first and unexpectedly found his master awake; he asked Dick why he was there. Dick said nothing and rushed to the bed, followed closely by the other three. Dick grabbed Rogus by the throat; the choking man tried to reach into his pocket but one of the other slaves stayed him. Rogus eventually fell motionless. Not convinced that they had killed their master, Dick and one of the women placed a length of homespun around his neck and pulled it until they were sure he was dead. One of the women planted a bottle of laudanum on the bed, to create the impression that Rogus had died from a drug overdose. The group went back to the field and pretended that nothing had happened. They had seized a perfect opportunity, but perhaps it was too perfect: a dead master with neck injuries and no other persons in the vicinity but his slaves provided the authorities with rather obvious suspects. <u>Under questioning, they all confessed, and the state executed them</u>.[32]

No matter how congenial relations appeared to be between master and slave, violence, even if only implied, maintained the relationship. In circumstances of such constant tension, violence could erupt unexpectedly, catching both assailant and victim by surprise. That is what occurred between Aaron and his mistress, Sheleneth Allums. Aaron had been a slave on the Allums plantation his entire life. His master's son described Aaron as an "obedient slave" who was of "entirely sound mind"; he was a "good nigger." This made the events of January 11, 1857, all the more shocking. Aaron had choked his mistress, bashed in her skull with a rock, and left her in a field to die. He had returned to the field a short time later and had found Allums trying to crawl home. He picked her up and helped her walk to the plantation house, then went to find a doctor. Mistress Allums died three weeks later. Aaron had attempted to kill his mistress because she was planning to destroy his animal traps; in a fit of anger, he lashed out. In that moment, Aaron could take no more of having someone else take every significant decision in his life. After the assault, he returned to being the apparently non-violent man he had been. The county executed Aaron. Slavery had cost two people their lives.[33]

Even children were not immune to the violence that plagued slave Georgia. On March 24, 1852, Burrell, an eleven-year-old slave belonging to Pliny Sheffield, took his master's four-year-old son John and four other slave children into the woods to play. This was probably not unusual; Burrell was John's nurse and had been since the boy was old enough to require one. Pliny Sheffield described Burrell as "a good nurse" who was both "sensible" and "shrewd." Exactly what happened in the woods we will probably never know, but John Sheffield ended that day with a fatal head wound. Burrell said John had been injured when a tree fell on him. Pliny, the elder Sheffield, did not believe the story and chained Burrell to a fence and whipped him. Burrell did not change his account. Sheffield beat him some more. Burrell continued to say a falling tree had killed John. The next day, Sheffield jailed Burrell without a warrant. He remained imprisoned for two months. The jailer and another white man both reported they had heard Burrell say on several occasions that he had killed his young master with an ax but that it was an accident. These confessions were supposedly made spontaneously, because the jailer never questioned Burrell; he did admit to beating the slave, but only once. At trial, a slave woman testified that Burrell did have an ax on the day of the incident. A doctor testified that if a tree had caused the wound, there would have been scratches on the dead boy's face; but there were none. Did John Sheffield die as a result of some boyish roughhousing, or a tree's falling, or had a black child, who was already psychologically overwhelmed by having to live his life as a human being and a thing, killed him in cold blood? A jury could not decide and acquitted Burrell.[34]

Violent assaults on whites in authority were relatively infrequent, but their impact on plantation communities was far greater than their actual numbers would suggest. Whites were paranoid about slave violence. The memory of a slave killing her mistress remained rooted in the community's consciousness for years, even if the murder had occurred in a neighboring county. Whites talked about it, and any instance of disobedience among slaves served as a reminder. This was especially true if the crime was of a particularly grisly nature.

On May 6, 1860, Joe, a Screven County slave, killed Reuben Blackburn, a white man. How Joe killed Blackburn certainly burned an indelible and horrifying image onto the psyches of white county residents and those whites nearby. Joe struck his victim in the head with an ax, causing a wound three inches long and two inches deep. The slave then proceeded to beat and strangle the already dying man, and concluded his bloody business by setting Blackburn on fire. Masters were clearly concerned about this kind of violence and alarmed when they learned of the murder of a fellow slaveowner or overseer, and yet, paradoxically, after a short while they reassured themselves that they were perfectly safe among their own slaves. Most routinely left doors unlocked, allowed slaves to possess firearms, axes, and other deadly implements, and even considered slaves their protectors against outside dangers.[35] Masters and mistresses had to convince themselves that their slaves were harmless and that they were themselves safe; thinking about the real possibility of violent death at the hands of their slaves would have made it impossible for them to rule over those they owned.

Insurrection

Even more than individual acts of slave violence, the specter of collective violence, insurrection, truly alarmed white Georgians. Between 1755 and 1865, counties indicted or charged four slaves with insurrection; juries acquitted three, and the governor pardoned one. No convictions occurred, because the acts had not met the statutory definition of the crime. In March 1861, the Wilkes County grand jury charged Willis with insurrection because he had attempted to "injure and kill" several white men using a handgun; Willis entered a plea of guilty to battery, and the court sentenced him to 195 lashes over the course of fifty days. There is only one documented incident of true slave insurrection in Georgia and it occurred in St. Andrew's Parish in 1774. Approximately one dozen newly arrived Africans killed their overseer and his wife and mortally wounded a white carpenter on the plantation of one Captain Morris. The band then proceeded to a nearby plantation and seriously injured its owner, Angus McIntosh. One of

McIntosh's slaves seized the opportunity to gain his freedom and joined the rebels. Moving on through the neighborhood, they attacked one Roderick McLeod and murdered his son. Apparently, the younger McLeod had seen the group coming and attempted to challenge them. Parties unknown ended the bloody march later that day.[36]

While only one insurrection had led to deaths of whites, a number of insurrection scares kept the white community's nerves on edge. On October 4, 1831, just two months after Nat Turner's slave uprising in Virginia, a rumor swept through Milledgeville, Georgia, that a large number of slaves were in rebellion less than a dozen miles from the city, en route to seize weapons from the state arsenal. The governor dispatched the militia, and private citizens armed themselves and took to the streets. Although the rumor proved to be unfounded, the sheriff arrested three slaves and a free black minister on suspicion of involvement in the conspiracy. Authorities released them later after no substantive evidence could be found to substantiate the insurrection or to link them to the plot. Two weeks after the Milledgeville scare, another occurred in nearby Dublin. Law enforcement officials arrested six slaves and accused them of attempting to stir their fellow slaves to revolt; four hanged. Four years later, authorities uncovered an insurrectionary plot along the Florida border; several lumbermen from Maine supposedly instigated that conspiracy.

In 1835, the mayor of Savannah investigated rumors that persons unknown were distributing insurrectionary literature to the slave population and that a mass uprising was imminent. Only a few pamphlets turned up at the post office. In that same year, Monroe County whites began to hear rumors that slaves in neighboring Macon possessed abolitionist tracts. Talk of insurrection commenced and continued into the fall. The gossip was given a measure of substance when a group of slaves at a camp meeting discussed loose plans to stage a revolt on the upcoming election day, when most white men would be preoccupied with voting and alcohol. The plot was discovered and its principal instigator hanged. In Augusta, in 1841, a slave hanged after authorities accused him of hatching a plot to seize the arsenal, fire the city, and massacre the citizenry. One of the most serious scares occurred in Crawford County in November 1860, when the prospect of Abraham Lincoln's election stirred whites' fears of slave rebellion. At the instigation of a local tinsmith, a group of slaves planned to rise up and take over the county while all the white men were in Knoxville, the county seat, casting their votes on election day. When one slave conspirator revealed the plan to the authorities, the tinsmith was hanged.[37]

The Politics of Black Criminality

Historians have long debated patterns of slave resistance, and many have stopped short of calling some acts legitimate resistance, because the acts lacked a political dimension, were not collective, or did not represent a threat to the entire slave regime. But, as the anthropologist James Scott observes, only "under the most extraordinary historical circumstances," when the "near total collapse" of existing structures of power and domination occurs, can truly open action or discourse from subordinates be expected to arise. Such conditions did exist from time to time in the Caribbean, seldom in North America. American slaves, unlike West Indian slaves, were usually outnumbered and outgunned; they had few areas like the mountainous regions of the Caribbean islands that could be used for permanent refuge. Most slaves knew that insurrection was a fool's errand.

Scholars have also viewed crime as a non-political activity. But Cesare Lombroso, the founder of modern criminology, defines political crime as "any action that attacks the legal system, the historical and social traditions of a society, or any part of the existing social fabric, and which consequently collides with the law." In a general sense, in my view, all crime against oppressors can be described as political resistance, because criminal prohibitions represent a society's effort to defend some of the most cherished values of those in power, as well as their interests and beliefs. The latter is especially true when those subject to the criminal laws are seldom protected by them and have had no voice in making them, as was the case with blacks in Georgia and elsewhere in the South in the colonial and antebellum years. But did this make every slave or free black who committed a crime a political rebel? Black political rebels are ordinarily compared to Gabriel or Denmark Vesey—oppressed blacks whose plots had clear and collective political agendas. The vast majority of black criminal defendants in Georgia did not display this kind of overt political consciousness. And yet this lack of collective political consciousness does not negate the political effects of criminal activity. The historian Philip Schwarz, for example, argues that legislatures enacted slave codes for political purposes, hence violations of those laws by blacks were "political in effect even when they were not politically motivated."[38]

If politics is considered the contestation of power within a sovereign body, acts of criminality on the plantation (viewed, conceptually and ideologically, as a sovereign entity and often functioning as such) were certainly political. Slaves engaged in behavior that threatened or altered the power arrangements on their farms or plantations clearly were engaging in political behavior, whether they conceived of it in such terms or not. Premeditated and collective murder of a master or mistress could well be so considered.[39] The political dimensions of the situation are apparent if we see the criminal justice system as white Georgians saw it. When they designed the criminal law for themselves, they created a dual system of obligations and protections, based on mutual consent. But in the system they created for blacks, they erected a system designed to keep blacks in subjection and to ensure a one-sided distribution of power. Lawmakers crafted the criminal law to control blacks, not to protect them as victims of crimes. The goals of the law were undisguised and explicitly political. Blacks who consistently broke this law threatened this power arrangement.

Slavery did not operate as whites hoped. Criminal acts by blacks forced whites to change the law and their own personal and collective behavior. When blacks and whites confronted each other in courtrooms and on plantations over violations of the formal and informal criminal law, they did so from diametrically opposed points of view. They faced each other in the majority of instances with divergent goals and values: whites, through law, force, custom, and tradition, sought to keep blacks in a perpetual state of personal and racial subordination; blacks sought to resist this dominion.[40] Black criminality was as political as white law.

"Negroes might cut the throats of our people and run to the Spaniards," said the Earl of Egmont in 1741, speaking of his fear of slave violence in Georgia.[41] This fear, in fact, had sustained his own opposition to slavery, because he knew that force maintained slavery and that some slaves—maybe many, if conditions were right—would meet force with force, and even kill to secure their freedom. Every day, whites and slaves confronted each other, with violence an ever present possibility. Legislators built a legal system to control black violence, one that was largely illegitimate to many blacks who came in contact with it. Enslaved men and a small number of slave women did assault and kill whites, a significant minority of them masters, mistresses, or overseers. This violence was often the product of conflicts that occurred when whites sought to discipline slaves, when slaves tried to free themselves, or when slaves were unable to contain their rage against the lack of control in the most important aspects of their lives—such as keeping themselves, their spouses, and children from being sold, or from being beaten, or worse.

Free blacks were responsible for few violent assaults or murders. Perhaps they saw little reason to resort to violence, since they were not subjected to the same brutalities and daily attempts at white control as slaves. Because they did not live on plantations, they no doubt had fewer occasions for inter-racial antagonism. They also knew that, unlike slaves, they had no one to protect them as an owner might protect the slaves who were the core of his economic worth and his source of political power, from irate individual whites or from vigilantes. Free blacks knew that it was probably best to steer clear of violent clashes or provocation of whites, which was difficult to do in a society dedicated to preserving racial dominion through force and violence.

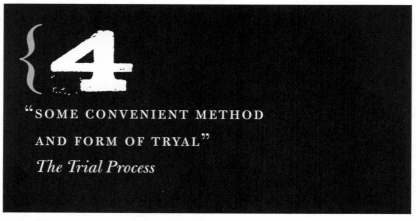

{4

"SOME CONVENIENT METHOD

AND FORM OF TRYAL"

The Trial Process

The worst system which could be devised . . .
—*Judge John Belton O'Neall,*
  South Carolina Court of Law and Errors, 1848

For white Georgians, the blacks in their midst constituted a dangerous internal enemy—one whose behavior had to be strictly controlled. Georgia legislators crafted a criminal justice system that charged masters with maintaining their slave forces in due subordination, and granted them wide latitude to enable them to do so. Slave owners detected crimes, adjudicated cases, and punished offenders with relatively little interference from the outside world. In this informal plantation justice system, offenders could be tried, convicted, and punished in a matter of minutes, with no avenue of appeal beyond the master's conscience. An elaborate formal criminal justice system awaited those bondspeople who violated interests outside their plantations or farms. By the late antebellum period, this formal system mirrored that of whites in almost every respect, but the consequences for black defendants were far different. Despite increasing legal protections, blacks were convicted at rates that far exceeded those of white defendants. Whites' commitment to slavery and to maintaining their superior racial position produced this disparate treatment.

{ The Plantation Trial Process

One Georgia ex-slave said, "I never heard of or knew of a slave being tried in a court for anything." Slaves were judged, but not by courts or juries. Slaveholders were the prosecutors, judges, and juries. Most former slaves queried by the WPA (Works Progress Administration) interviewers during the Great Depression could remember no instance (in the late antebellum period) of a slave on trial in a court or jailed by the government for a crime committed on the plantation, not even for murder. "Marster never had to take none of his Niggers to court or put 'em in jail neither; him and de overseer sot 'im right," said another Georgia ex-bondsman. With rare exceptions, farm or plantation crimes never made their way to state courts. The quality of justice slaves received depended on the sense of justice their masters and mistresses possessed.[1]

What actually happened to the thousands and thousands of slaves found guilty or innocent, punished by whipping or mutilation, or sold off the plantation by masters, no one can say for sure. Their "trials" took place on private property, beyond the prying eyes and review of the public. But South Carolina planter, politician, and proslavery ideologue James Henry Hammond boasted: "On our estates we dispense with the whole machinery of public police and public courts of justice. Thus we try, decide, and execute the sentences, in thousands of cases, which in other countries would go into the courts."[2]

The Old South ideal of mastery decreed that the planter/slaveowner was a judge—of a slave's productivity in work and in breeding; of a slave's deference, sociability, and health; and of all other matters related to the smooth functioning of his economic and social enterprise. The slaveholder's principal responsibility was to assess the behaviors of all his dependents, family and slaves alike, and to take preventative, corrective, or punitive action when the situation seemed to him to demand it. This process of largely unmonitored private judgment extended from the control of ordinary living to the acts of slaves who violated a plantation criminal code that the slaveholder himself had crafted; as its drafter, he was considered best qualified to interpret and implement it. The historian Philip J. Schwarz describes slaveowners and their agents, the overseers, as "the first rule-makers, the corrections officers, and even sometimes the executioners" in the plantation criminal justice system. Like monarchs, masters had to "answer to few people," ruled in "almost complete privacy," and were, in the end, the supreme authorities on their lands.[3]

Slave narratives in Georgia and elsewhere are replete with examples of masters and overseers who rendered judgment and sentenced slaves to the lash—or worse. In best-case scenarios, a trial of sorts took place. On one

Georgia estate, the master produced one or two of the involved parties as witnesses. The judge-master interviewed these people in the presence of the accused, then allowed the slave defendant to correct their testimony and to seek to establish innocence through other evidence. The slave driver was usually the one to provide such additional testimony; if the driver were absent, and the case an important one, the slaveowner postponed the hearing until the driver could be produced. After hearing the evidence on both sides, the master—as both judge and jury—announced his judgment as to guilt or innocence and promptly handed down and carried out the sentence, or ordered the driver, overseer, or another slave to do so. Slaves were expected to accept whatever verdict their owner delivered, because the master was, by definition, both "lawgiver and judge," and also, in the paradoxical paternalist ideal, "protector and friend."[4]

In rare cases, masters allowed slaves themselves to take part in the judging process. On Jefferson Davis's Mississippi estate, for example, no slave could be punished unless convicted by a jury of slave peers. Davis forbade his overseers to use the lash to correct recalcitrant bondspeople unless a slave jury had found them guilty at trial.[5] At the other end of the spectrum, masters and overseers dispensed with even the appearance of due process. If a slave committed an act in his presence, the judge-master responded immediately with the whip, with no allowance for arguments in rebuttal or mitigation. The historical record indicates that this mode of justice was the most common form in Georgia and the rest of the Slave South.

{ *The State Court Trial Process from 1755 to 1811*

If slave misconduct affected interests off owners' farms or plantations, the state courts held trials to judge those charged. On January 7, 1792, Will, a slave, appeared for trial in the courthouse at Washington County, Georgia, charged with the murder of his master, Philip Alston; we do not know how or the circumstances. A complaint had been made to a justice of the peace, and as the law required, four justices of the peace—Jared Irwin, John Watts, Benjamin Tennille, and Joseph Sessions—were summoned to preside over a jury of seven white freeholders (those who held title to real property). John Sheppard, Hugh Irwin, John Martin, Charles Sheppard, Alexander Irwin, John Stokes, and Benjamin Morrison were chosen. There were three witnesses present at the trial—one a juror, Benjamin Morrison; a Thomas

Ford; and Toney, a slave. Who these witnesses were, or what they testified to, is not known.

What happened during the trial itself is also not known, simply that "jurors sworn upon the Trial of the Prisoner at the Bar" found Will guilty.[6] The court pronounced the sentence: "You Negro Will; be remanded back to the gaol and between the hours or eleven and one o'clock you be taken out by the proper officer and be hung by the neck near the Courthouse till you be Dead, Dead, Dead and your head be cut off and stuck upon a pole near the place of execution."

Four months later to the day, on May 7, 1792, Sheriff William Brinson reported back to the court that he had hanged Will, decapitated his body, and placed his severed head on a pole near the courthouse; it would serve as a warning to would-be black murderers, and as reassurance for a nervous white populace.

The Georgia slave code of 1755 had set up "some Convenient Method and form of Tryal"—tribunals of justices of the peace and juries of freeholders—to try free blacks and slaves like Will. The most important people in the system of prosecution were the justices—in the colonial and antebellum periods seldom lawyers, but all white men, usually respected, middle-aged or older, whom their neighbors considered to share a strong sense of justice. One antebellum jurist called the post of justice of the peace "an honorable and responsible office [that] opens an ample field for a gentleman to exert his talents by maintaining good order in his neighborhood." Under the Georgia constitution of 1798, county inferior courts nominated justices of the peace and the governor commissioned them. They served on condition of "good behavior," and could be removed if indicted or convicted in superior court for "malpractice in office," or of any "felonious or infamous crime." The governor could also remove them with the consent of two-thirds of both houses of the general assembly.[7]

Justices had high social and civic standing. Baldwin County justice John Mathews served, at various times, as county sheriff, jailer, secretary pro tempore of the county commissioners, school board functionary, intendant (mayor) pro tempore, and state legislator. Fellow Baldwin justice John W. Devereux was commissioner of the state penitentiary and postmaster; Goodwin Myrick was a leader of the state militia. They were often men of diverse talents. Justice Blandford of the Georgia Supreme Court said of these men, "A justice of the peace is generally a man of consequence in his neighborhood; he writes the wills, draws the deeds and pulls the teeth of the people; also he performs divers surgical procedures on the animals of his neighbors."[8]

Hearings before the justices were irregular, informal, and social in their settings, often held not in courthouses but in private homes or outdoors under the trees. Hiram Warner, a Georgia supreme court justice, described one hearing in 1822 in the home of Justice of the Peace Little of Houston County: "The Court sat in the other room of the house, which was uncovered except by the blue sky. In one corner of his chamber was a barrel of whisky, with faucet inserted ready for drawing."[9]

Justices eschewed formality and technicality in their "courtrooms," in favor of what they considered common sense and fair play. The fates of defendants were determined less by law and more by what those taking part thought appropriate in light of their own or their community's standards of justice. But these standards necessarily included prejudicial notions about blacks, slavery, and white supremacy. U. B. Phillips notes that courts of justices and freeholders displayed "vices in plenty," since neither judges nor juries were trained in the law and all were subject to the passions of the community. But Phillips, as a historian who was also a champion of the Old South, argues that the fact that the men who ran these courts were "intimately and more or less tolerably acquainted with negro nature in general and usually doubtless with the prisoner on trial" mitigated such failings, though the "rambling, mumbling, confused and baffling character of plantation negro testimony" made their task more difficult. Neighborhood jurors would be more favorably disposed toward the defendant than any impartial panel of strangers would be, their judgment based more on common sense than on the "particularities of the law."[10] Phillips assumed that the paternalism of Southern white men, many of them slaveholders, would safeguard the rights and lives of black defendants, both enslaved and free. The prejudices and dedication to slavery that these justices embodied worked against blacks on trial.

A complete dearth of trial transcripts makes it impossible to assess the quality of performance of these Georgia justices of the peace during the colonial and antebellum periods, but the fact that several states required the concurrence of other white men before a justice could pass sentence suggests that the state may have questioned their judgment and competence, most likely because of their lack of legal training. After the colonial period, most states would not allow justices to preside over cases that carried a possible sentence of death. Antebellum masters would not permit their slaves—who were, after all, valuable property—to be put to death on the sole judgment of these generally honorable but largely untrained men. In his 1848 compilation of South Carolina slave laws, Judge John Belton O'Neall called that state's justice and freeholder court system "the worst which could be devised." He urged the legislature to get rid of it, on the grounds that the passions and prejudices of the neighborhoods in which the crime occurred unduly influenced courts, leading to the "condemnation" of "innocent" black defendants.[11]

The State Court Trial Process from 1812 to 1849

In 1811, Georgia's general assembly transferred jurisdiction for the trial of capital offenses from the justices of the peace to the inferior courts. The assembly itself appointed the justices of the inferior courts; the governor commissioned them. Justices held their office as long as they demonstrated "good behavior." The governor could remove a justice, but only with the consent of two-thirds of both houses of the legislature or if convicted of a crime. In 1819, the legislature amended the state constitution so that county citizens could elect inferior court justices directly—five justices for each county. Much of what has been said of justices of the peace can also be said of justices of the inferior courts; most were not trained lawyers, and county residents considered most of them upstanding members of their communities. During the early period, the state did not pay justices for their service. Later, the justices would set their own salaries—not less than $50 and no more than $200 a year—the salary commensurate with the part-time nature of the position.[12]

Although untrained in the law, like justices of the peace, justices of the inferior court were highly respected and often drawn on for posts of civic leadership. In Baldwin County, between 1812 and 1838, the seventeen justices of the inferior court held among them nine state offices, eight county offices, four citywide offices, seven leadership positions in the state militia, one national office, and six other positions of significant civic responsibility, such as minister and newspaper editor. What they lacked in legal training and acumen they made up, at least in the minds of their white constituencies, in character, good judgment, and leadership ability. After a stint in his youth as clerk to former governor William Stephens, David B. Mitchell, the most accomplished Baldwin County justice, was elected solicitor general of his militia district and state legislator, and appointed major-general in the state militia. In 1809, he was elected governor, and a few years later, President James Monroe designated him agent to the Creek Nation. Thereafter, Mitchell "retired" to become a justice of the inferior court.[13]

Justices of the inferior court were hardly competent to deal with complex legal issues, particularly those of black capital cases. In an 1849 message to the legislature, Governor George W. Towns put the problem this way: "The justices of this Court are usually selected from citizens of the respective counties without special reference to their legal attainments:—and to impose upon them the responsibility of deciding complicated and vexed questions of law involving human life, is, to my mind, unjust to them as a Court, and not the most reliable mode of attaining the ends of justice by a fair trial in the due course of law."[14]

The trial process in the inferior court began much as it had in the past. A victim or witness made a formal complaint before a justice of the peace, who then issued a warrant for arrest and notified two or more fellow justices to assemble for a hearing within three days of the complaint. But now the process began to differ significantly. The purpose of the hearing was no longer to determine guilt or innocence, but jurisdiction. After hearing witnesses and evidence, the justices would decide if the acts cited deserved the death penalty. If not, the justices could hand down other punishments, "not extending to the taking away of life or member." If the offense was a capital one, the law required that the justices file a notice with a justice of the inferior court within three days after the end of their own proceedings, stating that someone had committed a capital crime that fell within the inferior court's jurisdiction. (This notice also included a list of witnesses.) The justices would send the slave or free black to the county jail to await trial; there were no provisions for bail. The initial inferior court justice ordered the county sheriff, again within three days, to summon a jury of white men for trial.

At trial, the clerk of the court read to the defendant an accusation laying out the time, place, and nature of the crime charged. A jury was sworn, and both sides presented and cross-examined witnesses and evidence. Trials took place under the same rules of evidence as used in cases against whites.[15]

Slave defendants could not testify on their own behalf. The owners of slaves charged with capital crimes had a vested interest in making sure that their property did not take the witness stand and make admissions that could cost them their lives. In the Georgia capital cases that make up this study, only two slave defendants testified between 1755 and 1865, both slaves without masters who might have forbidden them to tell their stories. One was a runaway, and the other had allegedly killed his master. Black defendants on trial, unable to speak for themselves, had to rely on their masters and lawyers to speak for them. Eighty-one defendants (19.4 percent) went to trial with attorneys, one (0.2 percent) did not, and the status of legal representation of the other 335 (80.3 percent) could not be determined. Still, these figures are far from accurate because of the nature of the record keeping. Most clerks did not record whether counsel represented slaves on trial. Only when mention of attorneys is made in the record did I include those cases in my computations; however, I did include all cases appealed on technical legal grounds, under the assumption that most such appeals would have been made only by a lawyer. It is probably safe to assume that wealthy planters provided counsel for slaves accused of crimes, and that less well-to-do slave owners, who could not afford to hire lawyers for their slaves, did not provide them. The number of slave defendants with attorneys is probably more than assumed here, but most likely far from 100 percent.

Georgia law did not require masters to provide counsel for slaves. In _Lingo v. Miller_, in 1857, the Georgia Supreme Court assumed that any master who did not hire a lawyer for his slave must have had a sound reason, in view of the value of the slave as property. "There are laws that impose various obligations on the master, but this obligation [to provide counsel] is not among them. . . . _Every_ master has an interest to prevent his slave from being punished, an interest which increases with the increase of the punishment to which the slave is exposed."[16]

Perhaps the leading legal authority in antebellum Georgia, Thomas R. R. Cobb, disagreed with the supreme court's decision in _Lingo v. Miller_. What the supreme court considered an option, Cobb said, was an obligation derived from the master's responsibility as paternalist: "It being the duty of the master to protect the slave, and furnish him everything necessary to that protection, he cannot abandon him when charged with an offense." Georgia did not begin to provide counsel for slaves whose masters refused to do so until the 1850s, well after Tennessee and a number of other slave states decided to do so. Georgia at that time did provide lawyers to indigent white defendants, one of the few Southern states that did.[17]

The failure to provide legal counsel in capital cases clearly worked against the black defendant, particularly after the turn of the nineteenth century, when legal professionals began to administer the courts. The accused who had lawyers entered fewer guilty pleas and had more of their cases dismissed before trial than those without lawyers, or whose representation status is not known. Two and one-half percent of defendants with lawyers entered guilty pleas, compared to 7.8 percent whose representation status is unknown. The single defendant who went to court without legal representation entered a guilty plea. Nolle prosequi orders were entered in 8.6 percent of cases where defense lawyers were present, compared to 6.3 percent of cases in which it is not known whether they were or not. Juries convicted almost 62 percent of those with lawyers, a higher than average rate, but this figure is deceptive since it is largely based on appellate cases, thus skewing the figures toward those convicted (see table 3). This also explains the lower than average percentage of those not indicted.

Legal representation for black defendants was hard to come by. Most Georgia counties had no bar at all during much of the antebellum period. Circuit-riding lawyers, those who traveled from county to county to attend court sessions, were the only counsel. Because a number of counties had no courthouses or judges, superior court judges made the rounds as well. Judges and lawyers traveled together, ate together, and stayed at the same taverns; the bar became a brotherhood—a close-knit relationship between judges and lawyers that inevitably opened the door to improper influence and prejudice against slave and free black defendants.[18] When the person on trial was an alienated racial Other with little that bound that person to the network of men who controlled his fate, the prevalent camaraderie among lawyers and judges could tip the already shaky scales of justice that much closer toward injustice.

After the presentation of evidence, the jury would retire to decide on a verdict of guilty or not guilty. An acquitted defendant could not be tried again; thus there was no double jeopardy. A legislative act of 1803 provided that "no slave shall be put on trial twice for one and the same offence," a protection guaranteed to whites in the U.S. Constitution. If the jury convicted a slave or free black, the court immediately pronounced a sentence, of death or of a punishment "not amounting to death." The county paid all costs of the prosecution of slaves that resulted in a death sentence, plus the costs of the execution itself. In non-capital cases, the owner of the convicted slave had to reimburse the court costs.[19]

Theoretically, the most important of the new capital trial rights the legislature had granted to blacks in 1811 was the right to trial by jury, with a requirement of a unanimous decision for a finding of guilt. Joseph Henry

TABLE 3. DEFENSE COUNSEL AND DISPOSITIONS, 1755–1865

Defense counsel		Disposition							
		Unknown	Plea of guilty	Nolle prosequi	Verdict of guilty	Verdict of not guilty	Not indicted	Mistrials	Total
Unknown	Number of cases	47	26	21	145	58	37	1	335
	% within defense counsel	14.0	7.8	6.3	43.3	17.3	11.0	0.3	100.0
	% within disposition	88.7	89.7	75.0	74.4	80.6	97.4	50.0	80.3
Yes	Number of cases	6	2	7	50	14	1	1	81
	% within defense counsel	7.4	2.5	8.6	61.7	17.3	1.2	1.2	100.0
	% within disposition	11.3	6.9	25.0	25.6	19.4	2.6	50.0	19.4
No	Number of cases		1						1
	% within defense counsel		100.0						100.0
	% within disposition		3.4						0.2
Total	Number of cases	53	29	28	195	72	38	2	417
	% within defense counsel	12.7	7.0	6.7	46.8	17.3	9.1	0.5	100.0
	% within disposition	100.0	100.0	100.0	100.0	100.0	100.0	100.0	100.0

Source: See appendix.

Lumpkin, the first chief justice of Georgia's supreme court, asserted in *Flint River Steamboat Company v. Foster,* in 1848, that trials by juries of "twelve" of a defendant's "honest and impartial neighbors" were essential guarantors of liberty. "In criminal proceedings, trial by jury cannot be too highly appreciated or guarded with too much vigilance. So long as this palladium and *Habeas Corpus* remain unimpaired, life and liberty are safe from passion, prejudice or oppression, no matter from what quarter they emanate."[20]

Sir William Blackstone, perhaps the most renowned authority on the English common law, wrote that "the truth of every accusation, whether preferred in the shape of indictment, information or appeal, should afterwards be confirmed by the unanimous suffrage of twelve of his [the defendant's] equals and neighbors, indifferently chosen, and superior to all suspicion." To Blackstone, summary trials conducted by justices of the peace, courts of conscience, and commissioners of revenue, while more efficient, worked against this principle and hence against the liberties of an individual on trial.[21]

Americans, both North and South, considered juries of local men vital to a fair trial. The Massachusetts constitution of 1780, for example, stated, "In criminal prosecutions, the verification of facts, in the vicinity where they happen, is one of the greatest securities of the life, liberty, and property of the citizen." Local jurors were in the best position to assess the character of witnesses and the veracity of their testimony. James Wilson, a Pennsylvania delegate to the constitutional convention, said, "Where jurors can be acquainted with the characters of the parties and the witnesses . . . they hear everything that is alleged; they not only hear the words, but they see and mark the features of the countenance; they can judge of weight due such testimony." No less an advocate for liberty than Patrick Henry of Virginia argued that juries composed of men distant from the place of prosecution would be unjust. There would be "no neighbors who are acquainted with their [the defendants'] characters, their good or bad conduct in life to judge of the unfortunate man who may be exposed to the rigors of government."[22]

Colonial juries in the trials of blacks in Georgia were composed of freeholders. The law said nothing more about their qualifications or about how these freeholders were to be selected. After 1811, the requirements did become clear. During regular terms of the inferior court, the justices were to select a venire of no fewer than twenty-six or no more than thirty-six white men who were eligible to vote for state legislators. The statute excluded black men. On the day of a trial, the sheriff was to summon twenty-four men. If any failed to show up, men in and around the courthouse could be selected to replace them. The slave code allowed the "owner or manager" of the slave on trial to challenge seven of the jury pool of twenty-four; the prosecution, five. The slave defendant could not challenge any of the prospective jurors. The twelve remaining men became the trial jury.

The law did not specify who made jury challenges for free blacks; some may have taken these decisions for themselves, and others may have had them taken by their state-appointed guardians. A free black could apply to the superior court to have a willing "white person resident in the County" act as his or her guardian. Guardians of free blacks had the same powers as those necessary for "the management of the persons and estates of infants." All civil lawsuits "brought for or against" free persons of color would be in the name of the "guardian, in his capacity as guardian." Since the guardians of free blacks were responsible for filing appeals and pardons on behalf of their convicted wards, one can reasonably assume that these white guardians took the decisions regarding challenges and all other aspects of the defense.[23]

Georgia was unique in the early national and antebellum periods in not requiring that jurors in slave trials be slaveholders themselves; other Southern states did. North Carolina, South Carolina, Louisiana, Alabama, Mississippi, and Tennessee, at various times in those decades, mandated that some, if not all, jurors be slaveholders. The historian Daniel Flanigan considers tensions between slaveholders and non-slaveholders responsible for the requirement that only slaveholders sit on juries during the trials of slaves, because planters feared that class-based animosity of white yeomen against the more affluent slaveholding class would lead to convictions that would result in considerable losses in slave property. North Carolina supreme court chief justice John Taylor, in the 1826 case *State v. Jim,* provides one of the clearest explanations of the need for slaveholding jurors. The slaveholder jury requirement, he wrote in the majority opinion, was "intended to surround the life of the slave with additional safeguards, and more effectually to protect the property of the owner by infusing into the trial, that temperate and impartial feeling, which would probably exist in persons owning the same sort of property." Slaveholding jurors possessed this equanimity because they too "had property constantly exposed to similar accusations," and "would not wantonly sacrifice the life of a slave." In the opinion of the North Carolina Supreme Court, "The property of a man is more secure when he cannot be deprived of it except by a Jury, part of whom, at least, have the like kind of property to lose."[24]

Only in North Carolina and Florida did the law require all jurors to be disinterested parties. A North Carolina statute of 1793 mandated that jurors "shall not be connected with the owner of such slave, or the prosecutor, either by affinity or consanguinity," and an 1829 Florida statute read: "No person having an interest in a slave shall sit upon the trial of such slave." In other states, the law made no express provisions; presumably, jury challenges would resolve any question of inappropriate interest.[25]

Under the English common law, on which Georgia law was grounded, two kinds of challenges to persons selected as jurors were possible: principal challenges, that is, challenges for cause; and peremptory challenges, those not based on specific and stated reasons. Both the representative of the slave prisoner and the representative of the state could challenge for cause because the juror in question was *propter noris respectum, propter defectum, propter affectum, or propter delictum* (dishonorable, prejudiced, a criminal, or someone with other discernible defects). In criminal cases, counsel for the accused could raise thirty-five peremptory challenges, one short of three full juries. The rationale for this large number was to ensure that the prisoner's right to an unbiased jury would be fully indulged, while at the same time guaranteeing that the process would not delay the proceedings indefinitely. Two reasons could be cited for peremptory challenges. First, individuals could discern prejudices in others without being able to base that assessment on some legally acceptable fact. Blackstone argued that the common law allowed a defendant to strike such jurors on this basis because he was entitled to "have a good opinion of his jury, the want of which might totally disconcert him; the law wills not that he should be tried by any one man against who he has conceived a prejudice, even without being able to assign a reason for such dislike." Second, a juror challenged for cause but nonetheless accepted might harbor resentment against the defendant.[26]

Although masters and lawyers for black defendants in Georgia could challenge jurors, the 1811 act did not specify whether these challenges were for cause, peremptory, or a combination of the two. In 1850, after lawmakers moved capital trials of slaves and free blacks from the inferior court to the superior court, the number of peremptory challenges increased from seven to twenty for the defendant and from five to ten for the state. In the other Southern states, except for Tennessee, legislators did not permit challenges for cause in slave trials until the 1850s. Tennessee allowed black defendants the same number of peremptory and challenges for cause it allowed white defendants, with challenges for cause usually based on suspicion of juror bias or lack of qualifications. Outside Tennessee, states did not initially extend the right to raise peremptory challenges to slave defendants at all.[27]

Masters and counsel alike seldom used challenges for cause, because they had to live afterward in the same neighborhood as the challenged jurors, but this reluctance to challenge left the way open for courts to call and choose prejudiced jurors. Even with peremptory challenges, juries might include biased jurors simply because of the limited number of challenges and the common prejudices against slaves and free blacks. It was nearly impossible, in any case, under the law to field an unbiased jury; communities were small, and slave crime, or the accusation of criminality, was often of such a nature as to excite the passions of the neighborhood. Despite that, judges rarely granted changes of venue. In 1856, challenges exhausted the initial panel of twenty-four jurors in the trial of Bob, a slave, in Chatham County, and the trial judge summoned twenty-four new jurors. The jury found Bob guilty, and the court sentenced him to hang.[28]

Since the goal of antebellum jury selection was not an impartial jury but its opposite—one composed of individuals who knew something of the crime, the accused, and the community—many Georgian and other Southern juries would have been wholly unacceptable in a modern trial. On petit juries, individuals served who were related to each other, or relatives of justices, or persons who had been jurors in similar proceedings—or who had been victims themselves of criminal acts of which blacks had been accused, witnesses in prior proceedings, or even judges. Of juries selected for the trials of slaves in Baldwin County between 1812 and 1838, fourteen trials made it through the process of jury selection, and in these trials, six jurors had served or later did serve on more than one trial, often the very next slave trial before the court. A number of jurors in three trials had the same surname, indicating that they may have been related. Several jurors shared the surname Bivens with Justice William Bivens of the inferior court. Two justices, William Ball and Myles Greene, were jurors in cases before the inferior court, both before and after they had served as justices of that court. One justice, Appleton Rosseter, was the victim of a theft allegedly committed by a slave who was later convicted in the court on which he served. Rosseter later presided over other theft and burglary cases involving slave defendants. Similar instances of probable family connections occurred in other Georgia counties. On juries in Campbell, Hancock, Columbia, Jones, and Greene counties, several jurors had the same surnames.[29] In a jury selection procedure that sought impartiality, a number of those jurors would have been automatically disqualified.

Georgia followed regional practice in its jury selection process. The historian Michael Hindus, in his study of antebellum South Carolina, found that trials were "procedurally incestuous"—that court officials drew juries from a relatively limited pool of white men in each county. Although men were only supposed to serve on juries no more than once every few years, Hindus found a small group of the same men appearing regularly in the trials of blacks. Family members often sat together on juries; in other instances, jurors had the same last names as the magistrates, or as the victims in the cases. Arthur Howington, in his study of antebellum Tennessee, found no individuals on juries who might have been family members or related to the owners of the slave on trial. But he did find, in slave trials in Williamson County, significant repetition among the members of both court and jury, with eight justices appearing in more than one case.[30] In the eight trials Howington examined, thirty-two jurors could have been called, but only twenty-six were; two sat on three trials. Considering the racial prejudices of the time, and selection practices that allowed a considerable degree of potential partiality, the fairness of any jury verdict for a black defendant may be considered suspect.

Martha Dumas was headed home and walking along the road from Mr. Harvey's place when Charles, one of her mother's slaves, asked her if she wanted "a good watermelon." This is how Dumas began her testimony of October 31, 1836, before Jones County justices of the peace Nathan Passion, John Williams, and Jethro Walker.[31] Dumas accused Charles of raping her. Dumas said she wanted the melon Charles offered and asked him to give it to her, whereupon he replied, "If it was not worth coming after it was not worth having." He pointed to a place over a fence and said the melon was there; Martha climbed the fence and found nothing. Charles walked toward her and told her "what he intended to do." Dumas said she fainted and, as she fell, Charles caught her by the throat and began choking her, pulled up her dress, and pulled down his pants, all the while continuing to strangle her. When she came to, Charles was sitting beside her. He said he was sorry, "God knew he was sorry." Dumas could not stand and asked Charles to help her up. When she found she could not walk, she called on Charles to assist her in getting home. On the way, Charles asked her to tell no one what had happened, and she agreed because she thought Charles might kill her if she did. When they arrived near the house, Charles said "that she had his life in her hands and a little while ago he had her life in his hands."

This lurid testimony was enough to persuade the justices to issue an arrest warrant accusing Charles of "<u>feloniously ravishing</u>" Martha Dumas. They bound the case over for trial in the inferior court at Clinton. Later that day, jailer G. W. Chase arrested Charles, and on November 9, Charles stood before Justices Jonathan Parrish, Sterling Smith, and John Relloon, and a jury of twelve white men.

The trial began. Clerk Charles Macarthy announced that the state was charging Charles with the rape of Martha Dumas. How did he plead to the charge? "Not guilty," said Charles. Martha Dumas was the first witness. Her testimony is not recorded, but she no doubt repeated the story she had told the justices of the peace. Her mother, Charles's owner, Matilda Dumas, was the next to speak. Around sundown on October 13, her daughter had come home. Charles was with her in the kitchen. Martha immediately went to lie down on the bed; she seemed to have a chill. At about ten o'clock, her temperature began to rise; her eyes were "as red as blood," and her face was bruised. She had marks on her throat. Matilda Dumas believed that someone had choked her daughter. Martha could not walk for the next five days. Matilda Dumas ended her testimony by saying that Charles had been working on the road near the Harveys.

Charles did not take the witness stand. The justices and jury heard his story from others. William Barrow testified that, on the previous Wednesday, he and Frederick Miller had gone to the jail to see Charles. Barrow asked Charles why he was in jail. He admitted he had raped his young mistress. Barrow said he did not promise Charles anything for this information, nor did he threaten him. Frederick Miller confirmed Barrow's testimony. Then David Tye, a jail employee, said he had placed leg irons on Charles when a constable brought him to the jail and, like Barrow, had asked Charles why he was in jail. Charles again replied that it was for raping Martha Dumas, "at the corn field of his mistress." Had Dumas cried out? Charles said she had tried to, but he had choked her to keep her quiet. Charles said he told his young victim he would be "avenged on her" if she told anyone. He had been thinking for three months about assaulting her. When Tye asked him why, what had made him do it? Charles answered simply, "the Old Devil."

Neither the prosecution nor the defense called additional witnesses. The court then gave the case to the jury for deliberation, after which jury foreman Davis Duncan read the verdict: "We the jury find the prisoner guilty." The justices passed sentence on the spot. Charles was to be taken back to the county jail and kept there until November 18, when he was to be removed "to a convenient gallows erected near the town of Clinton" and hanged, between "ten o'clock in the forenoon and two o'clock in the afternoon."

The State Court Trial Process from 1850 to 1865

In 1849, at the insistence of Governor George W. Towns, the legislature moved the trials of slaves and free blacks for capital crimes from the inferior court to the superior court. The law still required all free and enslaved suspects to appear before justices of the peace for a preliminary hearing to determine if the offense charged was a capital or non-capital crime. If the offense claimed was punishable by death, the justices could not send the case to the inferior court for trial. Instead, they were to put the defendant in jail, and on the first day of the next term of the superior court submit to the attorney or solicitor general a report of their findings and the evidence in the case. As prosecutor for the superior court, the solicitor or attorney general prepared a bill of indictment to present to the county grand jury, and if no victim appeared to complain, the solicitor general himself made the case, relying on the report and evidence from the preliminary hearing. If the grand jury found a "true bill," the accused went on trial in the superior court, "the rules of evidence in the trials . . . the same as in the trials of white persons."[32]

When, in 1850, the general assembly transferred the capital trials of blacks to the superior court, the judges who handled their cases were generally men of considerable legal acumen, trained lawyers and members of the Georgia bar, elected to three-year terms. The governor could remove them only with the consent of two-thirds of both houses of the legislature or by conviction and impeachment. These men were not only jurists and leaders in the legal community; they were also state and national political leaders. Thirty-eight superior court judges represented Georgia in the U.S. House and Senate, with nine going on to become governor. Former judges William H. Crawford and Henry R. Jackson served as U.S. secretary of state, and James M. Wayne served as a justice of the United States Supreme Court for more than thirty years.[33]

The most important of the post-1850 trial rights granted to slave and free black defendants was the requirement that all persons accused of capital crimes be indicted by the county grand jury, and that indictments be based on probable cause. Blackstone himself considered the grand jury, like the petit jury, a principal pillar of liberty. "No man should be called to answer to the king for any capital crime, unless upon the preparatory accusation of twelve or more of his fellow subjects, the grand jury."[34] But in the Slave South, the grand jury, like its trial counterpart, was of mixed value to black defendants. On one hand, a true bill of indictment required more than a dozen individuals to agree—a vastly better protector of black lives than the judgment of three justices of the peace. Indeed, because the prosecutor had to convince this larger body of citizens of diverse classes to indict, it increased the odds that no formal charge would be brought. On the other hand, grand juries were subject to the same prejudices as trial juries, and just as likely to be biased in cases that outraged the general public. The antebellum grand jury was, in effect, the voice of Southern opinion and the protector of community values, and thus an advocate for slavery. Equal justice for black defendants was not its priority, its goal, or its result.[35]

On April 23, 1804, Judge Jabez Bowen Jr., a native New Englander and ardent opponent of slavery, delivered this charge to the Chatham County grand jury:

> Hear now my fellow-citizens, listen to what experience and wisdom suggest as the only means of rescuing you from the abyss which yawns beneath your feet and now, even now, opens its destructive and capacious jaws to ensnare and devour you! . . . . Impious wretches, cease your calumnies on that God whose decrees are just and immutable and who will confound your misinterpretations of his ordinances! How then does slavery exist not from the fiat of heaven, but from the municipal institution of base, degenerate man! . . . What then have we eventually to expect! What but blood, massacre and devastation![36]

Bowen ended his jeremiad against human bondage with a plan for gradual emancipation of all Georgia's slaves, but the grand jury, outraged by the charge, refused to publish it. Instead, it issued presentments excoriating Bowen. In response, the judge ordered the grand jury jailed, whereupon county justices of the inferior court issued a writ of habeas corpus ordering the jurors' release. Grand jury members swore out an arrest warrant against Bowen, on grounds that he had tried to incite slave insurrection. Authorities arrested the judge and locked him up in the same jail that had held the grand jurors. He remained there until his father, Jabez Bowen Sr.—a former chancellor of Brown University, deputy governor of Rhode Island, chief justice of the Rhode Island Supreme Court, and a friend of George Washington—arrived from Rhode Island to post bail. They left Georgia, never to return. In their absence, the state legislature formally impeached Jabez Bowen Jr., and the governor removed him from office.[37]

On the morning of November 19, 1853, John Goolsby entered the kitchen of his neighbor, Elijah McMichael. What he saw there, lying on the floor at his feet, was the lifeless body of the mistress of the house, Edna McMichael. Adding to the tragedy of the moment, Goolsby saw that Edna had been eight months pregnant. Goolsby found no one in the house except a slave girl, Ailey. Mrs. McMichael met her end as a result of what in a non-slave society would have been a trivial domestic dispute. Earlier that morning, Ailey had been weaving when Edna McMichael noticed that she had broken several stitches and asked why she had not tied them. Ailey said she had run out of thread. Her mistress said she would punish her if she did not mend the weaving and slapped her. Ailey stood up, grabbed her mistress by the throat, covered her nose and mouth, and threw her to the floor, holding her there for some time. Mrs. McMichael did not move, except for a hand or a foot.[38]

John Goolsby provided this account of Edna McMichael's death and the discovery of her body at Ailey's murder trial, held on April 28, 1854, in Jasper County Superior Court, after the grand jury's indictment of the eighteen-year-old slave girl for the murder of her mistress. The solicitor general's theory of the case was that Ailey had killed Edna McMichael in cold blood. Stephen Talmadge was the star witness in the case, testifying that Ailey had confessed to him in a jailhouse interview. The prosecutor introduced witnesses who provided evidence to corroborate the damning confession. Jailer Tilman Giblet testified that Ailey had admitted her guilt to him as well, one day after her commitment hearing, when he found her crying in her cell and asked what was wrong, and whether she "stuck up to what she had said in court" (her not guilty plea). "No," she said. Did she have anything to say? She said she had thrown "her arms around her mistress' neck & choked her to death." Giblet said neither he nor anyone else had made threats or promises to Ailey to elicit her confession.

John Goolsby testified that at about eight or nine o'clock on the morning of November 19 he had heard "hollering several times" from the McMichael house and had gone over to find his pregnant neighbor "lying stretched out on the kitchen floor dead." He saw fingerprints on her neck that were red at first, but turned purple while he was there; her hair was disheveled. Her body was still warm. Her face did not have red splotches, but when he placed a pillow under her head, her facial expression was natural and he saw that her lip had been cut.

The final prosecution witness was Dr. William Maddux, who had examined Edna McMichael's body the day after her death. He had found her face, neck, and upper torso "suffused with a blue tint," with scrapes on knees and elbows, several marks on her neck, and her hair in disarray. Could McMichael's bruises and fall have been caused by the onset of labor, the solicitor general inquired? Maddux replied that he did not think a fall could produce the elbow and knee scrapes, injuries most likely produced by "scurring around on her knees & elbows." Maddux saw nothing unnatural about her face, other than the bluish tint around her lips and mouth, symptoms consistent with what one might expect in a person who had been strangled to death.

Ailey's lawyer attempted to save his client's life by convincing the jury that she was not fully responsible for the crime—indeed, that Edna McMichael may have been killed as a part of a conspiracy between her husband, Elijah, and his slaves. In her confession to Stephen Talmadge, Ailey had said that Warren, another McMichael slave, had implored her daily to commit the crime, saying that if he were she and had the opportunity, he would kill their mistress. She told Warren she would be hanged if she did, whereupon Warren replied that she "would have but one time to die." In her "conversation" with Giblet, Ailey added that Warren said he would kill Edna McMichael if she would let him know when Mr. McMichael left for town.

Ailey's lawyer tried to raise doubt in the jury's mind about the facts surrounding the discovery of the victim's body and the cause of death. On cross-examination, John Goolsby admitted he had come to the McMichael house because Aimey, another of Elijah McMichael's slaves, had provided "information." (Ailey told Talmadge she had gone to Aimey and other slaves immediately after her attack on McMichael to confide in them.) On direct examination, Goolsby told the jury that he lived a quarter mile from the McMichaels, casting doubt on whether he could have heard yelling from the house. In his questioning of Dr. Maddux, Ailey's lawyer was able to get the physician to agree that marks on the victim's throat were consistent with those a handkerchief would make if used as a method of strangulation.

The evidence that should have given the jury the greatest pause in finding Ailey guilty of murder came from Elijah McMichael, the husband of the victim. On direct examination by the solicitor general, McMichael said that on the morning of the crime he had left for town with a Mr. Pye, riding by Jim, Aimey, and Warren as they headed off to the cotton patch. His wife, who was in "good health," stayed alone at home with Ailey. Before he had gone very far, Warren rode up to report on "the situation of his wife," whereupon he went back home and found his wife dead. During cross-examination, Ailey's lawyer revealed the suspicious and potentially inculpatory dimensions of Elijah McMichael's later behavior. Three weeks after his wife's death, he had Mr. Pye sell all of his slaves, including Warren, with whom he had been raised. The husband of the victim had gotten rid of key witnesses in the case—witnesses who might have been able to shed valuable light on the events of November 19. Would grief, anger, disgust, and distrust lead a normal, rational, and concerned husband and expectant father to dispose prematurely of witnesses who could secure the conviction of his wife's killer? Had Elijah McMichael conspired with his friends and slaves to rid himself of an unwanted, pregnant wife, and in the process had he exploited an impressionable slave girl? The jury did not think so. They took his testimony at face value and found Ailey guilty of the murder of her mistress. Judge Robert V. Hardeman sentenced her to hang.

The Role of Slavery in the Judicial Process

Most black defendants were bondspeople, and to whites, slaves were by race predisposed to violence, theft, and deception. Those who owned slaves, so North Carolina justice John Taylor argued, were in the best position to assess those racial differences and to pass judgment accordingly. Although black defendants after 1811 formally had most of the same due process rights whites enjoyed, the belief among whites of blacks' racial inferiority, as well as their value as property, inclined judges, juries, lawyers, and witnesses to disbelieve their trial testimony and to judge them differently.

In the South, power was based on land and the ownership of slaves, and the judges who administered the system were themselves slaveholders. In Baldwin County, for example, justices of the peace John Mathews, John W. Devereux, Nathaniel Waller, Goodwin Myrick, James Humphreys, and William Searcy were all slaveholders. A number of them sold slaves to satisfy personal debts. John Mathews sold a slave girl, Hannah, in 1815 to satisfy a public debt. In the same year, Devereux was forced to sell nine slaves to pay a creditor, and in 1817 he offered to sell the bondsman Job to satisfy a debt he owed to the state of Georgia. In 1818, he put his slave Phoebe on the auction block for similar reasons. Nathaniel Waller also resorted to the sale of slaves to fend off creditors; he sold a female slave in 1812 for that purpose. The justices handled slave sales for others as well. In 1818, Goodwin Myrick, as executor of the estate of a deceased Baldwin County woman, offered a number of slaves for sale.

Court-ordered sales of the kind engaged in by the Baldwin justices were extremely disruptive of slaves' family lives, far more so than commercial sales. If these men had any special regard for slaves that might manifest itself in court, it did not show itself in their treatment of their own slave families.[39]

Like their lower-court counterparts, the justices of the inferior court owned and sold human beings. The majority of the justices who presided over the trials of slaves in Baldwin County were slaveholders. Justices Amos Young, William Bivens, Harris Allen, Augustin Harris, William Rutherford, William Ball, Robert G. Crittenden, Myles Green, Thomas Moughan, Samuel Beecher, and David B. Mitchell were all slave masters. Moughan, the largest slaveholder, had fifty-eight slaves. Young had the fewest, with six slaves listed in his household in 1820. Justices of the Baldwin County Inferior Court also participated in the sales of slaves to satisfy personal debts, both as debtors and creditors. Daniel Wilson sold a slave to quash a levy. In 1821, Elias Harris sold one of his female slaves to meet a debt to his fellow inferior court justice Appleton Rosseter. Harris Allen lost a slave because of a debt owed to a resident of the county. Justice and former governor David B. Mitchell sold thirty-seven slaves to satisfy his creditors; William Carnes and Charles Williamson sold slaves for the same reason. Justice William Y. Hansell lost numerous slaves under the auctioneer's hammer as a result of personal debt.[40] There is no reason to believe that Baldwin County was exceptional among Georgia's counties in patterns of slave ownership by its judicial officials, which is clearly demonstrated by the ownership patterns of superior court judges.

By the 1850s, election to the superior court depended on legal acumen and social status, the status determined in large part by slave ownership. A random sample of sixteen superior court judges from around the state found fourteen of the sixteen as slaveowners, and the two judges I could not confirm as slaveowners may have been. Neither man appears at all in the Georgia census records of 1850 or 1860; it is thus possible that these men were slaveholders but were out of the state at the time of the enumeration. The slaveholdings of the judges ranged from a low of five slaves, in the households of Osborne Lochrane and Carlton B. Coles, to a high of thirty-six slaves, on the plantation of William Law of Chatham County.[41]

While the judges who presided over the trials of slaves owned slaves themselves, the jurors who sat in judgment generally did not. A random sample of approximately 10 percent of all cases that went to juries shows no jury with a majority of slaveowners. Additional evidence appears in the trial records of blacks in the inferior court of Baldwin County, where between 1812 and 1838 prosecutors and masters selected fourteen juries, none of which included more than six slaveowners. Two juries had no masters at all, and three only one slaveholder each. (The mode average for slaveowners serving on juries was three.)[42]

That Georgia juries were made up mostly of those who did not own slaves is not unusual when one considers the jury selection procedure. According to Georgia's 1798 constitution, the only requirements for voting for state legislators (the same requirements for jury service) were that individuals be "citizens and inhabitants of the state, and shall have attained the age of twenty-one years, and have paid all taxes which may have been required of them . . . for the year preceding the election." Each county had to maintain a list of all persons who met these qualifications; the clerks of the superior court and inferior court were responsible for correcting the jury lists each year. The clerk, in the presence or under the direction of one or more judges of the court, compiled a list of white men qualified to serve as grand and petit jurors. Each name was written on a separate slip of paper and put in the grand or petit jury compartment of a wooden "jury box." The box was locked, and the key kept by the clerk, a judge, or other designated person. Two months before the beginning of a trial term, the box was unlocked in the presence of the clerk and judges; twenty-three to thirty-six names were drawn randomly from the grand jury compartment, and from forty-eight to seventy-two from the petit jury compartment to make up the jury pool.[43]

Such a process would result in a random selection of jurors from the adult white male population at large, in Georgia a population that was overwhelmingly non-slaveholding. In 1860, there were 41,084 slaveowners in a total white population of 258,561 residents over twenty years of age. With the names of women excluded (no women could vote or serve on Georgia juries), the white male population consisted of 132,509 residents.[44] The

percentage of slave masters eligible for jury service could have been no
higher than 31 percent. The actual figure was certainly lower, because the
figures would have included female slaveholders and males who were not
yet twenty-one. The percentage of male masters over twenty-one in Georgia
was probably closer to 25 percent of the total white population. A random
selection from a population where only a quarter of the inhabitants held
slaves (even though some individual counties had more) would lead to juries that almost always had non-slaveholder majorities.

Georgia's reliance upon non-slaveholders to determine the guilt or innocence of slaves has considerable bearing on one of the great ongoing
debates in Southern historiography: the degree of conflict or cooperation
between masters and yeomen. Scholars have devoted a great deal of attention to class relations between slaveholders and yeomen, some arguing that
there was considerable conflict between the two groups, others that there
was significant congruency in interests and world views between them.[45]
In Georgia—at least in the antebellum period—the judicial system demonstrates a lack of conflict. By allowing the fates of slaves to be decided by yeomen, slaveholders in the state legislature were expressing confidence in the
common interests of all white men, a unity and consensus based on racial
supremacy and the economic well-being generated for all groups by slavery.
Potential conflict between masters and yeomen was muted no doubt, in part,
because both groups participated in the process of judging blacks. Yeoman
jury service also buttressed the cult of honor that was at the core of Southern
social relations.[46] Georgia's lawmakers were not alone in their confidence in
yeoman jurors. Most other slave states during the antebellum period did not
mandate that slave masters be included on juries for slave trials.

Race-based Differences in Conviction Rates

The very nature of the plantation system of justice ensured its speed
and efficiency: there were no jurors to be selected, no lawyers to be procured,
no mandatory continuances, no statutorily defined waiting periods between
conviction and execution of sentence, and no appeals. Masters or overseers
quickly tried and punished suspects, with the master's or mistress's mercy
the only means of mitigation or appeal. The system's true effectiveness—
from the white perspective—would be revealed if the ratio of slaves accused
of plantation crimes to those "convicted" could be known, but no records
exist for such a comparison. If the testimony of masters and ex-slaves is

accepted in lieu of documentary evidence, few slaves accused of committing prohibited acts that came to the knowledge of the overseer or master—acts that could be proved to the master's satisfaction—escaped unpunished.

The formal court system did produce records, which makes it possible to evaluate the treatment of black defendants. The first measure is the simple conviction rate: the ratio of guilty verdicts and pleas to the number of cases that reached the trial stage. If the system worked as it makers hoped, by weeding out weak and frivolous cases before trial, the simple conviction rate should have been relatively high. Between 1755 and 1865, the simple conviction rate for black defendants tried in Georgia courts, based on extant records, was an impressive 75.2 percent, a figure even higher at certain times or for certain crimes. Juries convicted nearly 94 percent of blacks put on trial between 1755 and 1811. Between 1812 and 1849, juries convicted blacks tried on charges of arson, attempted rape, murder, and attempted murder at rates of 80 percent, 80 percent, 86 percent, and 94 percent, respectively. Juries convicted every single black man charged with the rape of a white woman between 1812 and 1849. Conviction rates were considerably higher for those charged with crimes against persons than for those accused of property crimes and of crimes against public order.[47]

The sex and status of the slave or free black defendant had a strong impact on simple conviction rates. Slave men were the group most likely to be convicted in the period from 1755 to 1865, with a simple conviction rate of nearly 81 percent. Juries convicted slave women at a dramatically lower rate, 44 percent. This disparity is best explained, in part, by the difference in the types of crimes of which slave men and women were accused.[48] Although those accused of murder constituted the largest single group of women, a crime with a simple conviction rate of 81 percent, the majority faced charges of arson, burglary, and poisoning, which were difficult to prove and had conviction rates lower than the average of 75.2 percent.[49]

Differences in crimes alone do not, however, entirely explain the difference in conviction rates by sex. Apparently, there was a greater reluctance on the part of Georgia juries to convict women. In the six categories of crime for which both slave men and women were put on trial, juries convicted slave men at higher rates in four; they convicted women at a higher rate only for arson. The most telling statistic is that for murder, the most serious crime. For murder, slave men were convicted at a rate of nearly 85 percent; the simple murder conviction rate for slave women was 50 percent (see table 4). In hesitating, relatively speaking, to convict slave women and sentence them to death, juries may have been concerned that a dead slave woman represented a loss for the slaveholder not only of her labor but also of any children she might bear. Could juries have been loath to admit that the group they considered the least threatening was actually one of the most physically dangerous? Or perhaps white Georgia men were simply reluctant to see a woman of any color hanging from the end of a rope in the public square. While all of these factors probably played a role in the lower conviction rates for slave women, the most likely explanation is that slave women seemed less threatening than slave men because they seldom appeared in court. Years and years could go by between trials involving slave women. Local whites would have discerned no dangerous pattern of female criminality to which they had to respond.

If the disparity in conviction rates between slave men and slave women is remarkable, the difference between the enslaved and free is even more so. Juries found free black men guilty at the comparatively low rate of only 40 percent.[50] Free black women fared even better: neither of the two women brought before the Georgia courts between 1755 and 1865 was convicted. (The grand jury did not indict the first, and the trial jury acquitted the second.)

Once again, the disparity in conviction rates between free blacks and enslaved blacks is consistent with the differences in the crimes for which the state tried the two groups. Courts charged the majority of free black men and women with theft crimes and crimes against public order, both of which had lower than average conviction rates.[51] Low conviction rates reflect the fact that free blacks avoided, or had fewer opportunities to be part of, the kinds of violent confrontations with whites that led to higher rates of conviction.

Overall simple conviction rates in Georgia declined as time passed, from a high of nearly 94 percent in the colonial and early national periods, to a low of 71.1 percent in the period ending in 1865. The increased procedural safeguards put in place during the antebellum period no doubt explain the decline.[52]

Still, the simple conviction rate tells only part of the story. The effective conviction rate must be considered as well in assessing the treatment of black defendants. The effective conviction rate is the ratio of convictions to all indictments or accusations, a rate that represents the chance of conviction a defendant faces at the moment of appearance before a court accused of a crime. The difference between simple and effective conviction rates

TABLE 4. SIMPLE CONVICTION RATES BY CRIME AND DEFENDANT SEX AND STATUS, 1755–1865

Defendant status	Disposition		Murder	Attempted murder	Arson	Poisoning	Burglary	Larceny
								Crime
Slave male	Verdicts/pleas of guilty	Number of cases	82	47	8	1	26	2
		% within disposition	39.6	22.7	3.9	0.5	12.6	1.0
		% within crime	84.5	88.7	44.4	50.0	81.3	66.7
	Verdict of not guilty	Number of cases	15	6	9	1	6	1
		% within disposition	30.6	12.2	18.4	2.0	12.2	2.0
		% within crime	15.5	11.3	50.0	50.0	18.8	33.3
	Mistrials	Number of cases			1			
		% within disposition			100.0			
		% within crime			5.6			
	Total	Number of cases	97	53	18	2	32	3
		% within disposition	37.7	20.6	7.0	0.8	12.5	1.2
		% within crime	100.0	100.0	100.0	100.0	100.0	100.0
Slave female	Verdicts/pleas of guilty	Number of cases	5		3	2	1	
		% within disposition	45.5		27.3	18.2	9.1	
		% within crime	50.0		50.0	50.0	50.0	
	Verdict of not guilty	Number of cases	4	1	3	2	1	1
		% within disposition	30.8	7.7	23.1	15.4	7.7	7.7
		% within crime	40.0	100.0	50.0	50.0	50.0	100.0
	Mistrials	Number of cases	1					
		% within disposition	100.0					
		% within crime	10.0					
	Total	Number of cases	10	1	6	4	2	1
		% within disposition	40.0	4.0	24.0	16.0	8.0	4.0
		% within crime	100.0	100.0	100.0	100.0	100.0	100.0

Source: See appendix.

depends on pretrial factors that cause grand juries not to indict or prosecutors to abandon cases prior to trial. Among such factors are arrests without sufficient cause, frivolous prosecutions, or overcharging. By considering these factors and jettisoning weak cases before trial, grand juries and prosecutors in effect render pretrial acquittals, thereby avoiding the expense—in time and in money—of trying cases that, in all likelihood, would end in acquittal.[53]

In an ideal criminal justice system, the effective conviction rate would be relatively close to the simple conviction rate, because the pre-judicial screening process would filter out cases that had little chance of successful prosecution. The reality, of course, is different. Crowded dockets, reluctant witnesses or complainants, newly discovered evidence, and a host of other factors that cannot be calculated before a defendant is brought before the bar intervene, and, as a consequence, an effective conviction rate of at least 50 percent or more represents an "efficient" system. Georgia's overall effective conviction rate between 1850 and 1865 was 43.4 percent. Juries convicted close to half of the defendants who appeared before them, regardless of crime, status, or sex.[54]

It is impossible to calculate effective conviction rates accurately before 1850 because of the nature of the accusation process and record keeping during these years. For the colonial and early national periods, few trial records remain. For conviction data, I had to rely on appeals by convicted offenders to the legislature or executive, and on newspaper articles that recounted the executions of those convicted of capital crimes, both of which skew the analysis toward conviction. The dearth of court records in this period also makes it impossible to know how many defendants appeared before the courts but were never formally charged. The data for the early antebellum period is similarly flawed. From 1812 to 1849, complainants made initial accusations before justices of the peace; unfortunately, these courts were not courts of record, so clerks did not document the results of their proceedings. The only cases that appear in the record are those forwarded to the inferior courts for trial, again making it impossible to know with any degree of certainty the percentage of defendants never charged. The superior court records after 1850 do reflect both true and no bills, making it possible to calculate effective conviction rates.

As with simple conviction rates, effective conviction rates varied significantly by crime and crime type. The rate for post-1850 crimes against persons was significantly higher than for property crimes and crimes against public order. Nearly 60 percent of crimes against persons resulted in convictions, compared to 40 percent of property crimes and 30 percent of crimes against public order. Convictions for crimes against persons also accounted for 77.2 percent of all convictions (see table 5). There was also considerable variation among individual crimes. The highest effective conviction rate of all, 71.4 percent, was for rape, indicating the seriousness with which Georgia juries considered accusations of black carnal violations of white women. Murder followed rape in the rate of effective conviction; juries convicted nearly 55 percent of those whose cases prosecutors presented to grand juries on this charge. The lowest rates occur among the property crimes. The conviction rate for arson, for example, was a low 13.9 percent, reflecting the difficulty of identifying and prosecuting those who set clandestine fires. Arsonists were not only difficult to convict, they were also the hardest to charge, probably for similar reasons; grand juries failed to indict 33 percent of the arsonists brought before them (see table 6). Whites feared black violence more than violations of their property rights—except their slave property rights—a fear reflected in effective conviction rates.

Effective conviction rates in Georgia varied significantly with the sex and status of the defendant. Juries convicted slave men at a rate of 48.3 percent, a rate very near the average, but the effective conviction rate of slave women was just 21.6 percent, a rate more than two times lower than for enslaved men, and very close to the rate for white men. Perhaps most interesting in the effective conviction rate for slave women is the extremely low rate at which they confessed guilt: only 2.3 percent of slave female defendants, 1 in 44, entered guilty pleas, while 28 of 352 slave men, 8 percent, did so. Juries found free black men guilty at a lower rate than slave men and women, and free black women were not convicted at all. Only two free women ever faced criminal charges, and for relatively minor crimes; hence the conviction rate should not be considered to represent extreme lenience toward this group of defendants (see table 7). These differences in effective conviction rates by sex are explained by the same factors that account for gender differentials in simple conviction rates.

Simple and effective conviction rates in Georgia were similar to those in other states, North and South. The simple conviction rate for slave defendants in South Carolina was 70 percent; the highest conviction rates were for assault and related crimes, and the lowest rates were for property crimes such as burglary and arson, which were harder to detect and required eye-

TABLE 5. EFFECTIVE CONVICTION RATES BY CRIME TYPE, 1850–1865

		Crime Type			
Disposition		Persons crimes	Property crimes	Crimes against public order	Total
Unknown	Number of cases	37	15	1	53
	% within disposition	69.8	28.3	1.9	100.0
	% within crime type	12.8	14.7	4.3	12.7
	% of Total	8.9	3.6	0.2	12.7
Nolle prosequi	Number of cases	17	7	4	28
	% within disposition	60.7	25.0	14.3	100.0
	% within crime type	5.9	6.9	17.4	6.7
	% of Total	4.1	1.7	1.0	6.7
Verdicts/ pleas of guilty	Number of cases	173	41	7	224
	% within disposition	77.2	18.3	3.1	100.0
	% within crime type	59.9	40.2	30.4	53.7
	% of Total	41.5	9.8	1.7	53.7
Verdict of not guilty	Number of cases	39	24	9	72
	% within disposition	54.2	33.3	12.5	100.0
	% within crime type	13.5	23.5	39.1	17.3
	% of Total	9.4	5.8	2.2	17.3
Not indicted	Number of cases	22	14	2	38
	% within disposition	57.9	36.8	5.3	100.0
	% within crime type	7.6	13.7	8.7	9.1
	% of Total	5.3	3.4	0.5	9.1
Mistrials	Number of cases	1	1	0	2
	% within disposition	50.0	50.0	0.0	100.0
	% within crime type	0.3	1.0	0.0	0.5
	% of Total	0.2	0.2	0.0	0.5
Total	Number of cases	289	102	23	417
	% within disposition	69.3	24.5	5.5	100.0
	% within crime type	100.0	100.0	100.0	100.0
	% of Total	69.3	24.5	5.5	100.0

Source: Cases from 1850 to 1865 (see appendix).

TABLE 6. EFFECTIVE CONVICTION RATES BY CRIME, 1850–1865

					Crime					
Disposition	Murder	Attempted murder	Rape	Attempted rape	Arson	Poisoning	Attempted poisoning	Burglary	Man-slaughter	Larceny
Unknown Number of cases	20	13	1	1	5			6	1	2
% within disposition	38.5	25.0	1.9	1.9	9.6			11.5	1.9	3.8
% within crime	17.9	22.0	7.1	7.1	13.9			27.3	16.7	100.0
Nolle prosequi Number of cases	6	3	1	1	2	1		5	2	
% within disposition	25.0	12.5	4.2	4.2	8.3	4.2		20.8	8.3	
% within crime	5.4	5.1	7.1	7.1	5.6	16.7		22.7	33.3	
Verdicts/ pleas of guilty Number of cases	61	29	10	6	5	3		5	2	
% within disposition	48.8	23.2	8.0	4.8	4.0	2.4		4.0	1.6	
% within crime	54.5	49.2	71.4	42.9	13.9	50.0		22.7	33.3	
Verdict of not guilty Number of cases	15	6	2	5	11	2		4		
% within disposition	30.6	12.2	4.1	10.2	22.4	4.1		8.2		
% within crime	13.4	10.2	14.3	35.7	30.6	33.3		18.2		
Not indicted Number of cases	9	8		1	12		3	2	1	
% within disposition	25.0	22.2		2.8	33.3		8.3	5.6	2.8	
% within crime	8.0	13.6		7.1	33.3		100.0	9.1	16.7	
Mistrials Number of cases	1				1					
% within disposition	50.0				50.0					
% within crime	0.9				2.8					
Total Number of cases	112	59	14	14	36	6	3	22	6	2
% within disposition	38.9	20.5	4.9	4.9	12.5	2.1	1.0	7.6	2.1	0.7
% within crime	100.0	100.0	100.0	100.0	100.0	100.0	100.0	100.0	100.0	100.0

Source: Cases from 1850 to 1865 (see appendix).

TABLE 7. EFFECTIVE CONVICTION RATES BY DEFENDANT STATUS, 1850–1865

Disposition		Slave male	Slave female	Free male	Free female	Total
			Defendant Status			
Unknown	Number of cases	45	5	2		52
	% within disposition	86.5	9.6	3.8		100.0
	% within defendant status	18.9	13.5	18.2		18.1
Nolle prosequi ✓	Number of cases	19	3	2		24
	% within disposition	79.2	12.5	8.3		100.0
	% within defendant status	8.0	8.1	18.2		8.3
Verdicts/ pleas of guilty	Number of cases	115	8	2		125
	% within disposition	92.0	6.4	1.6		100.0
	% within defendant status	48.3	21.6	18.2		43.4
Verdict of not guilty	Number of cases	33	10	5	1	49
	% within disposition	67.3	20.4	10.2	2.0	100.0
	% within defendant status	13.9	27.0	45.5	50.0	17.0
Not indicted	Number of cases	25	10		1	36
	% within disposition	69.4	27.8		2.8	100.0
	% within defendant status	10.5	27.0		50.0	12.5
Mistrials	Number of cases	1	1			2
	% within disposition	50.0	50.0			100.0
	% within defendant status	0.4	2.7			0.7
Total	Number of cases	238	37	11	2	288
	% within disposition	82.6	12.8	3.8	0.7	100.0
	% within defendant status	100.0	100.0	100.0	100.0	100.0

Sources: Cases from 1850 to 1865 (see appendix).

witnesses. Juries found men guilty in 67.7 percent of cases that went to verdict; women were found guilty in 60.2 percent of cases.

In colonial New York, juries convicted nearly 69 percent of black bondsmen accused of crimes, an amazingly high effective conviction rate but not a surprising one, considering the dearth of available procedural protections at the time. The overall conviction figures for slaves in New York during the colonial period would have been even higher but for a low conviction rate of 55 percent for theft crimes. This was true of Georgia as well.[55]

Tennessee was an interesting contrast to Georgia, South Carolina, and New York; in Tennessee, the conviction rates were considerably lower. In Arthur Howington's study of 198 prosecutions of 160 slaves between 1825 and 1861, only forty (20 percent) ended in convictions in capital cases, and eighteen cases, or 9 percent, in convictions for non-capital offenses. Only 29 percent of prosecutions (of fifty-eight cases) ended with a conviction of any kind. Sixty-eight cases (34 percent) resulted in acquittals on the capital charge, either by the grand or petit jury. Twenty-eight percent of the cases (of fifty-five total) ended in acquittals. Courts dismissed sixty-five capital cases (33 percent) and declared fourteen (7 percent) mistrials. Twenty-two defendants out of 160 charged went to the gallows.

In Tennessee, the rates of conviction were highest in murder cases in which the victim was white. This conviction rate was only 50 percent, but the rate was considerably higher if the white victim was a master, mistress, or other authority figure. Eight slaves faced charges of murder or attempted murder of such persons; courts convicted and hanged six. Counties charged twenty-eight slaves with the murder of whites who were not figures in authority over the defendants; six were convicted of murder, and two were convicted of manslaughter. Twenty-six slaves were accused of attempting to kill other whites; juries found two guilty of attempted murder and two were convicted for lesser offenses. The figures are similar for free black defendants. For total crimes of violence against whites, the conviction rate was only 22 percent (of eighteen cases). Conversely, when the victim was black, the conviction rate of fifteen cases was 66 percent.[56]

In general, at the time of accusation blacks charged with capital crimes in Georgia stood a fifty-fifty chance of being convicted, but once the case reached the trial stage, the conviction rate jumped to approximately 75 percent. In isolation, these figures may not seem especially onerous, but when compared to those of white defendants, a disturbing pattern of disparate treatment emerges. The historian David J. Bodenhamer, who examined

4,007 criminal cases involving white defendants in four antebellum Georgia counties—Liberty, Murray, Bibb, and Musocgee—found that only 27 percent of all true bills ever reached a decision on the merits of the case; prosecutors dismissed the remaining cases (25.5 percent), or they simply disappeared from the record (47.5 percent). Felony cases made it to verdict more often than misdemeanors did, and the state prosecuted crimes against persons more vigorously than crimes against property. Once a case made it to trial, the defendant had little chance of acquittal; 70 percent of trials resulted in guilty verdicts. The simple conviction rate for misdemeanors was 73 percent, and it was 66 percent for more serious crimes. Those charged with crimes against persons were convicted in 74 percent of the cases; those charged with property crimes, 79 percent of the time. The effective conviction rate tells a different tale of system efficiency. Fewer than 19 percent of cases presented to the grand jury led to conviction, an effective conviction rate nearly thirty percentage points lower than that for black defendants.[57] In antebellum Georgia, a white person charged with a crime had little chance of ever being convicted of anything.

Bodenhamer offers several explanations for the low conviction rates of Georgia's criminal justice system for whites. First, he writes, the state's jails were in such poor condition, and their jailers so badly trained, that defendants simply escaped before trial. Second, courts met only twice a year, so cases that clogged the dockets simply fell through the cracks. A rapid expansion of civil litigation that squeezed criminal cases to the margins, Bodenhamer explains, compounded this overtaxing of the system. Third, tardy or defaulting jurors further delayed proceedings. Fourth, the process of initiating prosecutions resulted in inefficiency. All the law required to begin a criminal prosecution was for an individual to make a complaint. A magistrate determined if there was sufficient cause in the complaint to proceed, and if there was, he forwarded the case to the grand jury. The ease with which individuals could initiate prosecutions thus invited frivolous complaints. Once before them, grand jurors sent these bogus complaints to trial rather than no-billing them. Finally, Bodenhamer concludes, by shaming him in the community, the mere act of being charged with a crime served the social purpose of deterring the criminal; it was not necessary for the case to go to verdict.[58]

Bodenhamer's interpretation, by inference, helps to explain, in part, why conviction rates for blacks were so high compared to those for whites. First of all, many masters held their slaves in custody pending trial and were accountable for their appearance in court and fined if they did not keep the appointed hour. Hence, accused slaves were less often in jail, and less able to escape. Second, jailed slaves and free blacks found it much more difficult to escape to safety, as is clear from the difficulties experienced by runaway slaves generally.[59] Blacks were more easily identified, lacked resources, and had farther to travel to long-term or permanent freedom. Third, since capital trials for blacks were infrequent, dockets were rarely crowded, at least for black defendants. Also, before 1850 counties convened special tribunals to try each individual case. After mid-century, the few cases of black defendants took precedence over those of white defendants, as evidenced by the few continuances required to dispose of cases. Finally, since the cases in this study involved capital crimes with easily identified victims, there were few, if any, frivolous charges. Masters had a special interest in making sure that such accusations never made it to court, since the lives of their slaves—and hence a significant amount of their own money and property—were at stake.

Throughout the history of jury trials in England and America, the active participation of the community and the parties involved was key. Whether the parties testified directly against each other, as did individuals in the Dark Ages, or through private lawyers and state prosecutors, in America in the antebellum years, the essence of the trial was that of individuals actively engaging each other, telling their stories, and confronting one another in some fashion. Members of the communities in which the parties resided judged this adversarial process; they knew the parties and the standards of their communities. It was their responsibility to ensure that justice was done, both for the individuals and for society. Such active engagement on the behalf of the defendant and the defendant's peers was absent from the trials of blacks in Georgia. The result was injustice. Masters made all of the key decisions in the trial process; owners seldom allowed slaves to speak. The historical record does not allow us to assess accurately whether whites and the law similarly silenced and disempowered free blacks, but they probably did; even if free blacks could speak, community members, peers who shared their condition and interests, were not those who judged them. All of Georgia's judges were white men, as were the jurors over whom the judges presided. These men represented a set of concerns that conflicted directly with those of Negro defendants. Slavery, white supremacy, and white interests were the interests they were most committed to defending.

In Georgia, for most of the colonial and antebellum periods, the judges who presided over trials involving black defendants had seldom been trained to deal with the complex legal issues involved in capital cases. The results were conviction rates for black defendants that were considerably higher than for their white counterparts. All of this is evidence of the fundamentally unjust nature of the judicial process. Juries convicted slave men at the highest rates, reflecting both the degree of actual or perceived threat these men represented to whites and the more serious nature of the crimes they were accused of committing. Juries found slave women guilty at significantly lower rates, even when they committed, or were accused of committing, the same crimes as slave men. The lower rates were probably a product of white male notions of patriarchy and mastery, as well as of the infrequency with which women faced capital charges in individual jurisdictions. Juries did not see patterns of female criminality. Instead, they saw isolated anomalies and thus did not respond as they did with slave men. Free blacks rarely appeared in state courts, and when they did, juries found them guilty at lower rates than slaves, indicative of the fact that such convictions were for property crimes and crimes against public order, offenses with lower than average conviction rates.

Ironically, on plantations and farms, slaves could at least speak for themselves and confront their slave accusers directly; in rare cases, a jury of their slave peers could try them. Of course, the master had the final word, and his verdict and punishment would reflect his interests and sense of justice, not those of his chattel property. Beyond owners' self-interest and community disapprobation, no means existed to ensure the quality of the justice dispensed.

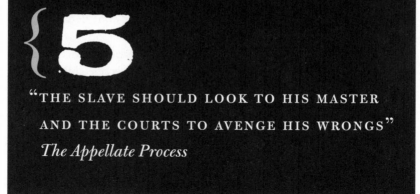

{.5}

"THE SLAVE SHOULD LOOK TO HIS MASTER AND THE COURTS TO AVENGE HIS WRONGS"
The Appellate Process

In all trials of slaves, the master shall control the defence of his slave.
—Code of the State of Georgia, 1861

"Subordination on the part of the slave is absolutely necessary, not only to the existence of the institution, but to the peace of the community. The policy of the law, therefore, requires that the slave should look to his master and the courts to avenge his wrongs."[1] In this uncompromising language, the Georgia jurist Thomas R. R. Cobb set forth the only means by which convicted slaves could challenge their convictions or ease their sentences.

From the colonial period forward, masters could apply to the governor for pardons or clemency for their convicted slaves. After 1798, slaveholders could challenge convictions in the superior courts and, after 1845, in the Georgia Supreme Court. But on the plantation, for slaves found guilty of breaking "plantation law"—that is, of disobeying rules of conduct established by the slaveowner—the only avenue of redress was the master's mercy, and there was no guarantee that mercy would be granted.

No free blacks, or their guardians, filed appeals, even though the law permitted them to do so. This failure to seek amelioration or redress may have been a consequence of cost; a free black might not have been able to afford a lawyer or the fees associated with filing an appeal, and his guardian—if he had one—might not have been able or inclined to assume the cost for him.

The right to appeal to a higher court was, in theory, the most important right available to slave defendants because it offered the possibility of a second trial and a chance to avoid execution if convicted of a capital crime.

Moreover, favorable precedents set in successful appeals could establish or reaffirm rules of criminal procedure that could protect slaves from arbitrary judgment and punishment. But this vital right did not belong to the slave. It was a right of the master alone.

According to the Code of the State of Georgia in 1861, "In all trials of slaves, the master shall control the defence of his slave (unless the court in its discretion pass an order directing the defence to be controlled by others), and all motions, demands, consents, bonds, bails, or other proceedings necessary to the defence, may be made by the master or his attorney." If a master chose not to appeal a capital conviction on behalf of his slave, there would be no appeal. The slave—the person with the most to lose—had no recourse or role in the process. Nor could a slave choose to accept responsibility and decide not to challenge a conviction and death sentence. A slave "had to look to his master and the courts to avenge his wrongs." Only his master determined when a wrong had occurred and what would be done about it. The right of appeal was thus a means for masters and mistresses to protect their interests and their property. In the best cases, a handful of slaves were the incidental beneficiaries of a master's sentiment or desire not to lose a valuable investment. In the worst cases, slaves were victims of their owners' penury, poor judgment, indifference, or cruelty.

Origins of the Right of Appeal

Across the South, the owners of slaves convicted of capital crimes generally had a right to appeal to the highest court in the county unless the trials had taken place in special tribunals, as in Virginia and South Carolina. After 1839, South Carolina law allowed a single judge of the supreme court to hear appeals for slave defendants; there was no right to a hearing by the full court. In Virginia, the law empowered a single judge of the supreme court to hear slave appeals, but the court heard only one case, and that not until 1865. Louisiana had no provision for appeal on technical errors, and in Maryland's entire history no court ever heard a slave appeal.[3]

In Georgia, legislators proposed an appellate process in the slave code of 1765, which the Board of Trade invalidated because it defined slaves as chattel. The act allowed a stay of execution in capital cases in order that the defendant's master might appeal his conviction and sentence to the governor or the governor's council. In 1770, the state legislature incorporated this procedure into the slave code and added a provision for bail release pending appeal. The law required the owner of the slave defendant to post a security bond to ensure his appearance in court and to cover the costs of the execution's delay.[4] This appellate process remained in place until 1811, when the legislature revised trial and punishment procedures for blacks.

Under the 1811 revision of the code, both the defense and prosecution had the right to appeal to the superior court any decision of the inferior court. The aggrieved party submitted an allegation of error to the inferior court; if the inferior court denied the appeal, the complaining party could appeal to a judge of the superior court. If this judge considered the complaint of error worthy of judicial review, he filed a writ (order) of certiorari to the inferior court commanding it to provide to the superior court, at the next term of the higher court, a certified copy of the trial record. When defense counsel filed the bill of exceptions (alleged errors) with the inferior court, that court suspended the sentence for forty days; after the superior court issued the writ of certiorari, the inferior court extended the suspension until the superior court rendered its final decision. If the superior court found in the defendant's favor, it granted a new trial, discharged the slave, or provided some other form of judicial relief. For those slaves whose death sentences the superior court upheld, one last avenue of reprieve remained. In 1816, the general assembly amended the code of 1811 to allow masters or guardians of blacks convicted of capital crimes to appeal to the governor for pardons, a pre-1811 right restored.[5]

The Creation of the Georgia Supreme Court

Georgia's legal system was of common law origin, so precedent played a significant role in the judicial process. However, the decisions of individual county superior courts and of state judicial circuits were not binding on each other; therefore, there was no uniform system of precedent. Supreme courts harmonized conflicting precedents in states that had them. Before the creation of its supreme court, Georgia attempted to solve the precedent problem through annual conventions of superior court judges, mandated by the Judiciary Act of 1799. Superior court judges met in these conventions to make rules for the administration of their courts and to set precedent. In 1801, the general assembly amended the judiciary act to end the practice of setting precedent, but judges continued to do so informally during rule-making sessions until the creation of the supreme court in 1845.[6] These annual meetings did not solve the problem of having multiple independent judicial bodies, a lack of uniformity of precedent that was both a blessing and a curse for blacks. Court decisions that had negative impacts on defendants in one county were not binding in others, which benefited some defendants. However, the same was true of salutary decisions; defendants in other counties were denied their advantages.

Many Georgia lawmakers had not wanted a state supreme court at all because they feared it would undermine their legislative prerogative, as the U.S. Supreme Court had done to Congress during the tenure of Chief Justice John Marshall. For decades, Georgia governors submitted proposals to the general assembly asking for a court of final appeal, and each year the assembly rejected those proposals, until 1834. In that year, the legislature passed a bill that amended the state constitution to allow for creation of a supreme court, but did not mandate its establishment; the general assembly did not pass legislation to require a supreme court until eleven years later, in 1845.

1845

The legislature appointed Georgia's three supreme court justices. One justice would sit for six years; a second, for four years; and the third justice, for two years. They served on good behavior and, like their counterparts in the superior and inferior courts, could be removed only by the governor with consent of two-thirds of both houses of the legislature, or on criminal conviction.

Only men licensed to practice law in the state for at least ten years were eligible for appointment to the supreme court.[7] John McPherson Berrien, U.S. attorney general during the Jackson administration and the legislature's first choice for chief justice, declined because the post required arduous circuit riding. Joseph Henry Lumpkin accepted the position. As chief justice, Lumpkin became the dominant figure on this first supreme court. Legal scholars credit him with shaping much of the state's law after 1845. Lumpkin was born December 23, 1799, and began his college education at the University of Georgia. After several years, he transferred to the College of New Jersey (Princeton), where he was graduated in 1819, and he was admitted to the Georgia bar a year later. In 1824-25, he represented Oglethorpe County in the Georgia House of Representatives, and he ran a successful law practice until he was appointed to the supreme court.

1st Chief Justice

Justices Eugenius Nisbet and Hiram Warner rounded out the first court.[8] Warner had been a schoolteacher, lawyer, state legislator, superior court judge, and, finally, a member of the United States Congress. Like Warner, Nisbet had been a lawyer, state legislator, and a member of Congress. A contemporary described the inaugural trio of Lumpkin, Nisbet, and Warner as an "Illustrious Triumvirate, founders of the jurisprudence of Georgia! Pioneers of a great work, they have done it well. Strongly and deeply the foundations are laid. The arch on which the structure of our written law reposes on three columns, each unique and dissimilar yet blending into harmonious unity Corinthian, Gothic, Doric. What a strong and beautiful composite they make!"[9]

Southern Judicial Culture

Like Northern jurists, Southern judges believed the law could serve as an instrument of social policy. While maintaining a firm grasp on the common law, judges nevertheless overturned selected time-honored doctrines and regularly created new ones to effect their vision of the good society. This level of judicial activism put Old South judges at odds with political figures who considered such initiative an attempt to curtail legislative power. Consequently, the Southern judiciary frequently clashed with lawmakers. Both Northern and Southern justices exercised their power of judicial review early and often, which exacerbated tensions with advocates of governmental decentralization, the principal Georgia example being the fight to create the supreme court.

Southern jurists did not differ from their Northern brethren on the judicial role, but they did differ on issues of race and slavery. Of the ten men who served as justices on Georgia's supreme court from its inception to the end of the Civil War, nine were slaveholders. Their slaveholdings ranged from the twelve of Charles J. McDonald to the thirty-seven of Eugenius Nisbet; the mean average was seventeen. Southern commitment to the "peculiar institution" and the animosity generated by sectional politics on this issue forced Old South judges to create doctrine on matters of race and property that varied sharply from the doctrines espoused by Northerners.[10]

According to the legal historian Timothy Huebner, "political sectionalism and legal nationalism" were at the core of the Southern judicial tradition. Even though the numbers of cases involving slavery were relatively small, Old South judges were preoccupied with questions of slavery and race. When slavery came under attack, whether through the initiative of blacks—as with Nat Turner's rebellion, or dissemination throughout the South of David Walker's *Appeal,* or abolitionist attacks during debates over the Missouri Compromise or the Wilmot Proviso—judges felt compelled to defend the institution in court. The paternalist ideal contained part of the rationale for this defense. Southern judges, like pro-slavery ideologues, argued that African peoples were biologically inferior and condemned by God to serve as the slaves of whites. Since blacks and whites were to be forever bound in this unequal relationship, it was incumbent on both parties to conduct themselves in a mutually beneficial manner. For their part, blacks were to submit and labor; whites were to take care of the material, emotional, and sometimes the spiritual needs of blacks in their charge. The ethos is best captured in the idea of benevolent stewardship.[11] AMAZING !

The person who perhaps best represented the ideal of the paternalist master and principled judge was Joseph Henry Lumpkin. Lumpkin was a slaveowner, and, if one of his former slaves is to be believed, a good one. Anna Parkes, whom the WPA interviewed in the 1930s, recalled, "Ole Marster and Ole Miss, dey took ker of us. Dey sho wuz good white folkses, but den dey had to be good white folkses, kaze Ole Marster he wuz Jedge Lumpkin, and de Jedge wuz bound to make evvybody do right, he gwine do right his own self 'fore he try to make udder folkses behave deyselves." Lumpkin encouraged his slaves "not to be 'shamed of'" their "race," because they "warn't no 'niggers.'" They were "Negroes," and he "'spected his Negroes to be de best Negroes in the whole land."[12]

Lumpkin's treatment of his slaves, attested to be humane, was the product of his commitment to social reform and paternalism. One of Georgia's most prominent jurists, Lumpkin was also an active leader of several social-reform movements. He had become a fervent evangelical after his conversion at a Methodist camp meeting in his twenties. Like that of Northern converts, Lumpkin's evangelicalism went hand in hand with a desire to improve society. After pledging to abstain from alcohol, he was elected president of the Oglethorpe County Temperance Society in 1829; he represented the state at the first National Temperance Convention. Lumpkin was a proponent of economic diversification. While fully supporting the South's cotton economy, Lumpkin believed the regional economy would be stronger if cotton mills were built to end Southern reliance on Northern mills. He even expressed early opposition to slavery, although he had completely reversed his position by the time he became chief justice. By then, he had come to believe that slavery was divinely ordained and a positive good for both races if both upheld the mutual obligations that were at the heart of his paternalistic vision.[13]

The legal scholars Mason Stephenson and D. Greer Stephenson Jr.

argue that, under Lumpkin's leadership, the Georgia Supreme Court was <u>"an active arm of government committed to the preservation of the slave system."</u>[14] It was before men like Lumpkin, men determined to defend slavery, that lawyers for black defendants appeared to plead for their clients' lives.

{ Issues on Appeal

Before the first day of each Georgia Supreme Court term, the defendant's lawyer submitted to each of the judges and the court reporter the following: a copy of the bill of exceptions (the list of alleged legal errors), a note on the points of law he intended to make at the hearing, a statement of the facts in the case, and a list of legal authorities on which he planned to rely.[15] The supreme court was now prepared to consider the case. Lawyers for black defendants challenged their clients' convictions on a number of different technical grounds. Most challenges were to the jurisdiction of courts, the form and substance of indictments and verdicts, the culpability of co-defendants, the admissibility of confessions, and the composition and impaneling of juries. Slavery and race were critical factors in many of these appeals.

In 1850, lawyers for Judge, a Houston County slave convicted of murder the year before, argued that the prosecution did not introduce any evidence that demonstrated that county justices of the peace had reviewed Judge's case and sent it to the inferior court, as the 1811 slave code required. The supreme court agreed and granted Judge a new trial.[16] In trying to keep capital trials of blacks and whites in separate jurisdictions, the legislature had created confusion that allowed the lawyer for a slave defendant to secure for him a second trial.

In 1851, the defense counsel for Anthony, a slave, argued that Anthony's conviction for the manslaughter of a free black man was invalid because proof of the preliminary proceedings had not been introduced at his trial in McIntosh County Superior Court. But in challenging the conviction in this way, Anthony's lawyer failed to grasp all of the ramifications of the 1850 transfer of black capital cases from the inferior to the superior courts. Allegations of capital wrongdoing still had to be made before the inferior courts, but once that court ruled the offense to be a capital one, the case was not automatically transferred to the inferior court but was sent instead to the solicitor general for presentation to the county grand jury. A true bill from the grand jury became the basis upon which trial in the superior court stood. The preliminary proceedings did not grant jurisdiction to the superior courts; the statute of 1850 did. The supreme court affirmed Anthony's conviction.[17]

William Blackstone, in his *Commentaries* on the common law, wrote that indictments required "precise and sufficient certainty." They had to state the "christian name, sirname, . . . and the county of the offender" to provide positive identification. The time and place of the crime had to be provided. These facts did not have to be exact; the indictment would withstand challenge as long as the place was within the court's jurisdiction and the time before the presentation of the indictment. There were occasions when the time had to be precisely rendered, as when a statute of limitations applied. Also, the offense itself had to be set forth with "clearness and certainty," in some instances with particular legal terminology in the indictment. For example, in treason cases, the acts must have been done "treasonably and against his [the king's] allegiance." Felony crimes had to be perpetrated "feloniously," and in cases of rape, the victim had to have been "ravished." In murder indictments, the length and depth of the wound had to be provided so the court could judge whether the injury had, in fact, been mortal. In larceny prosecutions, the court required the value of the stolen item or items, to determine whether the crime was a grand or petit larceny.[18]

In 1851, the Houston County grand jury indicted a slave named Stephen and charged him with the rape and attempted rape of Mary Daniel, a free white woman. His lawyer objected to the two-count indictment, arguing the prosecutor had to choose one charge or the other, because otherwise the jury would be asked to decide two different and distinct issues. The court decided in Stephen's favor, and the solicitor general chose to proceed on the rape charge. The jury found Stephen guilty on the lesser charge of "attempt to commit a rape." His lawyer then appealed the case to the Georgia Supreme Court, claiming the clerk should not have read the attempted rape charge to the jury. While the lawyer's reasoning is not stated in the record, one can deduce that he believed the reading of that count of the indictment planted the attempt charge in the jury's mind, and that but for this recitation, the jury would have acquitted Stephen. Chief Justice Lumpkin was not persuaded. He reasoned that the prosecution should not have been required to choose between counts, because "the two offenses charged in the indictment, being of the same nature, requiring the same plea, the same judgment and the same quantum of punishment, the State might have proceeded to trial on both counts at the same time." The two charges in this case were indeed sufficiently similar in nature—the attempt a lesser included offense within the rape—and the defendant had had ample notice to prepare a defense to both charges. Lumpkin did concede that the trial judge had erred by failing to address these issues before the clerk swore the jury and read the indictment, but that, "If the second count ought to have been permitted to stand, then it is no error in the Court to refuse to strike it out at any stage of the trial."

Stephen's lawyer next claimed that the indictment did not charge the defendant with "any crime of which a slave can be convicted"—that is, that the indictment simply charged rape, instead of rape of a free white woman. His focus on the language of the indictment sent Lumpkin into a diatribe of sorts: "Will the age of technicalities never pass away? Shall the law, affecting the dearest interests of men, their property, life and character, 'coming home to their businesses and bosoms,' never become a popular science?" He went on to say, "The Legislature, in 1833, declared that every accusation should be deemed sufficiently technical and correct . . . provided it stated the offense in the terms and language of the Code, or so plainly—(what a pregnant clause!) that the nature of the offense charged, might be easily understood by the Jury." In Lumpkin's view, the indictment against Stephen clearly met this criteria. The Houston County grand jury had charged Stephen with the rape of Mary Daniel, a free white female, on October 31, 1851, and with attempting to rape her on the same day. According to the chief justice, if the indictment were defective, it was because of "redundancy," stating in two places that the victim was a white female. "What man of rational understanding could fail to comprehend the offense for which this negro was prosecuted? And this alone is the criterion of sufficiency." On these particular grounds, the supreme court affirmed Stephen's conviction.[19]

In 1854, a Bibb County jury convicted John, a slave, of murdering a white man, Mark Swinney, of Bibb County. His lawyer argued that the conviction should be overturned because the indictment did not state that Swinney was a white man. Lumpkin ruled that, in Georgia, it was presumed that any slave or free black indicted for murder had been indicted for the killing of a free white person. The only time it was necessary for the status of the victim to be included in the indictment was in "the exceptional cases." (Lumpkin did not elaborate on these "exceptional cases.") The supreme court affirmed John's conviction.[20] In both cases, of Stephen and of John, defense lawyers had tried unsuccessfully to introduce differences in race and status between defendant and victim to overturn convictions.

In most slave states, courts routinely quashed indictments of slaves and free blacks because of technical shortcomings. Although the Georgia Supreme Court lamented such fastidiousness, as evidenced by Lumpkin's discussion in *Stephen v. State*, it too observed the technical rules of indictment drafting. Courts complained about technicalities but believed it was the responsibility of lawmakers to relax indictment requirements. During the antebellum period, the Tennessee legislature did do so, but few other states chose to follow suit before the Civil War.[21]

Lawyers for slaves like Anthony and Stephen also challenged their clients' convictions on the propriety of jury verdicts and on the reasonable doubt relied upon to achieve them. A grand jury had accused Anthony of murder in the death of a free person of color, and a petit jury had convicted him of the non-capital offense of manslaughter. Anthony's defense counsel, in addition to challenging the sufficiency of the indictment, also maintained that his conviction should be reversed since the superior court had no jurisdiction over the crime of manslaughter. After 1850, the superior courts did have jurisdiction over capital offenses committed by blacks, but since manslaughter was not a capital crime, the jury could not return a guilty verdict on that charge. Justice Nisbet, unmoved, reasoned that a grand jury had indicted Anthony for murder, a crime under the superior court's jurisdiction, and that it was entirely proper for a jury to convict on the lesser offense of manslaughter even though it had not been charged in the indictment. Acts of 1821 and 1850 had given the superior courts the authority to punish for manslaughter. Nisbet quoted the relevant part of the 1850 act: "That in case of conviction upon bill of indictment . . . the Judge shall pass sentence in conformity with laws now of force, imposing penalties and providing for the passing of sentence in such cases." Since the penal code did not address manslaughter committed by a black upon a black, courts should refer to an 1821 act that provided for punishment in such cases. Under that law, a slave or free person convicted of manslaughter was to be whipped and branded. This law was the only one that referred to manslaughter by slaves and was thus the law "of force" at the time of Anthony's conviction, making it proper for the jury to render a verdict and for the court to pass sentence.[22]

Stephen's defense counsel tried to have his conviction for attempted rape overturned on similar grounds. Just as they had challenged the indictment because it failed to state that the victim was a white woman, Stephen's lawyers argued that the verdict was not valid for the same reason. The court once again decided against Stephen, the justices ruling that the jury had convicted Stephen of attempted rape. Which rape? "Of course that charged in the indictment, on Mary Daniel, a free white female," a fact that, as the court pointed out in striking down the earlier challenge, appeared twice in the indictment. Stephen's defense counsel again attempted to argue that rape and attempted rape were distinct offenses that should have been tried independently, with separate verdicts rendered. For the second time, this argument proved unconvincing. The justices ruled that a conviction for attempt to commit a crime is proper if the jury has before it evidence that warrants such a finding.[23]

The ruling was in keeping with the precedent set in the 1849 case of *Alfred v. State*. The Cass County Inferior Court tried Alfred, a slave, for the rape of a four-year-old white girl. The trial judge believed that evidence to convict Alfred of rape was insufficient, and said, in his charge to the jury, "there would be no impropriety in a verdict of guilty of an assault and battery, if they thought he was not guilty of the crime charged." When the jury returned a guilty verdict on the rape charge, Alfred's lawyers appealed, claiming that the verdict was contrary to both law and evidence and the charge of the court. The supreme court sustained Alfred's conviction, holding that, as long as there was "some" evidence upon which the verdict might be based, it would be allowed to stand. The justices went on to say that, while they sympathized with Alfred's plight—apparently they thought the evidence against him especially weak as well—they could find no legal reason for setting aside the verdict and sparing his life. They suggested that he appeal to the governor for a pardon. Alfred hanged.[24] All legal authorities had agreed that there was insufficient evidence to convict Alfred of rape; the supreme court could have reasonably ruled that the guilty verdict was contrary to the evidence. Yet they chose not to, no doubt because of the seriousness with which white Georgia communities took the claim of black male sexual violation of white women. Juries convicted every black man charged with rape between 1812 and 1849, and the state executed every black man convicted of rape between 1755 and 1865.

Lawyers representing several slaves attempted to quash their clients' convictions by claiming that other parties participated in their crimes, making them innocent, or at least less culpable. Lawyers raised these challenges under the law of parties and accessories to crimes. According to Blackstone, under the common law, an individual could be convicted as either a principal or an accessory. Principals were in two degrees. In the first degree, the accused was the "actor, or absolute perpetrator of the crime"; in the second degree, the individual was "present, aiding, and abetting the fact to be done." Presence could be actual or constructive. Actual presence is self-explanatory. Constructive presence occurred when an individual was sufficiently close to the scene of the crime to be considered present, and also aided the principal in the criminal enterprise. Next in order of culpability were accessories, persons not present during the act but in "some way concerned therein, either before or after the act committed." An accessory before the fact "procured, counseled or commanded another" to commit a crime; an accessory after the fact knew a felony had been committed and "received, relieved, comforted or assisted" the felon, with the felony complete at the time the accessory gave assistance. For example, if "A" mortally wounded "B," and "C" rendered aid before "B" died, "C" was not an accessory to "B's" murder.[25]

In 1858, the Greene County Superior Court grand jury indicted Thornton, a slave, accusing him of procuring another slave to kill a white man. The jury found Thornton guilty of being an accessory before the fact in murder and the court sentenced him to death. His counsel appealed the verdict, arguing that a slave could not be convicted of accessory before the fact in murder because no such crime existed in the slave code. A lawyer was once again trying to save his slave client's life by arguing that slave status prevented legal rules from being applied in the customary way. The supreme court saw itself as having to answer two questions: Can a slave commit the crime of accessory before the fact in murder? And if so, is this crime punishable by death? In deciding the case, the court relied on the slave code of 1821 and the penal code of 1817. Under the 1821 code, the murder of a free white person was a capital offense when committed by a slave or a free person of color. (This offense had always been a capital crime, the 1821 law its most recent codification.) The court then proceeded to ask if the crime of murder included the crime of accessory before the fact; to answer this question, the justices turned to the penal code of 1817. The second division of this code indicated that those who aided or abetted the commission of crimes were principals in the second degree. The code provided no punishment for this crime, but Justice Benning declared that the omission did not mean that the legislature did not intend to punish those convicted of this crime. After all, it had devoted an entire division of the penal code to that crime. The court, turning to the common law, held that principals in the second degree should receive the same punishment as those in the first degree. This decision was in keeping with accepted doctrine, and the supreme court affirmed Thornton's conviction and death sentence.[26]

In 1859, a jury in Decatur County Superior Court convicted Hill and a second slave of the murder of a white woman named Margaret Saddler. Hill had not struck the fatal blow nor even touched the victim; his co-defendant had killed her. But in his instructions to the jury, the trial judge told jurors that if they were satisfied that the deceased had died at the hands of any person, the killing was murder, and if the defendant Hill had been present and aided and assisted in the killing, then he too was guilty of murder. In a short opinion upholding the conviction, Chief Justice Lumpkin simply restated the common law doctrine articulated in *Thornton:* "The stroke of one is the stroke of all. They are all principals in law and principals in deed." Hill's lawyers insisted that at most Hill was guilty as a principal in the second degree. Lumpkin ruled that this was a distinction without a difference, because the punishment for both was the same. Justice Linton Stephens dissented, arguing that, while it was true the difference in degrees was irrelevant when it came to punishment, it was vitally important in trial preparation. Hill's indictment simply charged him with murder. Stephens reasoned that by charging Hill as an accessory and not a principal in the second degree, the Decatur County grand jury had denied him sufficient information and notice to mount a defense. By way of example, Stephens pointed out that presence may be both actual and constructive: a man charged with murder appears in court without a defense because he knows he did not kill the victim nor was he in the victim's presence at the time of his death. But at trial he finds that testimony will be introduced that shows he spoke earnestly with the perpetrator before the crime and watched its commission. Had this hypothetical defendant been charged as a principal in the second degree, he would have known what to expect and prepared a defense. In Stephens's view, this was the situation in which Hill found himself. Unfortunately for Hill, Stephens's was the minority opinion.[27]

Georgia applied the law of parties in rather straightforward fashion when all concerned were black. An entirely different—and more complicated—state of affairs existed when one or more of the parties was white. Interracial criminal complicity raised the specter of class and racial upheaval and generated all sorts of questions about the relationship between law, slavery, and white supremacy. For example, the penal statutes for whites did not cover slaves; therefore, if a criminal conspiracy required a certain number of persons, and if the final conspirator were a slave, no involved white person could be prosecuted. If a riot required three persons and there were two whites and a slave, the whites could not be charged. A similar problem arose with the punishment of accessories. A white person could act as an accessory before the fact in a crime committed by a slave. Both the white person and the slave could be tried in separate tribunals, but a problem arose at sentencing. The common law punished an accessory before the fact as a principal. In many instances, the punishment for the principal was death when the defendant was black, but if the principal were white, the sentence would be a lesser one. For example, assault with intent to murder was a capital offense for a slave, but it only mandated imprisonment if committed by a white person.

In 1848, a jury in Putnam County Superior Court convicted Dudley Simmons, a white man, of receiving stolen goods from Bob, a slave, in violation of an 1840 act. Prior to Simmons's trial, Bob, accused of stealing the watch that Simmons had purchased, was acquitted of larceny. Simmons's lawyers argued at the supreme court that under the common law an accessory could not be convicted if a jury had found the principal not guilty. The prosecution countered by claiming that the 1840 act created a new offense, one in which neither common law principles nor those of the penal code on accessories applied. The supreme court disagreed, holding that the purpose of the act was not to change the rules regarding proof in cases involving parties, but to ensure that courts did not punish whites more severely than blacks. Under the slave code, larceny was punishable by corporal punishment that did not "extend to life or limb"; under the penal code, a white man could be sentenced to a prison term of two to five years. So if Simmons was to be convicted as an accessory to Bob's crime, he would have received, in the supreme court's opinion, a stiffer punishment than if he had committed the crime himself. (Of course, severe punishment would have made the point that complicity with slaves was more dangerous than similar criminal cooperation with whites.) Since legislators had enacted the 1840 law only to prevent such undesirable results, and not to change the common law principles regarding parties, those principles were applicable in Simmons's case. Under those principles, Bob's guilt had to be established before Simmons could be found culpable. The supreme court reversed his conviction.[28] By adhering to common law principles, the justices ensured that a white man would not be punished when a jury had acquitted his slave co-conspirator.

Problems also arose if an act was a crime for one status group but not the other. This scenario presented itself in *Grady v. State,* in 1852. In that case, a jury had convicted Thomas Grady, a white man, under an 1850 law of inducing a slave to run away to a free state with two other slaves. The law read, in relevant part, "If any free white person shall attempt to procure a slave to commit a crime . . . he shall be presented for such attempt, and if found guilty, shall incur the same punishment as if such free white person had committed the same crime, which he had attempted to procure the slave to commit." On appeal, Grady argued that his conviction was invalid because it was not a crime for one slave to steal another; therefore, being a party to such an act was likewise, no crime. The supreme court handled this argument by ruling that the legislators intended the 1850 law to refer to whites' criminal acts. Lumpkin believed the "very language of the law is the key to unlocking its meaning. It speaks of an attempt to procure a slave to commit a *crime;* but if the stealing of negroes, is not a crime by a slave, but is by a white man, then the Statute *ex vi termini* refers to such acts only as are by law, criminal in white men." Lumpkin went on to point out that this construction also prevented white people from being punished as blacks were. Grady's conviction stood.[29]

The criminal complicity of masters and their agents represented a special exception to the general law of parties. If a slave committed a non-capital crime at the command or under the compulsion of his master or the master's agent, the master or agent was punished and the slave held innocent as merely an extension of his master's will. According to Blackstone, this rule was similar to that regarding wives under the common law. Wives were not criminally liable for acts performed at their husbands' direction; this excuse, however, did not extend to servants. They were "as much free agents as their masters" and were therefore held accountable for their actions. (Blackstone does not comment on the liability of slaves, because the common law was "a stranger to slavery.") To be excused from criminal culpability, a slave had to be acting under compulsion; it was not enough that the master be aware of or have condoned the criminal behavior.

In 1850, a jury found Joseph Pannell, a white man, guilty of selling liquor to a slave. In his defense, Pannell claimed that the slave's master knew he had come to him for liquor, and that the overseer, the master's agent, was present during the transaction. The supreme court ruled that the only way Pannell would escape punishment was if the master had sent his slave to procure the liquor for him, and not for the slave himself. The supreme court affirmed Panell's conviction.[30]

Lawyers for slave defendants also based appeals on the rules of evidence, none as important as those regarding confessions. According to Simon Greenleaf, a nineteenth-century authority on evidence, "evidence of verbal confessions of guilt" was to be "received with great caution. For, besides the danger of mistake, from the misapprehension of witnesses, the misuse of words, the failure of the party to express his own meaning, and the infirmity of memory, it should be recollected that the mind of the prisoner himself is oppressed by the calamity of his situation, and that he is often influenced by motives of hope or fear to make untrue confessions." But confessions of guilt were among the most effectual proofs in the law if deliberate and voluntary. "A rational being will not make admissions prejudicial to his interest and safety, unless when urged by the promptings of truth and conscience," wrote Greenleaf in the 1892 edition of his *Treatise on the Law of Evidence.*[31]

Judges examined the circumstances surrounding incriminating admissions to determine their voluntariness. Courts asked witnesses if anyone had told the defendant it would be better to confess or worse if he did not. For Greenleaf, the key factor was whether interlocutors had obtained the confession "by the influence of hope or fear applied by a third person to the prisoner's mind." Despite this criterion, Thomas R. R. Cobb, one of Georgia's leading legal minds, was reluctant to accept the confessions of slaves. He acknowledged that courts regularly admitted slaves' confessions under the same circumstances as whites' but warned, "They should be received with great caution and allowed but little weight, especially when made to the jailor or arresting officers, for the habit of obedience in the slave compels him to answer all questions of the idlest curiosity, while his mendacious disposition will always involve even the most innocent in the most contradictory inconsistencies."[32]

In spite of Cobb's warnings, courts in the Slave South always deemed slaves' confessions admissible and considered them the best proofs of crimes if made deliberately and voluntarily. If their social betters awed slaves, as Cobb claimed, they seldom showed it by confessing. In eighteenth-century Virginia, only fifteen slaves confessed, and the numbers did not rise appreciably in the nineteenth century.[33] In Georgia, black defendants seldom confessed or pleaded guilty; only thirty entered guilty pleas during the entire colonial and antebellum periods. This unwillingness to admit guilt may have been the consequence of black intransigence and common sense, or of masters' refusal to allow slaves to do anything that might jeopardize their lives and value as chattel.

The Georgia Supreme Court first outlined the guidelines for the admissibility of slaves' confessions in 1852 in *Stephen v. State.* A jury had convicted Stephen of attempting to rape a mentally challenged ten-year-old white girl. Part of the evidence against him was a confession he had made to John W. Johnson, a white man in whose custody he had been temporarily left. Without prompting, so Johnson said, Stephen admitted to attempting to rape the victim but said another slave had talked him into it. Johnson cautioned that he should be "careful how he talked, for that it might cost him his life." Despite this warning, Stephen continued to unburden himself. There was no evidence that Johnson had made any threats or promises. In upholding the admissibility of this confession, Chief Justice Lumpkin articulated standard common law doctrine: "A confession, whether made upon official examination or in discourse with private persons, which is obtained from the defendant, either by the flattery of hope or by the impression of fear, however slightly the emotion may be implanted, IS NOT ADMISSIBLE EVIDENCE. For the law will not suffer a prisoner to be made the instrument of his own conviction." In the view of the court, no one had exerted such undue influence on Stephen at the time of his confession.[34]

In 1854, Jim, a slave, was convicted of murdering a white man in Lee County. While tied up at the plantation gin house, Jim confessed details of the crime to a white man. Jim's lawyers challenged the confession, arguing that, as a slave, Jim had to answer all questions put to him by a white man, especially if that man was in authority over him, and that being bound constituted undue duress. Justice Ebenezer Starnes refused to accept the proposition that slaves were required to answer any questions put before them regardless of the personal cost such responses might exact. "It may be true, that it is proper for a slave, always to answer, respectfully, the questions of a white man; but if this be so, it does not follow, that where no improper effort is made to extort confessions from him, he is obliged to make confessions to any white man who questions him." To do so "would lead to very troublesome and injurious consequences." Starnes did not specify what these "injurious consequences" might be, but slaves telling all that they knew to inquiring whites could not only negatively affect them, but also damage their owners' interests in any number of circumstances. In the context of a capital trial, a slave's confession could cost the slave her life and her master the considerable investment he had made in her. The court also did not believe the fact that Jim was tied up at the time of his confession constituted undue duress.

The justices avoided the defense's third contention, that slaves were required to answer all questions posed by authority figures. They concluded that no one had introduced evidence to show that the witness was such a person. In doing so, they upheld Jim's conviction and avoided an extremely thorny issue. If slaves were truly extensions of their masters' wills, as pro-slavery theorists argued, then how could these will-less creatures ever make voluntary confessions to masters, mistresses, or overseers? Cobb argued the slave is "bound, and habituated to obey every command and wish" of his master. "He has no will to refuse obedience, even when it involves his life. The master is his protector, his counsel, his confidant. He cannot, if he will, seek the advice and direction of legal counsel." Moreover, "the slave is always ready to mould his answers so as to please the master," so "no confidence can be placed in the truth of his statements." In Cobb's view, "such communications should be excluded from the jury."[35]

Southern jurists did not go as far as Cobb might have liked, but they were suspicious of slaves' confessions made to those with legitimate power over them. In *Wyatt (a slave) v. State,* the Alabama Supreme Court ruled that confessions made to masters should be considered with "caution, whether the confessions of guilt are made by a slave in interviews had with his master, or one having dominion over him, were not elicited or controlled by the relation, and predicated upon the fear of punishment or injury, or upon the hope of some benefit to be gained by making them." In *Simon (a slave) v. State,* the Florida Supreme Court urged similar prudence. The fact that the slave in this case made the confession to his master should be "entitled to the most grave consideration. The ease with which this class of our population can be intimidated, and the almost absolute control which the owner . . . [has] over the will of the slave, should induce the Courts at all times to receive their confessions with the utmost caution and distrust." The Mississippi Supreme Court took a different tack in *Sam (a slave) v. State,* accepting the admission by a slave, Sam, to his master that he had burned a gin house. The court held that "the relation which a slave bears to the master, is certainly one of dependence and obedience, but it is not necessarily one of constraint and duress. . . . It is not to be presumed that the master exercises an undue influence over his slave to induce him to make confessions tending to convict him of a capital offense."[36]

Exactly how far inquisitors in Georgia could go in securing confessions without putting the defendant under duress is revealed in *Sarah v. State.* In 1859, authorities suspected that Sarah, a slave, and a white man, probably

[handwritten margin note: Confessions by slaves were inadmissible in all southern states except Mississippi]

her lover, had attempted to poison her master and his family. Sarah was whipped and confessed the crime to her master. Later in the day, a white neighbor asked her about the crime; the presiding judge admitted Sarah's statements into evidence at trial. Sarah's experience was not unique. Slaves suspected of having committed crimes were routinely beaten, hanged by their thumbs, and tortured in other ways to extract information. Sarah's lawyers attempted to quash the confession by arguing she had given it under duress. Justice Lumpkin did not believe corporal punishment under these circumstances constituted undue duress. "What if the negro had been whipped by her master the morning before she made the confession, as proven by the witness, that does not make her voluntary confessions . . . subsequently objectionable." In Lumpkin's view, one act had nothing to do with the other; the chief justice provided no further explanation—other than that defense counsel should have raised its objection earlier in the proceedings. The decision in *Sarah v. State* was in marked contrast to the Alabama Supreme Court's ruling in *State v. Clarissa*. There the court ruled that a confession obtained by whipping was inadmissible even though three days had elapsed between the beating and the confession.[37]

Mason Stephenson and D. Grier Stephenson Jr. have strongly criticized Lumpkin's decision in *Sarah v. State,* maintaining that Lumpkin was a hypocrite, ignoring his own logic from *Stephen v. State* to arrive at a decision he liked. Lumpkin's reasoning was not entirely without legal basis. According to Greenleaf, under the common law, confessions were admissible if the influence of the promises or threats had been "totally done away with" before the confession was made or the evidence was received.[38] One wonders if the influence of numerous stripes of a cowhide whip could ever be "totally done away with." Lumpkin apparently thought so and Sarah was hanged. ✴

By far, the issue that was the subject of the largest number of appeals in antebellum Georgia was jury selection. Lawyers for thirteen defendants challenged their clients' convictions in the supreme court by claiming that jurors were biased or improperly selected. Since black defendants were members of a dishonored and subjugated race charged with violating the persons and property of the dominant racial group—some of whose members would sit in judgment at trial—it is not surprising that bias was possibly the central concern of their lawyers. In 1849, Alfred, a Cass County slave, appeared in the inferior court accused of attempted rape. Under the acts of 1811 and 1816, between twenty-six and thirty-six jurors had to be impaneled for capital trials. After the prosecution and defense had chosen twenty-three jurors,

Alfred's owner waived selection of the remainder and agreed that the first twelve men called would try his slave. After the jury found Alfred guilty, his owner appealed, asserting that his waiving of the remaining jurors had been improper. The lawyer for the owner argued that "the slave being property, and supposed to be merely passive, the Court is bound to see that he had the legal number of Jurors summoned for his trial, and that his owner could not waive his right." The supreme court held that in crafting the 1811 law the legislature wanted masters to select juries, as was clear from its having granted them the right to challenge jurors. The justices reasoned no master would knowingly and willingly make a decision against his slave, because "the interest which the owner has in his slave . . . [and] his personal attachment for him will always prompt him to be vigilant in securing and protecting all the rights of his slave." In this instance, the owner obviously thought that taking the first twelve jurors was the best way to secure those interests. The supreme court upheld Alfred's conviction.[39]

After the trial of Rafe, a slave, for murder, his lawyer on appeal objected to the jury selection procedure, arguing that the clerk of the inferior court had not properly compiled a list of qualified jurors, that the names of those chosen were not placed in the jury box in the presence of a superior court judge, that the names of the petit jury had not been drawn from the proper compartment of the jury box, and that the jury venire was not the one selected at the last term of the court. All of these acts were violations of the jury selection statute; to the defense, these violations made the impaneling of an impartial jury impossible. The defense also alleged that one juror had expressed a legally unacceptable bias against its client. Although Justice Charles McDonald acknowledged the technical violations of the law, he held that "the Statutes for selecting Jurors, drawing and summoning them, form no part of a system to procure an impartial jury to parties. They establish a mode of distributing jury duties among persons in the respective counties, subject to that kind of service, and of setting apart those of supposed higher qualifications for the most important branch of that service; they provide for rotation in Jury service." McDonald declared that the irregularities of the case did not defeat these goals, and that an act of 1856 ensured that biased jurors would not be chosen.

The 1856 act mandated that three questions be asked of jurors whose impartiality was suspect: "Have you, from having seen the crime committed, or heard any part of the evidence delivered on oath, formed and expressed any opinion in regard to the guilt or innocence of the prisoner at the bar?"

If the juror responded negatively, the judge asked, "Have you any prejudice or bias resting on your mind, for or against the prisoner at the bar?" If the juror also answered this question in the negative, the judge then asked, "Is your mind perfectly impartial between the State and the accused?" If he said "Yes," the court considered the juror competent as a matter of law. In capital cases, the judge asked a fourth question: "Are you conscientiously opposed to capital punishment?" Those who were unopposed were competent to sit on a capital jury. Either side could introduce evidence to prove that the prospective jurors' answers were false.[40]

At Rafe's trial, a juror said he had an opinion about the case but not from having seen the crime or having heard testimony under oath; it was solely based on rumor. The trial judge ruled the juror was qualified to assume his seat, whereupon defense counsel on appeal sought to overturn the conviction. Justice McDonald decided that as structured the act of 1856 was sufficient to ensure impartiality if followed, as it was in this case. Having a prior opinion about the case not based on personal knowledge or evidence was not, in and of itself, an impediment to jury service, because "men of the soundest heads and purest hearts, and without the slightest prejudice against the perpetrator of a crime might pass an hypothetical opinion in his case, predicated on a rumor, and still be competent to do ample justice upon hearing testimony falsifying the rumor." If the juror was willing to have his opinion changed based on evidence and testimony, he was fit to sit in judgment. Nor was this view of impartiality confined to Georgia. In Tennessee, courts dismissed jurors if they learned the circumstances of a case and used that knowledge to develop an opinion, but if jurors had based their opinions on rumor alone courts, did not excuse them.[41] The supreme court affirmed Rafe's conviction.

The questions of the 1856 act were the only ones that could be asked of a prospective juror to ascertain his level of partiality. In 1861, the Sumter County Superior Court tried Monday, a slave, for murder; his lawyer investigated a juror's level of bias by asking if he had spoken with the prosecutor and expressed an opinion about the case. The prosecutor objected, arguing that only the questions from the 1856 act could be asked. The trial judge agreed, and so did the supreme court.[42]

While the various mandatory questions might have been sufficient to discern bias a white juror might have against a white defendant, they did not even begin to uncover the kind of bias against blacks white jurors brought into jury boxes. This type of racial bias was so interwoven into the social fabric of the South that all participants in the process—from judges and prosecutors down to clerks, constables, and jury members—shared it. Perhaps that is why there were no direct questions on the issue. For white actors, it was not bias but reality, the way they understood blacks in their world. Jurors could truthfully answer that they had no "prejudice or bias" in their minds if they considered blacks naturally indolent, mendacious, or violent. Most others did, too.

Appellate Success Rates and Their Practical Effect

Superior and inferior courts convicted 224 blacks of capital crimes in Georgia from 1755 to 1865, as recorded in the data gathered for this study; the owners of thirty-eight filed appeals for them. These appeals led to new trials in eighteen cases, a success rate of nearly 50 percent (47.4 percent). Black defendants were more successful in having their convictions overturned than were whites, who secured reversals in only 43.8 percent of cases they appealed to the Georgia Supreme Court. Blacks were similarly successful in antebellum Tennessee. There, the supreme court sustained the causes of twenty-three of thirty-three slave defendants. The court reversed a higher percentage of black convictions than white, 70 percent compared to 53 percent. Indeed, in the Slave South as a whole, blacks achieved a higher level of success than whites in antebellum supreme courts. The legal scholar A. E. Keir Nash, in his study of nine Deep South states, found that between 1830 and 1860 blacks were successful in 57.6 percent of their cases, compared to only 30.9 percent for whites.[43]

In several influential articles, Nash offered reasons for the unexpected evenhandedness of antebellum appellate judges. First, judges were removed from politics that demanded strident defenses of slavery; they did not have to joust with Northern antislavery politicians, and they generally did not have to seek the votes of proslavery constituents. Second, as judges, they dealt with black defendants as individuals, making it far more difficult to ignore their humanity. Third, as jurists, they had a professional investment in the rule of law. But these characteristics of the judicial role were not enough to explain the behavior of Southern judges. For Nash, deep-seated, even unconscious, doubts about the morality of slavery in an increasingly liberal western world were also responsible for Southern judges' commitment to formalism and the rule of law. These doubts led judges to think about and recognize black defendants' humanity. Nash concluded that the tone of the opinions handed down displayed "genuine feeling," which meant that these judges wanted the "governmental structure" to consider blacks as human beings. Nash's conclusions in various publications in the 1970s challenged generations of scholarship, and historians of law and criminal justice produced works to support and challenge his thesis.[44]

Assuming that Nash's characterization of the motivations of Southern judges is correct—that they did recognize black humanity on some level—we must next consider the practical effect of this acknowledgment. The purpose of appellate rights, from the standpoint of the defendant, is to correct errors in the original trial and to secure an acquittal or some other form of judicial relief. But for blacks in Georgia, such relief seldom came. Of the eighteen slave defendants who received new trials, only six received acquittals or release because of mistrials. The majority of those who won their appeals may have been convicted. Of the remaining twelve slaves, nine can be accounted for: one received lashes; three, a combination of whipping and mutilation; five, hanging; and the fates of three remain unknown. Of 224 blacks convicted in Georgia's courts, the appellate process spared only six. Owners of slave defendants had the right of appeal; it just did those they owned very little good. Georgia and its appellate jurists could congratulate themselves on a seemingly fair and humane system and boast of it to the world. But appellate judges might also have been willing to commit to fairness and formalism because history had shown them that, in the end, slave defendants would be punished, just as their local communities had intended. The legal historian Kermit Hall reminds us, "Too much . . . can be made of fairness to slaves in criminal trial courts of the antebellum South."[45]

Free black defendants, or their guardians, and owners of slave defendants who did not file appeals, or whose appeals failed to exonerate them or ameliorate their punishments, had one remaining option: to turn to the governor for relief. But applying to the chief executive for a pardon or clemency was either a hopeless enterprise or a very successful one, depending on when masters and lawyers made the requests. During the colonial period, such pleas fell on deaf ears, but in the antebellum years, success was virtually guaranteed. The colonial governor's council did not grant the appeal of, or extend mercy to, a single slave whose owner appealed. In 1767, the master of a slave convicted of robbery asked the council to spare his slave's life; the council denied his plea. In 1768, Dickson's owner appealed the slave's conviction for the murder of a free black man; in a unanimous decision, the governor's council ruled that his death sentence should be carried out. In 1771, the master of a slave convicted of breaking into a store asked the council to allow him to transport the slave out of the colony; again, council members decided the slave should hang.[46]

The situation changed dramatically during the antebellum period, when owners of twenty-four slave defendants applied for some form of relief and all but one received it. Most defendants were pardoned outright, with no conditions; for others, portions of their sentences were reduced. In 1820, a jury convicted Hatten, a slave, of assaulting a white man with intent to murder and the court sentenced him to receive 100 lashes and to be branded on the cheek with the letter "A." The governor suspended the branding portion of the sentence. A court had likewise convicted Charles, a slave, of assaulting a white person and sentenced him to receive 117 lashes. Governor John Clark reduced the number of lashes to 39. Although whites received similarly lenient treatment, blacks fared better. Between 1836 and 1843, 112 whites petitioned governors William Schley and George R. Gilmer for pardons; the governors granted 96 of these requests. From 1854 to 1857, 211 whites asked to be pardoned; Governor Herschel V. Jenkins honored the requests of all but 49 of them. Jenkins granted pardons for a number of reasons: insufficient evidence of guilt, poor health, old age, extreme youth, or because convicts were from good families and could be expected to reform themselves.[47]

The situation was much different in Tennessee. Under that state's constitution, the governor had the right to dispense reprieves and pardons. Only three slave defendants received relief.[48] Georgia governors were probably generous in granting pardons and suspending punishments because such generosity was in keeping with the paternalistic ethos of the slaveholding leaders of the state. One of the most valued characteristics of the powerful paternalist was his ability to be merciful, to bestow favor on those beneath him when they were in no position to force the issue. This noblesse oblige is said to have guaranteed the loyalty of those who received it. Given the success ratio of antebellum pardons, it is surprising that so few owners of slave defendants saw fit to make use of them.

By the start of the Civil War, black defendants in Georgia had come to possess all of the same trial rights as whites. They could even have their convictions appealed to the state's highest court. At the supreme court, the justices rather evenhandedly applied accepted legal principles and reasoning to black cases. But these "rights" and the equanimity of appellate judges were of little practical value for the vast majority of slaves and free blacks. On plantations and farms, individual masters and mistresses determined the quantity and quality of the mercy slaves received and they decided the course trials would take for the relative handful of slaves who found their way into court; bondspeople played no role in the process. If masters were sufficiently concerned or self-interested, slaves could receive quality legal representation, all the way up to the supreme court. Once there, lawyers argued conscientiously on behalf of their enslaved clients—or more precisely, their masters—taking advantage of the same kinds of procedural loopholes available to white citizens. But this legal acumen did not benefit many blacks; juries acquitted perhaps just a half-dozen.

Ironically, those slaves whose masters appealed to the governor and to the paternalistic ethics of their slaveholding society fared better than those who relied on the law. Governors could afford to be benevolent because the pardons and clemency they provided did not threaten the socio-legal order as repeated appellate success would have. Individual gubernatorial relief did not set legal precedents that could potentially benefit scores of black convicts. Legal culture in Georgia demanded that the scales of justice tip in favor of slavery and white racial domination, and the appellate process complied with that dictate.

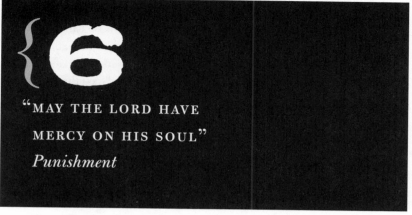

Joe . . . has been found guilty of the crime of murder. . . . On Friday
the thirtieth day of November . . . between the hours ten o'clock A.M. and
two o'clock P.M. at the place of capital punishment in said county—the
said Joe be by the Sheriff of Screven County hung by the neck until dead.
And may the Lord have mercy on his soul.
—Alpheus M. Rodgers, Georgia Attorney General, 1860

Punishment was the final act in the criminal justice process. The overwhelming majority of blacks sanctioned for crimes in the South received
their punishments on plantations, far beyond the eyes and ears of the public
and the present generation of historians. But, from available records, we do
know they were routinely whipped, mutilated, and occasionally killed for
violations of "plantation law."

George Washington Browning's owner was generally humane in whipping slaves, but on one occasion he lost his temper at Aunt Millie, a slave
woman whom he had caught stealing, and whipped her until blood ran in
streams down her back. Annette Milledge remembered, "Sometimes dey
would whoop dem terrible. Dey tied dem acros't a barrel and whoop dem
until de blood run out. De leas' little thing dey whoop de hide off 'em." Masters used various implements to facilitate corporal punishment. A whipping
pole used on one Georgia plantation was a shaft several feet in diameter with
a handcuff at the top to secure the slave while the master or overseer applied
the lash. One master had stocks built to serve as the site of punishment.
Owners punished other bad bondsmen with the "buck": the slave was made

to squat, a large stick was placed behind his knees, and his hands were tied to it. The slave was whipped in this incredibly painful position.[1]

When the whip failed to produce the desired results, masters turned to other forms of corporal punishment. One master hung recalcitrant slaves by their thumbs from an overhead beam; he branded others for breaking plantation rules. Another master drove nails into a barrel, placed the "prisoner" inside of it, and rolled it down a hill.[2]

Overall Distribution of Punishments

Trial records reflect criminal sanctions imposed by the state. Georgia hanged the majority of black convicts, 54 percent, and subjected 25 percent to punishments that combined whipping with branding—or some other form of mutilation and/or transportation—that is, sale outside the state. (I will refer to these punishments as combination punishments.) The state whipped the remaining 18 percent.[3]

Black hangings were public spectacles. Catherine M. Huey, a white woman, recounts the death of Henry Jackson, a slave convicted in the town of Decatur of raping a twelve-year-old white girl. Huey dressed up for the execution and joined the "great many people who thronged the streets and clustered around the weatherbeaten log jail." For several hours she was "pleasantly situated" in "good company," she wrote in 1853; "time passed almost imperceptibly" as she and the others waited for the event. The crowd was divided by race, with whites on one side of the street and blacks on the other. Huey found it "gratifying . . . to see the willingness of slaveowners to teach their slaves an important lesson" by compelling them to witness the hanging. Finally, the sheriff drove Jackson to the scene on an ox cart. He was "dressed in a suit of white . . . sitting by the coffin which was to encase his lifeless form." An unnamed black man "ascended the stand and sang a hymn." Jackson asked permission to speak to the audience, and the sheriff allowed him fifteen or twenty minutes. "His discourse was very affecting," wrote Huey. After the sheriff tied Jackson's hands and feet, he placed a white handkerchief over his face and the noose around his neck, then "drew the cart on which the convict stood, from under him, leaving the dangling form of the poor victim suspended in the air by a cord. When the form dropped from the cart, a loud groan went up from the people and they began to disperse."[4]

Georgia slaves who voiced objection to the death penalty usually did so on scriptural grounds. Former slave Mary Carpenter said, "I don't believe in hangin' an sich, cauz the word o' God says: Thou shalt not kill." Taking a human life, regardless of the justification, was a sin. Other ex-slaves said that in a world of sinners, no one was qualified to judge and punish others. That power belonged to God. Harriet Benton expressed this sentiment well: "As people sow, so shall they reap, it is not given to man to judge his fellow man." Anne Prather, who believed "divine punishment" awaited those who violated the criminal law, seconded Benton's assertion: man was in "no position to judge." Opposition to capital punishment and a belief in divine avenging did not, however, lead to slaves' opposition to all forms of retributive justice. One former slave, Robert Kimbrough, thought forms of physical and mental torture should be employed to compel the criminal to take his own life. "The culprit should bring his own blood down on his own head."[5] In a culture where mortal decisions most often went against them, it seems only natural for slaves to argue for divine protection, judgment, and punishment.

Executing the majority of convicted blacks suggests a clear lack of regard for their lives, but the reality was more complicated. Whites relied on hanging to send a message that serious black criminality would not be tolerated. Still, one important obstacle blocked full use of this crime-control technique: slaves' financial worth to their masters. Slaves were an extremely valuable commodity, so execution had serious financial consequences for masters. Thus, in sentencing, Georgia judges and juries had to weigh the property interests of slaveowners against the public's interest in safety. Over the course of the 110 years between 1755 and 1865, the scales tipped increasingly in favor of the property interests of the slaveholding class. Between 1755 and 1811, the state hanged 68 percent of convicted blacks, 54.5 percent between 1812 and 1849, and 51.7 percent by 1865. This approximately 26 percent decline in the use of the noose coincides with a number of factors that raised the costs of executing slaves. In 1770, Georgia lawmakers passed an act that required the colony to pay to the owners of executed slaves the slaves' appraised value, provided it did not exceed £40 sterling. This reimbursement was intended to encourage masters to ensure the presence of accused slaves for trial rather than attempt to hide them or to destroy or conceal important evidence. It had the corresponding effect of removing the principal barrier to the execution of slaves. The legislature repealed the compensation provision in 1793, raising the costs of putting slaves to death. With the closing of the slave trade in 1808, and the cotton boom that followed it, prices of slaves rose, making executing bondsmen a more expensive proposition. In 1830, a prime field hand could be purchased for $700; by 1860, the price had more than doubled, to $1,800.[6]

With their individual and collective prosperity depending on slaves, antebellum Georgia legislators, slaveowners, judges, and juries had a tremendous incentive to preserve slaves' lives. They provided bondspeople with greater procedural protections in court and used lesser forms of punishment. (Virginia chose to continue compensating owners and/or allowing owners to sell convicts out of state.[7]) This shift in punishment strategy is reflected in the increased use of flogging and combination punishments. From 1755 to 1850, flogging was the most frequent sanction after hanging; after 1850, combination punishments surpassed flogging, suggesting a desire to inflict a harsher punishment but one less severe than death, thus balancing public safety and slaveholders' property values. Fewer executions also conveyed to an increasingly critical North the impression that the slave system had become more humane.

Those blacks sentenced to the lash (alone or as part of a combination punishment) received a mean average of 179 lashes during the colonial and antebellum periods and a median of approximately 117. Moses, a Jones County slave convicted in 1822 of stealing $90 in bank notes during a burglary, received the lowest number, 25 lashes, and his owner removed him from the state. The greatest recorded number of lashes was laid on the back of George, an Emanuel County slave convicted of attempting to kill a white man in 1856. Each Tuesday for six months George received 50 lashes on his bare back, for a total of at least 1,200 lashes. He was branded on the right cheek with the letter "M" for murder and returned to his life in bondage.[8]

The number of lashes varied depending on the period in which the punishment occurred. During the colonial period, black Georgia convicts received a mean average of 123 lashes and a median of 75 lashes. After 1811, these numbers declined slightly, but rose by 1865 to mean and median averages of 220 and 195 lashes, respectively. This seesawing is probably best explained by an increase in certain serious crimes after 1850 and the resulting decision of Georgia judges to stiffen punishments. Between 1850 and 1865, prosecutions for murder increased from 25 percent of all crimes to 38.9 percent, and prosecutions for attempted murder increased from 17.7 percent to 20.5 percent. Rapes rose from 3.1 percent of all criminal prosecutions to 4.9 percent.[9] Courts punished these three crimes most frequently with death, but with the declining use of the gallows after 1850, they resorted to alternative means of punishment.

The state began to use combination punishments with the decline of executions after 1811. While this punishment seemed to be a suitable substitute for hanging, it had a point of diminishing returns. The intensity of these punishments could be heightened only through more extensive physical mutilation or by increasing the number of lashes. But more branding and ear-cropping (an extremely painful and disfiguring process in which a portion of the ear was cut off) and such punishments could ruin the value of a slave. The number of lashes could be safely increased by spreading the punishment over a longer period (as was done in the case of George) or by using whips made of materials that caused less damage than cowhide. In the late antebellum period, the state used the whip with greater frequency to augment combination punishments to a degree it considered sufficient to deter black criminals. During the colonial period, other slave states had used mutilation as a form of punishment, but Georgia may have been alone in its continued and consistent use of draconian punishments through the Civil War.[10]

Those convicts sentenced to combination punishments received a number of lashes, followed by branding (to identify the crime of conviction), cropping of their ears, or sale out of state. In 1862, a jury convicted Tom, a Columbia County slave, of murder. The court sentenced him to 50 lashes on six successive Mondays until he had received 300 lashes, after which he was to be branded on the right cheek with the letter "M" (for murder). Greene County slave Simon killed another slave in 1853, and a jury found him guilty of voluntary manslaughter. He received 39 lashes and was branded on the right cheek with the letter "M" and discharged. In 1850, King, a Fayette County slave, was convicted of arson. He received 50 lashes on four separate days in March and April, then was branded on each cheek with the letter "A." In 1861, a Talbot County jury found the slaves Jeff, Primus, and Bill guilty of burglary. Authorities branded them on the right cheek with the letter "B," so the public—and prospective buyers—would know of their dangerous characters, and cropped their left ears in the public square.[11]

Three Georgia slaves received other sentences—not hanging, whipping, or a combination punishment—in the colonial and antebellum periods. Caleb and Charlotte, convicted on April 18, 1865, in Oglethorpe County Superior Court of assaulting a white man and poisoning a white child, both with intent to kill, received no punishment at all. The court simply required their owners to pay unspecified costs. This extremely lenient and unusual sentence was undoubtedly a result of the fact that the Civil War was over and the convicts were no longer slaves. The end of slavery created profound problems for the Georgia criminal justice system. Courts never adjudicated a significant number of cases involving slaves in early 1865.

In 1863, a Bibb County jury convicted Milton, a slave, of attempting to rape a white woman. The court "authorized and directed" a committee of surgeons "to perform on the person of said Milton the surgical operation of castration as the penalty inflicted for the offense for which said boy stands convicted." It was the first and only time a Georgia court ordered removal of a black convict's testicles as punishment for a crime, a grisly punishment that was against Georgia law. A number of other states had made castration a penalty for rape or attempted rape during the colonial period. One newspaper editor in central Georgia wrote in 1827 that sexual mutilation and incapacitation were far too lenient a punishment for such a heinous crime.[12]

{ *Punishment and Crime Type*

The category of crime of which the defendant had been convicted significantly affected the severity of punishment in Georgia from 1755 to 1865. The state imposed the harshest penalty, death by hanging, most frequently on blacks convicted of crimes against persons, and reserved the least severe punishments for those who committed crimes against public order. Over 88 percent of those hanged were put to death for crimes against persons; courts sent only 10.5 percent of black convicts to the gallows for property crimes. No blacks hanged for offenses against public order. This distribution of capital punishments was similar to South Carolina's. Of the 296 slaves executed there between 1800 and 1855, nearly 72 percent lost their lives for crimes against persons. In colonial Virginia, in marked contrast to Georgia and South Carolina, most slaves were sentenced to death for property crimes. As the antebellum period progressed, this trend reversed itself, and almost 69 percent of those condemned to hang had been convicted of crimes against persons, aligning the state with Georgia and South Carolina.[13]

The use of combination punishments closely approximated that of hanging. Seventy percent of those so sentenced had been convicted of crimes against persons, compared to only 24 percent for crimes against property. Only three convicted of crimes against public order received combination punishment. Courts imposed flogging, the final sanction, more frequently

CASTRATION AS PUNISHMENT.

on those convicted of crimes against persons—nearly 67 percent of those whipped, compared to only 24 percent for crimes against property and 2.8 percent for crimes against public order.

It is clear from the distribution of punishments that Georgia's judges considered crimes against life more threatening to their society than crimes against property; their sentencing practices were no doubt a reflection of the values of a slave society. One of the greatest fears of any such society was of insurrection; by punishing crimes against persons most severely, whites hoped to curb or eliminate what they considered slaves' tendencies toward violence. Southern masters had also come to accept a certain level of property crime, especially various forms of theft, as one of the costs of maintaining a slave economy. These societal priorities are even more evident when one examines punishments for individual crimes.

Despite the dozens of crimes of which they could have been convicted, blacks in Georgia courts were convicted and sentenced for only twelve types of criminal offenses: murder, attempted murder, rape, attempted rape, poisoning, manslaughter, robbery, arson, burglary, larceny, insurrection, and aiding runaways. The state punished two slaves for unknown offenses, and two for offenses against persons that did not fit into other categories of crimes against persons (mayhem is an example). The seriousness with which white Georgians regarded these crimes is reflected in the punishments inflicted on those who engaged in them. Murder, the most serious crime, merited the most serious punishment: hanging. Nearly 55 percent of those hanged were executed for murder, and 69.5 percent of those so convicted went to the gallows—an execution rate for murder that was more than three times higher than that of South Carolina, where murder accounted for only 28.6 percent of all executions.[14] Attempted murder, the next crime on the hierarchy of seriousness, accounted for 14.3 percent of all state-sanctioned killings in Georgia; nearly 36 percent of all blacks convicted of attempted murder hanged. Just over 11 percent of all capital sentences were handed down for rape, and all black defendants convicted of rape were hanged. While convictions for rape were far from certain, the punishment was not. The state executed single-digit percentages of blacks for attempted rape, arson, burglary and poisoning (see table 8). No defendants convicted of manslaughter, larceny, insurrection, or aiding runaways lost their lives. This distribution of punishments in Georgia further demonstrates that whites considered crimes against persons far more serious than those against property and public order.

Table 8 also demonstrates that the hierarchy of perceived seriousness was evident in the administering of combination punishments. Forty-two percent of those who received combination punishments had been convicted of murder; a little more than 25 percent of all defendants convicted of this crime were whipped and branded or mutilated in some other fashion. Courts sentenced nearly one-quarter of those convicted of attempted murder to combination punishments, accounting for 20 percent of all combination punishments. Almost 32 percent of all burglars faced combination punishment, accounting for 14 percent of the total. Arson closely followed burglary in the category, making up 10 percent of the total punishments. Judges clearly preferred combination punishments in arson cases; they punished over 62 percent of the arsonists in this way. The state sentenced only one black convict to combination punishment for attempted rape, and a few received the same sentence for manslaughter, other crimes against persons, and aiding runaways.

Counties used whipping, the least severe punishment, infrequently for serious crime. Authorities only applied the lash to the backs of 4.9 percent of those convicted of murder, and used it not at all for those found guilty of rape or attempted rape, arson, poisoning, or manslaughter. Flogging primarily awaited those convicted of burglary and serious but non-lethal assaults, accounting for 19.4 percent and 44.4 percent of punishments in the category, respectively. While the use of the whip for a lesser property offense, like burglary, is understandable, its use in cases of attempted murder is less so. The most likely explanation for this paradoxical outcome is that judges took account of the nature of the specific injury and the status of the victim in individual cases before passing sentence. A slave who cut another slave across the chest could expect the lash; one who stabbed his master in the stomach could not.

Punishment and Victim Status

Logic dictates that in a society based on racial slavery, crimes against the dominant race would be most severely punished. This logic held true for Georgia. Over 65 percent of all punishments were administered for crimes against whites in the period from 1755 to 1865. For capital punishment, the pattern was even more pronounced. Seventy-six percent of black convicts hanged for victimizing white men, women, and children, clearly indicating the premium placed on their lives. Conversely, blacks who victimized other

TABLE 8. PUNISHMENT BY CRIME, 1755–1865

Crime (the final two columns, "Poisoning persons crime" and "Aiding runaway", fall under the heading *Other*)

Punishment		Unknown	Murder	Attempted murder	Rape	Attempted rape	Man-slaughter	Arson	Burglary	Poison-ing	Poison-persons crime	Aiding runaway
Lashes	Cases	2	4	16					7		2	
	% within punishment	5.6	11.1	44.4					19.4		5.6	
	% within crime	100.0	4.9	38.1					31.8		66.7	
Hanging	Cases		57	15	12	7		3	8	2		
	% within punishment		54.3	14.3	11.4	6.7		2.9	7.6	1.9		
	% within crime		69.5	35.7	100.0	77.8		37.5	36.4	66.7		
Combination	Cases		21	10		1	2	5	7		1	3
	% within punishment		42.0	20.0		2.0	4.0	10.0	14.0		2.0	6.0
	% within crime		25.6	23.8		11.1	100.0	62.5	31.8		33.3	100.0
Other	Cases			1		1				1		
	% within punishment			33.3		33.3				33.3		
	% within crime			2.4		11.1				33.3		
Total	Cases	2	82	42	12	9	2	8	22	3	3	3
	% within punishment	1.0	42.3	21.6	6.2	4.6	1.0	4.1	11.3	1.5	1.5	1.5
	% within crime	100.0	100.0	100.0	100.0	100.0	100.0	100.0	100.0	100.0	100.0	100.0

Source: See appendix.

blacks accounted for only 13.3 percent of all executions. No black convict hanged for having committed a serious crime against a free black, suggesting that this group was not of great societal value. If justice for a free black victim meant depriving a master of his slave, the odds were against such justice.[15]

In patriarchal Georgia, the sex of the victim played a significant role in punishment. The most consistently severe punishment awaited those who committed offenses against white men; nearly 45 percent of those who lost their lives did so for crimes against white men. Nearly 25 percent of hangings were of blacks whose victims were white women. The high value placed on the lives of white women is evidenced by the fact that more than 86 percent of those who committed crimes against them hanged, the highest percentage of any group. The state executed twice as many blacks for victimizing white men, but death was far more certain for any black who criminally violated a white woman.[16]

Among black victims, those who killed slave men accounted for 11.4 percent of the executions; this execution rate, just below the rate for those convicted of crimes against white women, certainly makes sense in light of the economic value of enslaved men. A prime male field hand usually cost one-fifth more than his female counterpart, though these statistics might underestimate the value of slave women: in Georgia, only two slave women fell prey to crime, and in both cases the perpetrators hanged, suggesting that Georgia courts considered slave women as valuable as slave men, perhaps more so.[17] A definitive answer awaits additional study.

An integral part of the victim's status was the relationship to the convict. In the bulk of Georgia's cases, the exact nature of the relationships is unknown, but enough is known to suggest strongly that who the victim and convict were to one another had a significant effect on the punishment administered. The two most important relationships were between slave convicts and whites in authority over them, and between slaves and fellow bondsmen. Fear of black-on-white violence, especially violence directed at the master class or its surrogates, was perhaps the overriding concern of the criminal justice system. While masters, mistresses, overseers, and other white authority figures account for only 20.9 percent of victims, the punishment of those who violated the personal and property rights of this class was severe. Over 75 percent of those convicted of crimes against members of the authority class hanged. Another 18.2 percent were recipients of combination punishments; only 6.1 percent received the lash. Protection of the bodies, virtue, livelihoods, and property of the master class and its agents was of paramount interest to Georgia's criminal justice apparatus.

These statistics are deceptive, however, since they underestimate the number of victims from this class. Nearly 61 percent of all victims were whites whose relationship to the convicts is unknown. Certainly some of these white men and women were in positions of authority over their victimizers. In Virginia, the majority of whites killed by slaves were authority figures.[18] While this study cannot shed definitive light on the magnitude of slave-on-master crimes, it does demonstrate that Georgia judges and juries took such crimes quite seriously.

The next most important type of relationship was that which existed between slave offenders and slave victims. The overriding concern from the master class's point of view was the protection and preservation of slave property. This could be accomplished by executing those slaves who killed or disabled others, but such executions would represent the loss of more slave lives and their value as laborers. In 1941, the Mississippi newspaper editor Hodding Carter described in these words how black-on-black murders should be handled to safeguard the South's race-based labor system: "If a man had two fine mules running loose in a lot and one went mad and kicked and killed the other he certainly would not take out his gun and shoot the other mule, but would work it."

What was required to accomplish the masters' goal was a pattern of punishment that balanced severity with a concern for slaves' lives. Georgians achieved this balance by hanging approximately half of the slave convicts and subjecting the remaining half to combination punishments and flogging. It is important to note that the state only used the lash in slightly more than 7 percent of the cases, suggesting that courts did not take lightly crimes against the lives/property values of slaves, and would punish offenders to the limits of economic feasibility.[19] Punishing a slave too harshly could diminish or eliminate value entirely, but failure to punish slaves for assaults that might lower the value of their slave victims could encourage such assaults, or at least make the costs of perpetrating them acceptable. Combination punishments represented a workable compromise.

Any conclusions about victim status and punishment must also take account of the types of crimes committed against particular classes of victims. If a group found itself the victim of crimes that were subject to harsher punishment, the crime, and not the status of the victim, may have determined punishment.

In crime categories where both blacks and whites were represented, offenders who victimized whites were punished more severely than those who committed crimes against blacks. For example, blacks who killed white men were executed in 96.3 percent of the cases. For white women, the figure was even higher: every Negro who killed or raped a white woman hanged. As with previously cited statistics, these clearly demonstrate that courts considered the lives and bodies of white women the most sacred. No convict ever received the lesser punishment of lashes for the murder of a white man or woman. Combination punishment was used in only one case where the victim was a white man, and in none where the victim was a white woman.

Negroes convicted of killing slave men were put to death in only 42.3 percent of the cases; half received combination punishment, and a small percentage received only the lash. The picture is quite different for the two slave men who killed slave women: the state executed both of them. No black hanged for killing a free black, once again suggesting the minimal value Georgia placed on the lives of those who were of comparatively little pecuniary value to its slaveholding society.[20]

Punishment and Defendant Sex and Status

Slave men received the largest share of all punishments dispensed by the criminal justice system. More than 93 percent of those executed were enslaved men; they also received 94 percent of all combination punishments, and 86 percent of the floggings. Although slave men were the principal group hauled into court, convicted, and punished, and with much greater frequency and severity than slave women, women received no greater leniency in punishment. Once convicted, courts punished slave women in a like manner to men in most cases. Roughly 55 percent of both groups hanged; 18.2 percent of women faced the lash, compared to 17.4 percent of men. A significant difference appears in combination punishments; slave men received this punishment in 26.4 percent of cases, bondswomen in only 18.2 percent, a discrepancy that may be explained by the fact that juries convicted slave men of a greater number of crimes for which combination punishments were administered.[21] These punishment-distribution figures suggest that judges thought female convicts were as dangerous as their male counterparts, a contention borne out by an examination of punishments for individual crimes.

Courts in Georgia convicted both slave men and women of committing only four crimes: murder, arson, poisoning, and burglary. Murder was the most serious, and women convicted were punished at a higher rate than men. Eighty percent of females convicted of murderer were hanged, compared to only 70.7 percent of men. These figures suggest that juries may have considered female murderers a greater threat to society. The same was true in South Carolina, where courts punished slave women who committed crimes against persons more severely than men. The figures for arson are comparable for both sexes; 40 percent of enslaved male arsonists were executed, 33.3 percent of females. The execution rate for men was thus 6.7 percent higher than that for women. The combination-punishment rate, however, was higher for women than for men, by exactly that percentage number. Given the small numbers involved—five men and three women—the discrepancy is statistically insignificant, making it safe to assume that judges considered both groups of arsonists equally menacing.[22] (A comparison of burglary figures would not be productive, since only one female slave was convicted of that crime.)

County courts convicted only four free blacks of crimes in the colonial and antebellum periods, making it impossible to draw statistically valid conclusions about their punishment. Two of these convictions were for murder or manslaughter; one defendant was whipped, and the other received a combination punishment. And two defendants received convictions for attempted murder and burglary, respectively; the first hanged, and the second was whipped. If South Carolina was representative of Georgia and the other Old South states, then courts punished free blacks less severely than slaves.[23]

The status or sex of blacks did not make a significant difference in their punishment. Women appeared before Georgia courts less frequently and were convicted less often than men, but once found guilty, judges punished them as severely as their male counterparts. At present, it is impossible to say whether judges and juries treated free blacks any better or worse than slaves, since the numbers of free black convicts is too small for clear patterns of punishment to emerge.

In Georgia, during the colonial and antebellum years, criminal justice officials hanged, whipped, and mutilated slaves and free blacks convicted of crimes. Surprisingly, in the late eighteenth century, whites endured the same kinds of punishments, for the same crimes and for the same reasons. By the second decade of the nineteenth century, black convicts alone generally suffered brutal physical punishments, and slavery and white supremacy were responsible for this disparate, unjust state of affairs.

{ *Whites in the Colonial Scheme of Punishment*

Colonial Georgians, like other early Americans, considered criminal behavior to be the consequence of humankind's sinful nature. After Adam and Eve's fall from grace, it was impossible for humans to eliminate or control their evil and antisocial tendencies. Crime, like the poor, would always be with us, and therefore the emphasis in punishment was not on reform but on retribution, suffering for one's sins. The purpose of punishment was not to change the character of offenders but rather to terrorize them so they would not consider engaging in prohibited acts. The body, not the mind or the soul, was the focus of punishment.[24] To the extent that punishments had psychological dimensions, the goal was to inflict psychic pain and not to reform the offender.

Fines and whipping were the most common forms of punishment for whites—fines for those with property, and whipping for those without it. Courts combined the stocks, branding, and banishment with fines to punish minor offenders. The stocks had the advantage of inflicting both physical and psychological pain, holding miscreants up to ridicule by members of their own, close-knit communities. Shaming was a powerful punishment. So, too, public shaming was the rationale for compelling offenders to wear letters that informed the community of the nature of their crimes. The law required adulterers to place a red letter "A" around their necks; drunkards had to wear the letter "D." Branding offered similar physical and psychological advantages. Courts also used branding and whipping in conjunction with banishment to punish strangers and remove them from the community. Georgia also subjected white criminal offenders to ear-cropping.[25]

Courts did not regularly use imprisonment as a form of punishment; they used jails simply to house those awaiting trial or to repay debts. Colonial jails were generally in private homes. The jailer and his family usually lived in the gaol and often took meals with the prisoners. Jailers did not chain or restrain inmates, and the inmantes did not wear uniforms. They were free to roam about the jail/house as they pleased. Indeed, jails were so much like private residences that some feared they would attract inmates. Colonial officials were also reluctant to use incarceration, because of the cost of constructing and maintaining proper jails. Georgia officials regularly lamented the poor condition of the few existing jails and the shoddy construction and overcrowding that made escapes frequent.[26]

Execution, the final and most severe sanction, served the dual purposes of incapacitation and deterrence. The offender was forever deprived of the opportunity to commit other crimes, and his death served as a grim warning to others. The state executed white Georgians for horse and cattle theft, "negro stealing," counterfeiting, robbery, murder, and a host of other crimes. Even ordinary theft and disrespect for parental authority could be capital offenses.[27]

Blacks in the Colonial Scheme of Punishment

In the colonial period, whites considered blacks volitional beings capable of moral choice and burdened by as much temptation to sin as they themselves were, possibly more. In a 1727 letter to colonial slaveholders, Edmund Gibson, Bishop of London, instructed masters and mistresses to "consider Them, not merely as slaves, and upon the same Level with the Labouring Beasts, but as *Men*-Slaves and *Women*-Slaves, who have the same Frame and Faculties with yourselves, and have Souls capable of being made eternally happy, and Reason and Understanding to receive Instruction in order to do it." On the shared humanity of blacks and whites, a missionary, Morgan Godwin, remarked, "Methinks that the consideration of the shape and figure of our Negroes Bodies, their Limbs and Members, their Voice and Countenance in all things according with other Men's together with their Risibility and Discourse (man's Peculiar faculties) should be sufficient conviction." In *The Negro Christianized*, the famous Puritan divine Cotton Mather described Africans as "Rational Creatures" whom God had made the servants of others. Thomas Jefferson, who considered slaves inveterate thieves, believed that any moral shortcomings slaves exhibited were the product of their circumstances, and not of any innate propensity for immorality.[28]

The Georgia trustees considered slaves part of their religious universe, and, in the colony's first slave code, mandated that slaves be exposed to "all the spiritual benefits of Christianity." Masters had to ensure that, "at some time on the Lords Day," slaves receive "instruction in the Christian Religion." Failure to comply led to a fine of £10 sterling.[29] Some whites objected strenuously to this egalitarian view of African moral capacity and argued passionately in favor of black inferiority, but no government official or legislator suggested that blacks should not be held accountable for their criminal behavior.

Given this view of blacks as sinful people incapable of true reform, like everyone else in that regard, it is not surprising that during the colonial period in Georgia, and in the rest of British North America, blacks were subject to the same sorts of punishments as whites. States whipped, transported/banished, and hanged black convicts, and did the same with white offenders. These punishments would not have been unfamiliar to African slaves, since they were staples of criminal justice in West Africa as well. Blacks were not subject to fines or the shaming punishments. Colonial slaves did not possess significant sums of cash, so they could not be fined. While individually and collectively bound to the community, blacks—slave or free—were not a part of the web of reciprocal communal obligations and benefits to which white citizens belonged; accordingly, shaming mechanisms did not apply to or work to chastise them. As persons who were "socially dead," slaves—and by association and extension, free blacks—had no honor to protect, and therefore no shame to cultivate. The historical sociologist Orlando Patterson writes that, to the master class, slaves could have no honor, because they lacked the social independence upon which honor depends. The slave "had no name to defend. He could only defend his master's worth and his master's name."[30]

Like their white counterparts, black convicts were not imprisoned for crimes, but the state did establish a prison-like institution for them. In 1763, Georgia lawmakers authorized the building of a workhouse "for the custody and punishment of Negroes." The workhouse served as a place of confinement and punishment for "obstinate and disorderly" Negroes and a temporary holding facility for unidentified or unclaimed runaway slaves. Once slaves were inside the walls of the workhouse, staff clapped them in irons, subjected them to "moderate whipping," and put them to work.[31]

To all appearances, then, it would seem that black Georgians were in fact imprisoned and punished in the workhouse, but this was not so. The state did not sentence blacks to the workhouse as punishment; it was masters who sent them there, at their own discretion. This high level of private involvement suggests that the state used the workhouse to further the interests of masters far more than as a mechanism of criminal justice, and was in keeping with a legal culture that gave priority to the needs of slaveholders. This conclusion is also evident from reports of actual practices at the workhouse.

Most black prisoners were runaways who were being held until their masters could come to reclaim them, or slaves detained for what was euphemistically called "safe-keeping": masters brought troublesome slaves to the workhouse to be whipped. The workhouse was a useful place for the corporal punishment of slaves: it permitted squeamish slaveholders to avoid being the immediate cause of pain—to avoid laying on the lash; and it protected those who did not want to dirty their hands, and also those who did not wish to sully their reputations by association with the severe floggings that might be required to bring recalcitrant bondsmen back in line. The short period most confined blacks spent in the workhouse also suggests that punishment through incarceration was not its raison d'être. The sole extant record of workhouse confinements shows that the average prisoner stayed there for less than a month, most for about one week, even those awaiting trial on serious charges of violent crimes.[32] Such short-term deprivations of "liberty" could hardly have been thought of as punishment for men and women already permanently denied their freedom through bondage. Courts did not send free blacks to the workhouse, because they used it as an extension of the plantation system of criminal justice.

Race-based Differences in Punishment

When punishment in colonial Georgia differed between blacks and whites, the difference was largely a matter of degree and not of kind, with blacks receiving somewhat more of the barbaric punishments that courts meted out to convicted whites. Whites deemed this heightened degree of severity necessary because they saw black criminality as especially dangerous, potentially auguring the beginnings of slave unrest and rebellion of the sort experienced in the St. Andrew's Parish Revolt in 1774, when a dozen fugitive slaves injured or killed six whites. To make the point that such dangerous behavior would not be tolerated, Georgia whites burned several slaves for their crimes, including two involved in the St. Andrew's Parish insurrection. It was occasional practice in that period to display the heads of executed slaves on poles near the scenes of their crimes as a deterrent to others.[33]

White Georgians chose burning and decapitation as methods of execution and deterrence because their English forebears had used these same sanctions to punish, disgrace, and dishonor persons convicted of treason. During the colonial period, when murder was "committed (in the estate Oeconomicall) upon any subject, by one" who was "in subjection, and oweth faith, duty and obedience, to the party murdered," the crime was petit treason. Petit treason most closely approximated the crime committed when a slave killed his master, but the colonial law did not generally consider this type of homicide petit treason, because petit treason required a relationship of mutual trust and obligation and no such existed between slave-murderer and master-victim. Colonial lawmakers knew that slaves' obedience depended on force, and not on the paternalistic system of mutual obligations that characterized, or was said to have characterized, antebellum master-slave relations. Therefore, judges and lawmakers never fully articulated and codified in statutes the application of the law of petit treason to slave–master murders. Nevertheless, colonists punished a great many slaves who killed their masters as if they had, in fact, committed petit treason.[34]

These particular executions and public displays were certainly more grisly than the average run of executions for whites, but they must be considered against the backdrop of an Atlantic World in which some European women believed to be witches were burned at the stake, and white European criminals were condemned to be "hanged, others to having their hands cut off or their tongues cut out or pierced and then to be hanged; others for more serious crimes, to be broken alive and to die on the wheel, after having their limbs broken; others to be broken until they die a natural death, others to be strangled and then broken, others to be burnt alive after first being strangled; others to be drawn by four horses, others to have their heads cut off, and others to have their heads broken."[35] Immolation and postmortem decapitation seem almost humane in comparison to this litany of horrors.

In sum, blacks possessed the same sinful natures as whites, and courts accordingly punished them in the vast majority of cases in the same ways. The whip was the most common instrument of punishment for non-felony offenders of both races, and the gallows awaited both blacks and whites convicted of serious crimes. Authorities occasionally burned slaves and mutilated their bodies postmortem, in cases whites deemed particularly offensive to their communities but not as a matter of course.[36] Punishment of both blacks and whites was usually a very public, very bloody affair. These rituals of blood ended for whites by the turn of the nineteenth century. For blacks, these rituals would continue for generations.

The Birth of the Prison

By the last third of the eighteenth century, both public corporal and capital punishment fell into increasing disfavor in the West for several practical and ideological reasons. First, these punishments failed to produce the desired results. Public executions, designed to awe spectators and force them into docile submission, had the actual effect of repelling crowds, fostering identification with the criminal, and promoting hatred of the state. Riots and other disruptions began to increase during executions, disturbances hardly likely to produce social harmony and tranquility. Brutal public sanctions led to an overall downturn in incidence of punishment.[37]

The late eighteenth century also witnessed the European Enlightenment, a revolution in social, political, and economic thought that profoundly altered conceptions of crime and punishment. The historian Peter Gay has described the Enlightenment as "a vastly ambitious program . . . of secularism, humanity, cosmopolitanism, and freedom, above all, freedom in its many forms—freedom from arbitrary power, freedom of speech, freedom of trade, freedom to realize one's talents, freedom of aesthetic response, freedom, in a word, of moral man to make his own way in the world." Immanuel Kant saw the Enlightenment, in Gay's view, as "man's claim to be recognized as an adult, responsible being."[38] The Enlightenment's emphasis on secularism, human reason, personal accountability, and empiricism undermined the central pillar of colonial punishment theory: sin. No longer were humans considered the hopelessly depraved creatures John Calvin had maintained they were, but rational beings capable of boundless improvement. If human beings were not innately criminal, their criminality must have other causes, perhaps outside themselves. It became clear to thinkers on crime that the external environment played a far more significant role in the development of socially deviant behavior patterns than they had previously surmised.

This revelation compelled criminal justice reformers to devise a means of controlling the environmental factors they now regarded as responsible for antisocial behavior. They could change society itself, removing the privations and temptations that forced or lured men and women into crime. Such societal remodeling would be, if possible to achieve, an ultimate solution to the problem of crime, but was clearly impractical in the short term. Or they could attempt to change the individual to face the environment without turning to crime. The initial step would be removing offenders from chaotic environments and placing them in strictly controlled contexts where the work of personal transformation could be accomplished. This place of isolation and reform was the penitentiary.

While the prison movement began in the Northeast, in Pennsylvania and New York, Georgia was one of the first Southern states to consider erecting a penitentiary. In 1804, state representatives proposed the first legislation;

in 1816, after lengthy debate and political wrangling, builders completed the prison. Maryland followed suit, opening the gates of its penitentiary in 1829. Between 1834 and 1837, Louisiana and Missouri constructed prisons, and within the next five years, Alabama and Mississippi did so as well. Of the Deep South states, only the Carolinas and Florida failed to join the prison-building movement.[39]

The emergence of the prison as the dominant means of punishment led, in turn, to campaigns against corporal and capital sanctions. Crusades against these physical punishments were part of larger nineteenth-century reform movements that considered immoderate physical punishment, slavery, war, dueling, and other forms of violence as atavistic holdovers from an unenlightened past. Reformers saw excessive corporal punishment as violating the human and civil rights of those on whom courts inflicted it. They did not believe in abandoning corporal punishment altogether, but rather in ensuring that it not be arbitrary or extreme. The most important goal of reform was a well-ordered society; if whipping was necessary as a last resort to achieve this goal, then so be it.

Reformers saw the lash as especially appropriate for certain groups; moral conditioning alone would not remake them. Among such groups were those from impoverished backgrounds considered products of poor parenting and corrupting influences. And while society considered women, by nature, to be repositories of virtue and gentleness, those who prostituted their bodies or otherwise engaged in criminal behavior forfeited this positive presumption. One inspector (at Sing Sing prison in New York State) considered black women uniquely "depraved and abandoned," for example.[40] Reformers, no doubt, thought the same of black men.

Northerners associated whipping with slavery and the oppression the institution visited on blacks; it was not a fit punishment for free, democratic, white men. The lash reduced white men to the status of slaves. This negative association is captured in author Richard Henry Dana's experience as an antebellum seaman, in his captain's views on flogging: "You see your condition! You see where I've got you all, and you know what to expect! . . . I'll make you toe the mark, every soul of you, or I'll flog you all, fore and aft, from the boy up! . . . You've got a driver over you! Yes, a slave driver,—a nigger driver! I'll see who'll tell me he isn't a NIGGER slave!" In 1850, Congress prohibited flogging in the United States Navy, bringing to an end an age-old seafaring tradition. By the 1850s, Northern prison officials used the whip and related instruments less frequently. Middle-class families and public schools, too, reduced their use of corporal punishments against small children and adolescents.[41]

During congressional debates on the abolition of naval flogging, Southern representatives fought to continue the practice. The historian Myra C. Glenn argues that this was an outgrowth of the sectional rivalry over slavery, that Southern men saw attacks on flogging as veiled assaults on slavery and responded by characterizing opponents as radicals and fanatics, in terms similar to those they used for abolitionists. Living with slavery fostered a more cynical view of human nature. In the Southern view, if individuals were not wholly rational creatures, fear and physical punishment were the only means to ensure that each remained in the place assigned. Whipping was a necessary and convenient way to maintain the ideal hierarchical society.[42]

The rise of penal discipline itself accelerated reform movements of the late eighteenth century to limit or abolish the death penalty. In 1794, Pennsylvania made death mandatory only for first-degree murder; many other states followed suit, ending the practice of sentencing offenders to death for petty and less serious crimes. After opening its own prison, Georgia reduced its number of capital offenses from 160 to 20. Pennsylvania, again in the forefront of reform, banned public executions in 1834; Rhode Island, New York, Massachusetts, and New Jersey did so by 1835. States now gave juries the option of imposing sentences other than death for murder, starting with Tennessee and Alabama in 1841. In 1846, Louisiana adopted a similar practice for all capital crimes. Antebellum reform reached its peak when Michigan made death the compulsory penalty only for treason, and eliminated the penalty altogether in 1846. Wisconsin and Rhode Island followed suit, abolishing capital punishment in 1852 and 1853, respectively.[43] By the 1850s, prison, and not the gallows, was the destination for whites convicted of serious crimes; their minds and spirits, not their bodies, were the foci of punishment. For whites, punishment was far less severe by mid-century than in the colonial period.

Punishment of Blacks in the Antebellum Period

In the main, Southern blacks failed to benefit from the salutary criminal justice reforms of the Jacksonian era. For them, corporal and capital sanctions remained staples of punishment, and courts did not incarcerate most blacks for their criminal acts. The reasons for not imprisoning slaves and free blacks were more practical than ideological. While criminal justice reformers engaged in debate about the proper goals and means of punishment, racial theorists argued about the true nature of African peoples. Proslavery ideologues contended vociferously that blacks were inferior to whites, and would remain so forever. They did not suggest that blacks had become more inferior morally than in the colonial period; they had the same moral capacities that they always had, and therefore the corrective methods of prison discipline would have worked, at least at the level of theory. But most blacks in Georgia, and elsewhere in the South, were there for one purpose and one purpose only: to work for whites. Whites did not long tolerate anything that interfered with that objective. Quite simply put, incarcerating blacks would take them from the fields, kitchens, and shops, and their labor was vital to the Southern economy, culture, and identity. White Southerners, moreover, viewed imprisonment itself as a republican punishment for white men; imprisoning even free blacks would imply an equality that would have undermined the state's race-based socioeconomic system.[44]

Southern whites believed that imprisoning blacks would not have been punishment in their eyes. Thomas R. R. Cobb wrote in 1858, "To deprive a freeman of his liberty, is one of the severest punishments the law can inflict; . . . But to the slave this is no punishment, because he has no liberty of which to be deprived." The New South patrician William Alexander Percy wrote in 1941 that, while white men viewed work and industry as virtues, "None of them [blacks] feels that work per se is good; it is only a means to idleness." Hence, blacks could consider prison not as punishment but as a refuge, "a place to lounge about with other loafers."[45] Percy was referring to blacks during the era of Jim Crow, but his point would not have been lost on antebellum Southerners.

With prisons off-limits to slaves, Georgia's judicial authorities had no choice but to continue the corporal and capital punishments of the colonial era. But this was entirely appropriate. Cobb explained it this way: "The condition of the slave renders it impossible to inflict upon him the ordinary punishments, by pecuniary fine, by imprisonment, or by banishment. He can only be reached through his body, and hence, in cases not capital, whipping is the only punishment which can be inflicted." With "death and whipping, being the only available punishments," it was necessary for slave codes "to throw all offenses under the one or the other."[46]

With only their bodies to offer up on the altar of punishment, blacks were subject to a much wider range of corporal and capital punishments than whites. By the mid-1850s, according to the abolitionist George Stroud, there were no crimes for which death was the *mandatory* penalty for whites in Alabama (there were six crimes for which they *could* be executed), but there were at least eighteen such offenses for slaves. In Tennessee, whites could be put to death for two offenses, slaves for eight. Kentucky slaves could be executed for eight crimes; whites for only half that number. For slaves and whites in South Carolina, the comparable numbers were thirty-six and twenty-six, respectively. Statutes in North Carolina provided the death penalty for bondsmen convicted of forty offenses; whites could be sentenced to death for thirty-six crimes. Georgia had twenty capital offenses for blacks (both free and enslaved) and thirteen for whites. Virginia topped all other Southern states in capital punishments for slaves: there were *sixty-eight* capital crimes for slaves, but only one, first-degree murder, for whites. Courts subjected blacks to capital punishment for a wider variety of crimes in all slaveholding states, and they also faced whipping, branding, castration, and other forms of physical punishment—although to a lesser degree than in the colonial period—long after the courts ceased meting out these punishments to whites.[47] The criminal justice process had once again been perverted to serve slavery and white supremacy.

White Georgians constructed a criminal justice apparatus designed to protect their interests in general and slavery in particular. The ways masters and courts punished blacks for their crimes reflected these priorities. The most severe punishments were administered to those slaves and free blacks who threatened or took the lives of whites, especially those of white women, slaveowners, and authority figures. Among blacks, as far as available records reveal, the lives of slave men were most prized; they were the most valuable workers. The criminal justice system sanctioned with greater severity those who killed slave men than those who victimized slave women or free blacks. The 194 men and women whipped, branded, and hanged at the command of Georgia courts were only the public tip of a large glacier of criminal punishment, since masters, mistresses, and overseers beat, branded, tortured, and killed countless others on farms and plantations throughout the state. The details and circumstances of their individual stories will remain forever unknown.

We are ready to die and would as soon be dead as to live in torture.
—Unnamed Georgia convicts leased to the Dade Coal Mines, 1886

The criminal justice system in Georgia functioned for more than a century to protect the prerogatives of slavery and white racial domination. When the Confederacy collapsed in the spring of 1865, Georgia's criminal justice system for blacks fell apart with it. Prosecutions for murder, rape, arson, burglary, and other capital offenses simply disappeared from the historical record. On Georgia's farms and plantations, now former masters no longer acted as solitary judges, juries, and executioners.

But that dead system of "justice" for blacks was seldom just, as we can see from the prosecution of a slave man, the average defendant in the state court system. In April 1861, a Sumter County grand jury indicted Monday and charged him with assault with intent to murder a white man, Andrew Bass. The state accused him of violating laws that he had no role in crafting, laws intended to secure the interests of those who would judge him. Endangering the interests of whites was the surest way for a black person to end up on trial, especially if the crime charged involved a serious physical assault, as this one did. Had Monday committed a similar assault against a Negro, it would have been considered homicidal assault—the only capital crime one black could commit against another—but the state even charged that crime most often when the victim was the slave property of a white Georgian. An all-white, all-male grand jury charged Monday. A white lawyer represented him, and not one of his choosing; his master chose the lawyer for him. A petit jury of white men his master selected, not one of his peers, would decide whether Monday would live or die. The judge who presided over the case was a slaveholding white man. Lawyers for the prosecution and defense made their arguments during proceedings in which Monday did not utter a word besides denying the charge against him; in all likelihood his master would not have allowed him to speak if he had wanted to. At the end of its deliberations, the jury returned a verdict of guilty. The judge sentenced Monday to hang—the same end that awaited most black convicts—on June 7, 1861, between ten o'clock in the morning and three o'clock in the afternoon.

Monday's owner appealed the case to the Georgia Supreme Court and arranged for a defense lawyer. The lawyer argued that a number of violations of legal rules and procedures had occurred during the trial. As it did in almost half the cases brought before it involving Negroes, the supreme court agreed and ordered a new trial. The Sumter County Superior Court tried Monday a second time and found him guilty a second time, just as were most other Negroes whom appellate courts granted new trials. In the entire period studied, from 1751 to 1865, only six blacks ever received retrial acquittals. But this time, the trial judge reduced the sentence and spared Monday's life. The court sentenced him to 117 lashes and to branding on the cheek with the letter "M."[1]

Monday received all of the due process protections a white man would have received. But there were crucial differences. He did not exercise these rights himself; the man who owned him did. And those who judged him surely acted on behalf of their own racial and status interests, which were not his. Monday was also subject to punishments no white faced. Whites charged with crimes in state courts were seldom convicted, but nearly half of all blacks who were even *accused* of crimes were convicted. Once a case reached the verdict stage, courts convicted approximately 75 percent of all defendants. Courts convicted those accused of certain crimes against persons, such as murder, attempted murder, and rape, in nearly 90 percent of mid-antebellum cases. Juries convicted those who victimized masters, mistresses, and overseers 87 percent of the time, compared to 73 percent for whites not in authority over the defendants.[2]

Had Monday been tried on his home plantation, the procedural safeguards of a formal trial would not have been available to him. In court, the rules of evidence and criminal procedure and the skillful machinations of trained lawyers protected black lives to a degree. No such safeguards existed on the farms and estates of Georgia masters, where individual slaveowners decided how alleged violations of their criminal "law" would be handled and what procedures, if any, would be followed. In most such cases, justice was swift: a master or overseer observed a violation of "law," or learned of it from informants, and established culpability based on the testimony of witnesses and other evidence, or his own knowledge or sense of the character of the "defendant." The time from act to conviction could be a matter of minutes. Once a master established the identity of a "suspect," nothing stood between the offender and the master's justice.

For the slave "defendant" on the plantation, that justice might have meant being whipped or branded, confined in a plantation guardhouse, or rolled down a hill in a barrel into which nails had been driven from the outside, or worse.[3] Only the master's conscience and imagination, and the law's bar against murdering slaves, limited punishment. Murder is the most difficult crime to conceal, but there is no way of knowing how many owners or overseers killed slaves without being discovered, charged, or convicted. As ex-slaves remembered, masters and overseers did, on occasion, kill their bondspeople, as in 1853 when an overseer beat a thirteen-year-old Dougherty County slave girl, Mariah, to death. If a master killed a slave, said she died of natural causes, and buried her without examination, who could prove otherwise? Certainly not slave witnesses, who were forbidden to testify against whites.[4]

Most blacks knew of and experienced the master's plantation justice firsthand. Only a small fraction of blacks found themselves facing the state's machinery of justice, but the formal and informal criminal justice systems worked together to ensure that crimes were handled with deadly dispatch. For blacks, the criminal justice system was seldom more than another type of chain designed to keep them ever more securely bound.

Legislators established the dual system of law to ameliorate the tensions in relations between masters and the state. For the state to optimally restrict black criminality, it would have had to severely impinge upon the rights of masters; for masters to fully exercise their power, they would have had to have been beyond the authority of the state. A system that split responsibility between masters and the state for the control of black criminality, or alleged criminality, seemed an expedient solution. Masters retained responsibility for behavior within their boundary lines, and the state assumed jurisdiction over behavior beyond them. Georgia's strong commitment to its bifurcated system of criminal justice is reflected in the fact that, in the period studied, there are no court cases of serious slave-on-slave crime occurring on the same plantation or farm. If the recollections of ex-slaves and the trial records of other states are to be believed, slaves on the same plantations certainly assaulted and killed each other, but in Georgia the law allowed masters to handle these cases themselves.

Free blacks occupied a position in the criminal justice system that was in several respects worse than that of slaves. They were subject to the same criminal laws and trial procedures as slaves and they could be whipped like slaves, as was Michael Davis, the Newton County free black man who killed Milledge Gay in 1857 to prevent the white man Gay from beating him a second time. Free blacks had many of the social and legal liabilities of slaves, but they lacked the personal and legal protection of any white person's self-interest. Georgia law is not clear on who made decisions for free blacks in criminal court; the only extant references are to white guardians filing appeals and acting for their black wards in civil law suits. The implication is that some white person had to act for free blacks in court, which was in keeping with the expected role of guardians throughout the Slave South. But white guardians did not have the same kind of financial and personal interests in their free black wards that masters had in their slaves. Free blacks were free, but they probably played limited roles in their trials—for example, none ever appealed a conviction.

Because slaves were valuable properties, their lives had value the criminal justice system recognized. Free blacks' lives did not have such value, so the state punished crimes against them with the least severity of any group, reflecting their low societal worth. With an essentially unprotected position in communities, it was in the best interests of free blacks to avoid serious infractions of white personal and property rights, and they apparently did, since few of them appeared in state courts. Free blacks also had fewer occasions for violent confrontations with whites; counties generally charged them with less serious offenses against persons and public order, crimes that led to lower levels of conviction and less severe punishments.

Throughout the formal criminal justice process, the law extended protection to blacks only to the degree necessary to protect the interests of whites. The intelligence, will, hopes, desires, and fears of black defendants mattered not at all within the system. Black defendants played no role in the process; they were simply subject to it. The system was a venue for white conflict resolution when slaves threatened or damaged interests beyond those of the people who owned them. It was also an attempt to cloak exploitation with the legitimacy of the law in a western world increasingly opposed to human bondage. To confer this legitimacy, lawmakers and jurists created a system that granted blacks most of the legal safeguards enjoyed by whites. It was a concession with the potential to undermine slavery itself, but only if the system was equitably administered and recognized fully black humanity, in theory and in practice. Judges and juries used their discretion, deliberately or unconsciously by habit, to ensure that this kind of justice was not done.

Critics might argue that judges and juries did not engage in a cold-blooded racial and economic calculus of the kind I am proposing, that these actors had—at least on some level—a genuine concern for justice and black defendants, as A. E. Kier Nash and others have argued. Judicial actors certainly did not openly debate property values and racial supremacy before rendering judgment; these determinants, operating on a subconscious level, were products of socialization within a legal culture based on the priorities of a slave society. Paternalism represents such unconscious denial. Paternalistic masters and mistresses convinced themselves that they genuinely loved and cared for their slaves and they acted on this belief; as a result, material conditions for slaves improved. But more benevolent treatment did not represent a genuine and complete recognition of slaves' humanity. Masters still separated families, and white men still raped slave women or otherwise coerced them into unwanted sexual relationships. Whites still denied black intelligence and free will. Paternalism protected slavery, in effect, by allowing masters and mistresses to claim to themselves and the world that their socioeconomic system was humane and just. It enabled them to assuage any individual and collective guilt to create the only self-reproducing slave population in the hemisphere, with the consequent multiplying of profit from labor or sale. Slaves were incidental beneficiaries of paternalism, and the same was true of the salutary aspects of the criminal justice system.

The legal scholar Derrick Bell has argued that the American legal system has historically pursued equality for blacks only when that pursuit has also benefited whites, that is, when there has been a convergence in the interests of the two groups. When these group interests diverge, the legal system quickly backs away from its commitment to racial equality.[5] A problem in using Bell's theory of interest convergence as a tool of analysis is that it is necessary to determine which interest the legal system is acting on behalf of when interests come together, and it is often difficult to do so. Perhaps the system is operating in the interests of blacks, with the convergence with white interests coincidental. In the case of slaves and the criminal law, how does one know whether a judge and jury were protecting the interests of masters and themselves or expressing genuine concern for blacks as human beings, or all of these? One way to answer this question is to see how courts responded when the interests of masters and slaves, whites and blacks, diverged.

When Reconstruction began, white Southerners in Georgia and else-where faced a world that war and political change had turned upside down. Blacks were no longer a population of slaves but free people, ostensible equals in the eyes of the law. But whites in the South did all in their power to create a reality that was as close to the one they had lost as possible. This was especially evident in matters of criminal justice. Under slavery, the law sublimated the demands of justice to the dictates of white supremacy and the slave economy, with the economic value individual slaves repre-sented for their masters muting the most cruel and exploitative aspects of the system. During Reconstruction and the age of Jim Crow, this shield of individual economic value to whites fell away; the interests of masters and slaves ceased to converge. Blacks could now be exploited ruthlessly, and the criminal justice system was complicit in this exploitation. In the colo-nial and antebellum periods, blacks had been the principal source of labor, and whites employed the law in the postbellum period to ensure that they remained so, despite Emancipation. State legislatures enacted Black Codes that criminalized freed blacks' attempts to relocate or to pursue vocations outside of agriculture. These legislatures also created the convict lease system.

When the Union general William Tecumseh Sherman began his march to the sea in 1864, Georgia governor Joseph E. Brown freed all prisoners in the state penitentiary at Milledgeville, in exchange for their promise to help move state property to safety and to fight for the Confederacy. By 1865, the dilapidated prison held just four inmates, a considerable waste of revenue in the cash-strapped state. Governor Brown wanted to abolish the penitentiary system altogether and return to the corporal punishments and executions of the eighteenth century—the punishments Negroes had always endured. But rather than subject whites to the same brutal punishments as blacks, the legislature decided to lease convicts to private parties. Georgia became one of the first states to do so.[6]

Convict leasing allowed states to punish criminals and have a seemingly endless supply of workers for the region's economic reconstruction. There was no mention of race in the statute that created Georgia's convict leasing system, but before long 90 percent of those caught in its grasp were black.[7] This was not by mere chance. Sheriffs, judges, and jurors conspired to con-vict Negro defendants. Lessors rented men, women, and children to private citizens at low prices for whatever labor the lessees required. Shorn of sig-nificant oversight and legal responsibility for the welfare of these convicts, lessees worked them in horrendous conditions, to the point of exhaustion and death. In Georgia, convicts labored in 60° water in coal mines; others worked seven days a week, at night, and often without adequate food, water, or shelter. Medical care was almost non-existent. Even slaves had not been regularly abused and used up in this fashion. Commissions empanelled to investigate conditions invariably discovered these abuses and recommended reform, but the reforms never came. The excesses of the system finally produced national public outrage that led, in turn, to its abolition in some states at the turn of the century. Georgia continued its leasing of convicts until 1908.[8]

The end of convict leasing did not, however, end the use of the criminal justice system for the economic exploitation of blacks. The prison farm replaced the private convict lease. These state-run farms were little more than antebellum cotton plantations. In 1897, Georgia had opened its own, two miles west of Milledgeville. All of the key features of slave life were there, from cotton-picking quotas, overseers, and drivers, down to whips and wardens who lived in Big Houses attended by black house servants.[9] As with the convict lease system, white actors acted in corrupt concert to funnel blacks into the prison farm complex. To provide sufficient numbers of convict workers, courts routinely ignored the rules of criminal procedure. Black defendants and convicts had fewer protections than they had enjoyed as slaves—and those were the ones lucky enough to land in court. In the age of Jim Crow, the South experienced the highest levels of lynching and extralegal mob violence in the nation's history. Georgia was one of the states most deeply implicated in this racial reign of terror.[10]

The American legal system is based on precedent. If the slave-era system of criminal justice in Georgia had been grounded in a legal culture possessed of a genuine commitment to justice for black defendants, the system of naked economic exploitation and racial violence that emerged in the New South would not have done so, at least not as quickly as it did. The postbellum criminal justice system was not new, but a mere continuation of the age-old practice of subordinating the requirements of justice to the dictates of racial and economic self-interest.

In the near century and a half since the end of slavery, blacks and their allies have fought to end the injustice that permeated and corrupted the criminal justice system. Tremendous strides have been made, but the picture remains bleak. In 1990, the nonprofit Sentencing Project reported that "on an average day in the United States, one in every four black men ages 20-29 was either in prison, jail or on probation/parole." Matters were even worse in the nation's capital. On an average day in 1991 in Washington, D.C., 42 percent of black men between the ages of eighteen and thirty-five were in jail, prison, or under some form of judicial supervision. The Sentencing Project estimated that approximately 75 percent of all eighteen-year-old black men in the nation's capital would be jailed at least once before age thirty-five. By the mid-1990s, the United States was spending in excess of $200 billion annually on crime control, most of it directed at black and other minority populations.[11]

Instances of police brutality against blacks remains disturbingly high, and racial profiling—the practice of stopping and even arresting blacks largely based on race—is just now receiving significant social and political attention. Blacks are convicted and sentenced to death at levels far out of proportion to their numbers in the population, especially in the former slave states. While historians certainly cannot lay the current tragic state of affairs firmly on the doorstep of colonial and antebellum criminal justice systems, we cannot ignore the fact that—like much else about race relations in America—slavery and white supremacy had a significant role to play. As we reach the end of this first decade of the twenty-first century, blacks are still searching for legal justice.

APPENDIX

The following cases were used to create the statistical analyses in this book, including the data presented in tables 1 through 8. Unless otherwise noted, the case files are housed at the Georgia Department of Archives and History (GDAH) in Atlanta.

	Defendant's Name	County	Year	GDAH Location (drawer/box/page)
1	John	Baldwin	1862	140/58/120
2	Stephen	Baldwin	1862	140/58/150
3	Becky	Baldwin	1864	140/58/217
4	Sam	Brooks	1863	178/58/230
5	Bill	Burke	1853	114/34/266
6	Gibbs	Bulloch	1863	10/44/39
7	Isabella	Campbell	1860	107/73/343
8	Mason	Campbell	1861	107/73/402
9	Burke	Campbell	1862	107/73/450
10	Elisha	Carroll	1858	15/46/168
11	Sarah	Carroll	1859	15/46/239
12	Sam	Cherokee	1864	12/68/315
13	Sam	Cherokee	1864	12/68/315
14	Turner	Clay	1857	16/78/166
15	Georgia	Clay	1860	16/78/413
16	Daniel	Clark	1852	98/21
17	Jim	Columbia	1843	192/25/57
18	Henry	Columbia	1850	192/26/23
19	John	Columbia	1852	192/26/61
20	Elias	Columbia	1858	192/26/318
21	George	Columbia	1860	192/26/401
22	John	Columbia	1860	192/26/401
23	Tom	Columbia	1862	192/26/123
24	Sam	Columbia	1862	192/26/173
25	Margrett	Coweta	1858	172/57/412
26	Emiline	Crawford	1860	121/76
27	Rene	Dade	1858	131/57
28	Jesse	Decatur	1856	130/1

	Defendant's Name	County	Year	GDAH Location (drawer/box/page)
29	Jacob	Decatur	1856	130/1
30	Hill	Decatur	1859	130/1
31	Griff	Decatur	1859	130/1
32	Thom	Decatur	1859	130/2/40
33	Pallas	Decatur	1860	130/2/82
34	Dolly	Decatur	1860	130/2/82
35	Coleman	Decatur	1860	130/2/82
36	Samuel	Dekalb	1853	177/9/144
37	Riley	Dekalb	1853	177/9/144
38	George	Dekalb	1854	177/9/161
39	Frank	Dekalb	1853	177/9/217
40	Lige	Dekalb	1854	177/9/394
41	Sefe	Dekalb	1854	177/9/396
42	Jack	Dooley	1862	183/2/332
43	Henry	Dougherty	1863	149/18/4
44	Peter	Early	1854	31/6
45	Lwan	Early	1858	31/8/25
46	Bob, a.k.a. Robin	Emanuel	1850	113/17/205
47	Council Cullers	Emanuel	1855	113/17/288
48	George	Emanuel	1856	113/18/92
49	King	Fayette	1850	94/27/73
50	Hanah	Floyd	1856	136/2/127
51	Tyler	Floyd	1857	136/2/135
52	Joe	Floyd	1857	136/2/190
53	John	Fayette	1865	94/11/546
54	Lank	Franklin	1853	177/17
55	Jerry	Franklin	1853	177/17
56	Daniel	Franklin	1854	177/17
57	George	Fulton	1864	106/55
58	Henry	Fulton	1864	106/55
59	Rubin	Fulton	1864	106/55
60	Scott	Greene	1851	33/66/311
61	Edward	Greene	1852	33/66/496
62	Simon .	Greene	1853	33/67
63	Thornton	Greene	1858	33/68/361

	Defendant's Name	County	Year	GDAH Location (drawer/box/page)
64	Tom	Greene	1860	33/68/613
65	John	Greene	1858	33/69/634
66	Martin	Greene	1858	33/69/638
67	Becky	Greene	1860	33/70/102
68	Henry	Greene	1864	33/70/370
69	Aleck	Greene	1857	34/6/147
70	Maria	Greene	1858	34/6/226
71	Isaac	Greene	1858	34/6/377
72	Mib	Greene	1864	34/6/617
73	Albert	Gordon	1852	137/59
74	Henry	Gordon	1852	137/59
75	Joseph	Gordon	1860	137/60
76	John	Gordon	1863	137/60
77	Nelson	Habersham	1852	178/28
78	Peter	Habersham	1852	178/28
79	Billy	Habersham	1853	178/28
80	John	Habersham	1853	178/28
81	Sarah	Harris	1858	165/16/248
82	Bill	Harris	1860	165/16/372
83	Mitch	Harris	1863	165/16/468
84	Amanda	Harris	1863	165/16/468
85	Lewis	Harris	1865	165/16/500
86	Hattie	Henry	1861	9/51
87	Henry	Henry	1863	9/51
88	Seaborn	Henry	1863	9/51
89	Isaac	Houston	1851	158/37/295
90	Judge	Houston	1849	158/37/283
91	Jerry	Houston	1853	158/38/212
92	Stephen	Houston	1851	158/38/16
93	Mike	Houston	1854	158/38/319
94	Bill	Houston	1855	158/38/56
95	Charles	Houston	1856	158/38/267
96	Wiley	Houston	1857	158/38/292
97	Aggey	Houston	1858	158/38/376
98	Gabriel	Houston	1858	158/38/376
99	West	Houston	1860	158/39/337
100	Heywood	Houston	1863	158/39/462

	Defendant's Name	County	Year	GDAH Location (drawer/box/page)
101	Randolph	Houston	1853	158/39/462
102	Ailey	Jasper	1854	35/61/232
103	Moses	Jasper	1862	35/61/166
104	Anthony	Jones	1857	154/56/393
105	Prince	Jones	1859	154/56/458
106	Henry Hord	Jones	1859	154/56/458
107	John	Jones	1860	154/56/484
108	Samuel	Laurens	1865	123/60/130
109	Dick	Laurens	1861	123/60/96
110	Josephine	Laurens	1861	123/60/96
111	Caroline	Laurens	1861	123/60/96
112	Bibb	Laurens	1861	123/60/96
113	Nelly	Laurens	1861	123/60/96
114	Edward	Laurens	1863	123/60/138
115	Jack	Lee	1861	181/1/521
116	Jim	Liberty	1852	30/47/267
117	Willis	Liberty	1853	30/47/328
118	Rafe	Liberty	1856	30/47/388
119	Betty	Liberty	1858	30/47/496
120	Adam	Liberty	1858	30/47/496
121	Isaac	Liberty	1863	30/48/122
122	Amos	Lincoln	1854	88/55
123	Bill	Lowndes	1858	291/62/46
124	Andy	Lumpkin	1856	149/50/54
125	Aleck	Lumpkin	1856	149/50/54
126	Sampson	Lumpkin	1857	149/50/54
127	Marion	Lumpkin	1856	149/50/54
128	Elias	Macon	1864	164/19/583
129	Ben	Macon	1864	164/19/586
130	Sam	Macon	1864	164/19/586
131	Redmond	Macon	1864	164/19/586
132	Sam	Madison	1858	177/41
133	Peter	Madison	1862	177/41
134	David, a.k.a. Davy	Marion	1855	141/71

	Defendant's Name	County	Year	GDAH Location (drawer/box/page)
135	Jim	Marion	1856	141/71/14
136	Bill	Marion	1863	141/71/284
137	Rhoda	Marion	1863	141/71/284
138	Nathan	Meriwether	1850	12/59/479
139	Monroe	Meriwether	1850	12/59/482
140	Noah	Meriwether	1850	12/59&60/647
141	Henry	Meriwether	1860	12/60/302
142	Sarah	Meriwether	1858	12/60/48
143	Johan	Monroe	1857	2/33/172
144	William	Monroe	1856	2/33
145	Caleb	Monroe	1854	2/33/105
146	Perry	Monroe	1857	2/33
147	Jane	Morgan	1850	41/58/599
148	William Setner	Murray	1853	93/65/155
149	Jarrett	Muscogee	1851	80/64/336
150	Neil	Muscogee	1853	80/64/318, vol. 2
151	William, a.k.a. Bill	Muscogee	1855	80/65/162
152	Elbert	Muscogee	1856	80/65/345
153	Andrew	Muscogee	1856	80/65/136
154	Jeff, a.k.a. Jeffrey	Newton	1850	11/2/240
155	Michael Davis	Newton	1859	11/3/384, vol. 2
156	Albert	Newton	1863	11/4/447, vol. 3
157	Elbert	Newton	1863	11/4/447, vol. 3
158	Willis	Oglethorpe	1850	46/25/194, vol. 2
159	Pressley	Oglethorpe	1855	46/26/582, vol. 2
160	Hamit	Oglethorpe	1863	46/28/488
161	Caleb	Oglethorpe	1865	46/28/530
162	Charlotte	Oglethorpe	1865	46/28/531
163	Ned	Oglethorpe	1862	46/29/407
164	Arthur	Oglethorpe	1862	46/29/408
165	Catherine	Polk	1852	132/64/13
166	Randall	Pulaski	1853	39/18/144, vol. 2

	Defendant's Name	County	Year	GDAH Location (drawer/box/page)
167	John	Pulaski	1856	39/18/348
168	Jerry	Randolph	1853	143/16
169	Lewis	Randolph	1853	143/16
170	Lott	Randolph	1853	143/16
171	Allen	Randolph	1855	143/16
172	Joe	Richmond	1852	141/48/350, vol. 2
173	Jim	Richmond	1860	141/50/632
174	Sarah	Richmond	1863	145/15/228
175	Patrick	Richmond	1862	145/15/237
176	George	Richmond	1863	145/15/283
177	Tucker	Richmond	1864	145/15/406
178	Jack	Richmond	1865	145/15/450
179	Ned	Richmond	1865	145/15/450
180	Sawney	Richmond	1865	145/15
181	Eleeta	Richmond	1864	145/15/341
182	Joe	Screven	1860	112/4/199
183	Edmund	Spaulding	1860	163/62/352
184	Ned	Spaulding	1863	163/62/520
185	Edmund	Spaulding	1863	163/62/520
186	Mat	Stewart	1860	54/68/28
187	David	Sumter	1853	133/5/311
188	Rachel	Sumter	1853	133/5/311
189	Robin	Sumter	1853	133/5/358
190	Ted	Sumter	1853	133/5/367
191	Randal	Sumter	1854	133/20/105
192	Kinchen	Sumter	1855	133/20/314
193	Alfred	Sumter	1855	133/20/314
194	Sampson	Sumter	1855	133/20/314
195	Monday	Sumter	1861	133/8/41
196	Elbert	Sumter	1863	133/8/262
197	Ned	Talbot	1853	126/6/507
198	Morris	Talbot	1861	126/7/27
199	Jeff	Talbot	1861	126/7/30
200	Bill	Talbot	1861	126/7/30
201	Primus	Talbot	1861	126/7/30
202	Priscilla	Talbot	1864	126/7/141

	Defendant's Name	County	Year	GDAH Location (drawer/box/page)
203	Andrew	Talbot	1864	126/7/141
204	Bob	Taliaferro	1858	109/37/287
205	James Floyd	Taliaferro	1858	109/37/62, vol. 2
206	Rose	Taliaferro	1861	109/37/149, vol. 2
207	George Moss	Taliaferro	1861	109/37/166, vol. 2
208	Shadrack	Tatnall	1854	84/56
209	Jesse	Tatnall	1863	84/56/267
210	Edmund	Taylor	1856	164/43/212
211	Ted	Taylor	1862	164/43/484
212	Mat	Terrell	1858	142/1/74
213	Joe	Terrell	1858	142/1/74
214	Wade	Thomas	1852	4/45/236
215	Burrell	Thomas	1852	4/45/239
216	Francis	Thomas	1854	4/45/5, vol. 2
217	Washington	Thomas	1855	4/45/28, vol. 2
218	Jerry	Thomas	1855	4/45/102, vol. 2
219	Henry Green	Thomas	1855	4/45/113, vol. 2
220	Henry	Thomas	1857	4/45/243, vol. 2
221	Jacob	Thomas	1861	4/46/435
222	Plummer	Thomas	1862	4/46/484
223	Aaron	Thomas	1862	4/46/491
224	Bill	Thomas	1864	4/46/531
225	Susan	Troup	1850	155/19/205, vol. 2
226	Wiley	Troup	1856	155/19/419, vol. 2
227	Aaron	Troup	1857	155/20/687
228	William	Troup	1859	155/21/975
229	Willis	Troup	1863	155/22/47
230	Rhoda	Upson	1850	144/9/315
231	Phil	Upson	1859	144/10/9
232	Jack	Upson	1859	144/10/111
233	Samson	Upson	1860	144/10/163
234	Henry	Upson	1862	144/10/316
235	Ned	Walton	1863	127/42/314

	Defendant's Name	County	Year	GDAH Location (drawer/box/page)
236	Luke	Warren	1853	103/43 & 44
237	Green	Warren	1853	103/43
238	Julia Ann Loach	Warren	1861	103/44/477
239	Loach	Warren	1861	103/44/477
240	Bonner	Warren	1861	103/44/499
241	Jeff	Warren	1862	103/44/506
242	Willis	Wilkes	1861	42/72/90, vol. 2
243	Tom	Wilkes	1862	42/72/139, vol. 2
244	Margaret	Wilkes	1860	42/72/61, vol. 2
245	Allen	Bibb	1851	183/12/208, vol. 5
246	William	Bibb	1851	183/12/389, vol. 5
247	Johnson	Bibb	1852	183/12/527, vol. 5
248	John	Bibb	1853	183/13/479, vol. 6
249	Cain	Bibb	1855	183/13/408, vol. 7
250	Jacob	Bibb	1858	183/15/136, vol. 9
251	Becky	Bibb	1860	183/15/612, vol. 9
252	Robert, a.k.a. Bob	Bibb	1860	183/15/613, vol. 9
253	Eugene	Bibb	1863	183/16/286, vol. 10
254	Jack, a.k.a. John	Bibb	1863	183/16/264, vol. 10
255	Gilbert	Bibb	1863	183/16/292, vol. 10
256	Stephen	Bibb	1863	183/16/423, vol. 10
257	Milton	Bibb	1863	183/16/621, vol. 10
258	Gracia	Bibb	1863	183/16/625 vol. 10
259	Gilbert	Bibb	1864	183/16/776, vol. 10
260	Tom	Bibb	1865	183/16/844, vol. 10
261	William	Bibb	1865	183/16/844, vol. 10
262	Henry	Bibb	1865	183/16/844, vol. 10
263	Elias	Bibb	1865	183/16/843, vol. 10
264	Tom	Bibb	1865	183/16/849, vol. 10
265	Mary	Bibb	1865	183/16/849, vol. 10
266	Floyd	Bibb	1865	183/16/864, vol. 10
267	George	Bibb	1865	183/16/867, vol. 10
268	Charley	Bibb	1865	183/16/867, vol. 10

	Defendant's Name	County	Year	GDAH Location (drawer/box/page)
269	Bob	Chatham	1856	68/42/112
270	William	Chatham	1857	68/42/338
271	Willis	Chatham	1860	68/42/365, vol. 2
272	Peter	Chatham	1863	68/43/444
273	Edwin	Chatham	1862	68/43/452
274	Adam	Chatham	1862	68/43/453
275	Guy	Chatham	1862	68/43/453
276	Frank	Chatham	1862	68/43/456
277	Edward	Chatham	1862	68/43/441
278	York	Chatham	1862	68/43/458
279	Thomas	Chatham	1862	68/43/474
280	Samson	Chatham	1861	68/43/269
281	George	Chatham	1864	68/43/184, vol. 2
282	Sylvester	Chatham	1864	68/43/185, vol. 2
283	Lucinda	Chatham	1864	68/43/178, vol. 2
284	Frank	Hancock	1843	121/46/1, vol. 2
285	Israel	Hancock	1849	121/46/8, vol. 2
286	Pamer	Hancock	1849	121/46/20, vol. 2
287	Warren	Hancock	1850	121/46/29, vol. 2
288	Bob	Bryan	1800	25/23
289	Tim	Bryan	1800	25/23
290	Charles	Bryan	1804	25/43
291	Tom	Bryan	1804	25/43
292	Ben	Putnam	1813	1/17
293	Jack	Putnam	1814	1/17
294	Eldridge	Putnam	1817	1/17
295	Cato	Putnam	1819	1/17
296	Sophia	Putnam	1819	1/17
297	George	Putnam	1821	1/17
298	John Boon	Putnam	1822	1/17
299	Harry	Putnam	1822	1/17
300	Jake, a.k.a. Jacob	Putnam	1824	1/17
301	Jerry	Putnam	1824	1/17
302	Jacob	Putnam	1824	1/17
303	Jim	Putnam	1824	1/17

	Defendant's Name	County	Year	GDAH Location (drawer/box/page)
304	Stanley	Putnam	1826	1/17
305	Dick	Putnam	1831	1/17
306	Jim	Putnam	1838	1/17
307	Charles	Putnam	1843	1/17
308	Allen James	Taliaferro	1857	109/8/1
309	William Lesley	Taliaferro	1857	109/8/2
310	Wilson Lloyd	Taliaferro	1857	109/8
311	Moses	Jones	1822	76/72
312	Harry	Jones	1834	76/72
313	Adam	Jones	1835	76/72
314	Charles	Jones	1836	76/72
315	Claiborne	Jones	1845	76/72
316	Shadrach	Jones	1845	76/72
317	Thomas, a.k.a. Tom	Jones	1846	76/72
318	Peter	Elbert	1837	2/76
319	Edmond	Elbert	1839	2/76
320	Wesley	Elbert	1847	2/76
321	Adeline	Elbert	1849	2/76
322	Guy	Screven	1844	37/32
323	Bob	Lincoln	1848	37/32
324	Bob	Lincoln	1814	81/23
325	Pollard	Lincoln	1818	81/23
326	Hall	Lincoln	1818	81/23
327	Tobe	Lincoln	1819	81/23
328	Buck	Lincoln	1819	81/23
329	Jesse	Lincoln	1823	81/23
330	Moss	Lincoln	1828	81/23
331	Randol	Lincoln	1834	81/23
332	Elick	Lincoln	1838	81/23
333	Carter	Chatham	1813	90/33
334	Jim	Chatham	1813	90/33
335	Elijah	Chatham	1813	90/33
336	Dick	Chatham	1814	90/33

	Defendant's Name	*County*	*Year*	*GDAH Location (drawer/box/page)*
337	Sampson Whitefield	Chatham	1817	90/33
338	John Baxton	Chatham	1817	90/33
339	William Ford	Chatham	1818	90/33
340	Julia	Chatham	1818	90/33
341	Adam	Chatham	1819	90/33
342	Benjamin Lee	Chatham	1819	90/33
343	George Flyming	Chatham	1820	90/33
344	Titus	Chatham	1820	90/33
345	Reuben Williams	Chatham	1820	90/33
346	Susan	Chatham	1821	90/33
347	Hardtimes	Chatham	1821	90/33
348	Thomas	Chatham	1821	90/33
349	Dick	Chatham	1822	90/33
350	Robin	Chatham	1822	90/33
351	Shadrach	Chatham	1822	90/33
352	Molly	Chatham	1824	90/33
353	Ben	Chatham	1824	90/33
354	Harry	Chatham	1825	90/33
355	Harry	Chatham	1827	90/33
356	Major	Baldwin	1812	199/25
357	Fanny Micklejohn	Baldwin	1815	199/25
358	Tom	Baldwin	1815	199/25
359	John	Baldwin	1816	199/25
360	Aluk	Baldwin	1818	199/25
361	Rodney	Baldwin	1819	199/25
362	Peter	Baldwin	1821	199/25
363	Edmond	Baldwin	1821	199/25
364	Dave, a.k.a. Davy	Baldwin	1822	199/25

	Defendant's Name	County	Year	GDAH Location (drawer/box/page)
365	John	Baldwin	1822	199/25
366	George	Baldwin	1825	199/25
367	George	Baldwin	1825	199/25
368	Stephen	Baldwin	1825	199/25
369	Ellick	Baldwin	1826	199/25
370	Martin	Baldwin	1832	139/62
371	Caroline	Baldwin	1829	139/62
372	Charles	Baldwin	1838	139/62
373	Will	Washington	1792	Georgia Slave Trials, Telamon Cuyler Collection, University of Georgia
374	George	Burke	1793	Georgia Slave Trials, Telamon Cuyler Collection, University of Georgia
375	Jack	Washington	1796	Georgia Slave Trials, Telamon Cuyler Collection, University of Georgia
376	Jerry	Washington	1796	Georgia Slave Trials, Telamon Cuyler Collection, University of Georgia
377	Sam	Washington	1796	Georgia Slave Trials, Telamon Cuyler Collection, University of Georgia
378	Orange	Washington	1796	Georgia Slave Trials, Telamon Cuyler Collection, University of Georgia
379	Lewis	Chatham	1797	Georgia Slave Trials, Telamon Cuyler Collection, University of Georgia
380	Frank	Camden	1797	Georgia Slave Trials, Telamon Cuyler Collection, University of Georgia
381	Abram	Camden	1797	Georgia Slave Trials, Telamon Cuyler Collection, University of Georgia

	Defendant's Name	County	Year	GDAH Location (drawer/box/page)
382	Lewis	Chatham	1795	Georgia Slave Trials, Telamon Cuyler Collection, University of Georgia
383	Unknown	Chatham	1767	*Colonial Records of Georgia*, 10:245
384	Dickson	Chatham	1768	*Colonial Records of Georgia*, 10:631
385	Unknown	Liberty	1771	*Colonial Records of Georgia*, 10:305
386	King	Chatham	1791	*Georgia Gazette*, May 5, 1791
387	Unknown	Chatham	1794	*Georgia Gazette*, February 6, 1794
388	Unknown	Chatham	1794	*Georgia Gazette*, February 6, 1794
389	Unknown	Chatham	1794	*Georgia Gazette*, February 6, 1794
390	Pressley	Oglethorpe	1855	19 GA 192
391	Jim	Lee	1854	15 GA 535
392	Anthony	McIntosh	1850	9 GA 264
393	Alfred	Cass	1849	6 GA 483
394	George	Chatham	1806	*Georgia Decisions*, 1:80
395	Peter	Richmond	1842	*Georgia Decisions*, 2:46
396	Peter	Elbert	1803	50/45/215, vol. 1
397	Tom	Unknown	1804	50/45/458, vol. 1
398	Peter	Clarke	1805	50/45/29, vol. 2
399	Joe	Elbert	1805	50/45/53, vol. 2
400	Walley	Jefferson	1805	50/45/207, vol. 2
401	Sam	Hancock	1808	50/46/110, vol. 2
402	Solomon	Elbert	1809	50/46/309, vol. 2
403	Jack	Jackson	1809	50/46/417, vol. 2
404	Tom	Richmond	1809	50/46/428, vol. 2
405	Harry	Liberty	1809	50/47/95, vol. 1
406	Sam	Clarke	1811	50/47/33, vol. 2
407	Bob	Montgomery	1817	50/48/197, vol. 3
408	Hatten	Hancock	1820	50/48/115, vol. 4

	Defendant's Name	County	Year	GDAH Location (drawer/box/page)
409	Charles	Richmond	1820	50/48/128, vol. 4
410	George	Chatham	1820	50/48/152, vol. 4
411	Dick	Hancock	1820	50/48/180, vol. 4
412	Surry	Richmond	1831	50/50/226, vol. 1
413	John	Screven	1831	50/50/283, vol. 1
414	Harry	Dooly	1832	50/50/457, vol. 1
415	Dick	Jasper	1827	50/49/332, vol. 2
416	Dennis	Oglethorpe	1837	Executive Minutes, 1836-43, GDAH
417	Caesar	Muscogee	1825	Executive Minutes, 1822-27, GDAH

NOTES

INTRODUCTION

1. Christopher Waldrep, *Roots of Disorder: Race and Criminal Justice in the American South, 1817–80* (Urbana: University of Illinois Press, 1998), 2.

2. Scholars of the general history of slavery often write on matters of criminal justice using a narrative interpretive approach rather than attempting to quantify these data. Narrative studies are certainly valuable, but without quantification it is impossible to discern patterns in criminal justice over time. Four classic works on Southern slavery define the non-quantitative approach to slaves and free blacks and criminal justice. They are Ulrich Bonnell Phillips, *American Negro Slavery: A Survey of the Supply, Employment and Control of Negro Labor as Determined by the Plantation Regime,* 2d ed. (Baton Rouge: Louisiana State University Press, 1966); Stanley M. Elkins, *Slavery: A Problem in American Intellectual Life,* 2d ed. (Chicago: University of Chicago Press, 1968); Kenneth Stampp, *The Peculiar Institution: Slavery in the Antebellum South* (New York: Vintage Books, 1956); and Eugene G. Genovese, *Roll, Jordan, Roll: The World the Slaves Made* (New York: Pantheon, 1976). Each of these books provides significant insight into slaves and criminal justice, and each has influenced subsequent state and local studies of slavery and criminal justice. Georgia studies that follow the narrative approach are Ralph Betts Flanders, *Plantation Slavery in Georgia* (Cos Cob, Conn.: John E. Edwards, 1967); Donald L. Grant, *The Way It Was in the South: The Black Experience in Georgia,* ed. Jonathan Grant (New York: Carol Publishing Group, 1993); Joseph P. Reidy, *From Slavery to Agrarian Capitalism in the Cotton Plantation South: Central Georgia, 1800–1880* (Chapel Hill: University of North Carolina Press, 1992); Julia Floyd Smith, *Slavery and Rice Culture in Low Country Georgia, 1750–1860* (Knoxville: University of Tennessee Press, 1985); Betty Wood, *Slavery in Colonial Georgia, 1730–1775* (Athens: University of Georgia Press, 1984); and Jonathan M. Bryant, *How Curious a Land: Conflict and Change in Greene County, Georgia, 1850–1885* (Chapel Hill: University of North Carolina Press, 1996). A. E. Keir Nash inaugurated the study of appellate decisions with the following articles: "Fairness and Formalism in the Trials of Blacks in State Supreme Courts of the Old South," *Virginia Law Review* 56 (1970): 64–100; "A More Equitable Past? Southern Supreme Courts and the Protection of the Antebellum Negro," *North Carolina Law Review* 48 (1970): 197–241; "The Texas Supreme Court and the Trial Rights of Blacks, 1845–1860," *Journal of American History* 58 (1971): 622–42; and "Reason of Slavery: Understanding

the Judicial Role in the Peculiar Institution," *Vanderbilt Law Review* 32 (1979): 7–218. Nash argued that Southern appellate courts provided black defendants with a surprising degree of procedural fairness. Numerous works emerged to support and challenge his conclusions about appellate courts, including Mark V. Tushnet, *The American Law of Slavery, 1810–1860* (Princeton, N.J.: Princeton University Press, 1981); Daniel J. Flanigan, *The Criminal Law of Slavery and Freedom* (New York: Garland Publishing, 1987); Daniel J. Flanigan, "Criminal Procedure in Slave Trials in the Antebellum South," *Journal of Southern History* 40 (1974): 405–24; Patrick Brady, "Slavery, Race and the Criminal Law in Antebellum North Carolina: A Reconsideration of the Thomas Ruffin Court," *North Carolina Central Law Journal* 10 (1978): 248–60; and A. Leon Higginbotham Jr., *In the Matter of Color: Race and the American Legal Process: The Colonial Period* (New York: Oxford University Press, 1978). (I will discuss Nash and his supporters and detractors in greater detail in chapter 5.) A number of monographs have used quantitative approaches to provide a more detailed picture of criminal justice for blacks, among them Jack Kenny Williams, *Vogues in Villainy: Crime and Retribution in Antebellum South Carolina* (Columbia: University of South Carolina Press, 1959); Michael Hindus, *Prison and Plantation: Crime, Justice and Authority in Massachusetts and South Carolina, 1767–1878* (Chapel Hill: University of North Carolina Press, 1980); Edward L. Ayers, *Vengeance and Justice: Crime and Punishment in the 19th-Century American South* (New York: Oxford University Press, 1984); Arthur F. Howington, *What Sayeth the Law: The Treatment of Slaves and Free Blacks in the State and Local Courts of Tennessee* (New York: Garland Publishing, 1986); Donna J. Spindel, *Crime and Society in North Carolina, 1663–1776* (Baton Rouge: Louisiana State University Press, 1989); Derek N. Kerr, *Petty Felony, Slave Defiance and Frontier Villainy: Crime and Criminal Justice in Spanish Louisiana, 1770–1803* (New York: Garland Publishing, 1993); Waldrep, *Roots of Disorder;* and James M. Denham, *"A Rogue's Paradise": Crime and Punishment in Antebellum Florida, 1821–1861* (Tuscaloosa: University of Alabama Press, 1997). The study that best combines quantitative and narrative approaches in the examination of slave crime is Philip J. Schwarz, *Twice Condemned: Slaves and the Criminal Laws of Virginia, 1705–1865* (Baton Rouge: Louisiana State University Press, 1988). It is also the only study that is entirely devoted to slave crime. None of these studies attempt to integrate appellate court decisions and procedures and plantation justice into their quantitative models in a systematic way. The best work on slave patrols to date is Sally E. Hadden, *Slave Patrols: Law and Violence in Virginia and the Carolinas* (Cambridge, Mass.: Harvard University Press, 2001).

3. Hindus, *Prison and Plantation,* 33–35.

1. "MY LORD THEY ARE STARK MAD AFTER NEGROES"

1. James Oglethorpe to the trustees, January 13, 1733, Phillips Collection of Egmont Manuscripts, University of Georgia Library, Athens, quoted in Phinizy Spalding, *Oglethorpe in America* (Chicago: University of Chicago Press, 1977), 1.

2. Spalding, *Oglethorpe in America*, 2–4; Harold E. Davis, *The Fledgling Province: Social and Cultural Life in Colonial Georgia, 1733–1776* (Chapel Hill: University of North Carolina Press, 1976), 4.

3. Allen D. Candler, ed., *Colonial Records of the State of Georgia* (Atlanta: Franklin Printing and Publishing, 1904), vol. 1, p. 11. Volume and page numbers are generally the only descriptors I provide for items in the *Colonial Records* because documents are often not titled. This style of citation is conventional among historians of colonial Georgia.

4. Davis, *Fledgling Province*, 8.

5. Ibid., 8–9; the quoted material is from the colonial charter (Candler, *Colonial Records*, vol. 1, p. 11).

6. Candler, *Colonial Records*, vol. 1, p. 21.

7. Trevor Richard Reese, *Colonial Georgia: A Study in British Imperial Policy in the Eighteenth Century* (Athens: University of Georgia Press, 1963), 41.

8. Ibid., 41–42; Davis, *Fledgling Province*, 11–12.

9. Reese, *Colonial Georgia*, 29–30.

10. James Edward Oglethorpe, *A New Account of the Provinces of South Carolina and Georgia* (London: Bible and Dove, 1732), in James Edward Oglethorpe, *Publications of James Edward Oglethorpe*, ed. Rodney M. Blaine (Athens: University of Georgia Press, 1994), 213–16.

11. Peter Gordon, *Journal of Peter Gordon 1732–1735*, ed. E. Merton Coulter (Athens: University of Georgia Press, 1963), 3, 39; Spalding, *Oglethorpe in America*, 12–13; Betty Wood, *Slavery in Colonial Georgia, 1730–1775* (Athens: University of Georgia Press, 1984), 4.

12. Wood, *Slavery in Colonial Georgia*, 16; Spalding, *Oglethorpe in America*, 61–62.

13. Wood, *Slavery in Colonial Georgia*, 16–17; Spalding, *Oglethorpe in America*, 62.

14. Wood, *Slavery in Colonial Georgia*, 13–14.

15. Phinizy Spalding, "Colonial Period," in *A History of Georgia*, ed. Kenneth Coleman, Numan V. Bartley, William F. Holmes, F. N. Boney, Phinizy Spalding, Charles E. Wynes (Athens: University of Georgia Press, 1977), 21.

16. Candler, *Colonial Records*, vol. 1, pp. 19, 22.

17. Francis Moore, *A Voyage to Georgia* (London: Jacob Robinson, 1744), 26, quoted in Spalding, *Oglethorpe in America*, 15.

18. Reese, *Colonial Georgia*, 19–20.

19. Spalding, *Oglethorpe in America,* 15; Gordon, *Journal of Peter Gordon,* 49–51; Reese, *Colonial Georgia,* 27.

20. Spalding, *Oglethorpe in America,* 16–17.

21. Wood, *Slavery in Colonial Georgia,* 18–21; Earl of Egmont, *The Diary of Lord John Percival, First Earl of Egmont, 1730–1747* (London: Historical Manuscripts Commission, 1920–23), 2:204–5.

22. Gordon, *Journal of Peter Gordon,* 53.

23. Wood, *Slavery in Colonial Georgia,* 24–25.

24. Candler, *Colonial Records,* vol. 1, pp. 49–52; Wood, *Slavery in Colonial Georgia,* 5–8; Benjamin Martyn, *An Account Shewing the Progress of the Colony of Georgia in America from Its First Establishment* (London: n.p., 1741), in *The Clamorous Malcontents* (Savannah: Beehive Press, 1973), 190–92.

25. Martyn, *An Account,* 191–92.

26. Ruth Scarborough, *The Opposition to Slavery in Georgia prior to 1860* (1933; repr., New York: Negro Universities Press, 1968), 21.

27. Wood, *Slavery in Colonial Georgia,* 19–20.

28. Patrick Talifer, Hugh Anderson, and Davis Douglas, *A True and Historical Narrative of the Colony of Georgia in America, 1741* (Charlestown, S.C.: P. Timothy, 1741), in *The Clamorous Malcontents,* 69–70.

29. Wood, *Slavery in Colonial Georgia,* 26–27.

30. Spalding, "Colonial Period," 27.

31. Reese, *Colonial Georgia,* 46.

32. Davis, *Fledgling Province,* 148–49.

33. Candler, *Colonial Records,* vol. 20, pp. 139, 203; vol. 21, pt. 1, pp. 173–74.

34. Gordon, *Journal of Peter Gordon,* 56–59.

35. Talifer, *A True and Historical Narrative,* 75–78.

36. Wood, *Slavery in Colonial Georgia,* 29.

37. Talifer, *A True and Historical Narrative,* 89–90.

38. Egmont, *Egmont Diary,* 2:65, 492.

39. James Edward Oglethorpe, "Negro Insurrection," in *Publications of James Edward Oglethorpe,* 253–55; Wood, *Slavery in Colonial Georgia,* 31.

40. Egmont, *Egmont Diary,* 2:473–74.

41. Ibid., 3:31, 78–79, 81; Candler, *Colonial Records,* vol. 2, pp. 271, 336; Reese, *Colonial Georgia,* 43–44.

42. Wood, *Slavery in Colonial Georgia,* 39–40.

43. William Stephens, *A State of the Province of Georgia* (London: W. Meadows, 1742), in *The Clamorous Malcontents,* 3–5.

44. Ibid., 11–12, 14.

45. "The Remonstrance of the Inhabitants of the Town and County of Sa-

vannah, and the Rest of the Inhabitants of the Province of Georgia in America, To the Honourable Trustees for Establishing that Colony. Sign'd 22 Nov. 1740 Copy'd 2d Dec 1740 Rec'd 22 May 1741," Egmont Papers, 14205, University of Georgia Library, quoted in Wood, *Slavery in Colonial Georgia,* 41–43. The biggest local thorn in the sides of the Malcontents was Johann Martin Bolzius. His persistent claim that Georgia could be successfully planted without slave labor, and the example of Ebenezer to support this assertion, continually buttressed the trustees' belief in the soundness of their social and economic plan. Bolzius had to be eliminated or neutered as a critic of the Malcontents. The pro-slavery forces launched a campaign to discredit Bolzius, arguing that he used his influence as the Salzburgers' spiritual leader to coerce his followers into signing petitions against the introduction of Negroes. As for the apparent success of Ebenezer, the minister simply lied. In an October 1741 visit to Ebenezer, Thomas Stephens was able to get three Salzburgers to sign an affidavit supporting the Malcontents' view of their minister and his machinations (Wood, *Slavery in Colonial Georgia,* 70–72). The three Salzburgers—Christopher Ortman, John Michael Riser, and Thomas Bicher—said that as the "oldest settlers" in Ebenezer, they had "never yet been able to support themselves and Families by Cultivation"; nor did they "know an Instance of it, among all the said Inhabitants." Far from opposing the introduction of slaves, "the Inhabitants in general of the said Ebenezer, are desirous of Negroes." The only reason they signed a petition to the contrary was that Bolzius "would have been angry with them, if they had refused to do so." They would sign a petition in support of slavery, "were it not that Mr. Bolzius . . . who exercises an arbitrary power over us, might make them very uneasie." A fourth Ebenezer resident, John Speilbeigler, expressed similar sentiments in a separate affidavit (Thomas Stephens, *A Brief Account of the Causes That Have Retarded the Progress of the Colony of Georgia in America* [London: n.p., 1743], in *The Clamorous Malcontents,* 306, 308).

46. Talifer, *A True and Historical Narrative,* 56–57, 120–21; Candler, *Colonial Records,* vol. 4, supp. 201.

47. Wood, *Slavery in Colonial Georgia,* 32–35.

48. Ibid., 37, 47–48, 52–53; Thomas Stephens, "The Hard Case of the Distressed People of Georgia," in *The Clamorous Malcontents,* 266–67.

49. Trevor Reese, "Introduction," in *The Clamorous Malcontents,* xiv–xv.

50. Stephens, "The Hard Case," 268–69.

51. Egmont, *Egmont's Diary,* 3:265; Wood, *Slavery in Colonial Georgia,* 54–55.

52. Wood, *Slavery in Colonial Georgia,* 56–57; Candler, *Colonial Records,* vol. 1, pp. 398–99.

53. Davis, *Fledgling Province,* 125–26.

54. Wood, *Slavery in Colonial Georgia*, 77–79; Egmont, *Egmont's Diary*, 3:265; Candler, *Colonial Records*, vol. 25, p. 289.

55. Candler, *Colonial Records*, vol. 25, pp. 72, 295; Scarborough, *Opposition to Slavery*, 47.

56. Scarborough, *Opposition to Slavery*, 50.

57. Candler, *Colonial Records*, vol. 25, pp. 236–37.

58. Scarborough, *Opposition to Slavery*, 50; Candler, *Colonial Records*, vol. 21, pp. 161–62.

59. Candler, *Colonial Records*, vol. 1, p. 57.

60. Ibid.; Davis, *Fledgling Province*, 126.

61. Candler, *Colonial Records*, vol. 26, pp. 415–16; vol. 37, p. 141; Wood, *Slavery in Colonial Georgia*, 89; *Agriculture of the United States in 1860 Compiled from the Original Returns of the Eighth Census* (Washington, D.C.: Government Printing Office, 1864), xciv, 247; *Population of the United States in 1860 Compiled from the Original Returns of the Eighth Census* (Washington, D.C.: Government Printing Office, 1864), 198, 518.

62. Wood, *Slavery in Colonial Georgia*, 2.

63. Gordon, *Journal of Peter Gordon*, 46–48.

64. Candler, *Colonial Records*, vol. 4, supp. 271–72.

2. "FOR THE BETTER ORDERING AND GOVERNING NEGROES"

1. Allen D. Candler, ed., *Colonial Records of the State of Georgia* (Atlanta: Franklin Printing and Publishing, 1904), vol. 1, pp. 57–60. For the role of South Carolina slaveholders in Georgia, see Betty Wood, *Slavery in Colonial Georgia, 1730–1775* (Athens: University of Georgia Press, 1984), 85–86, 111–12.

2. Candler, *Colonial Records*, vol. 18, pp. 105–7, 131.

3. Ibid., vol. 18, pp. 136–37; Wood, *Slavery in Colonial Georgia*, 116.

4. Candler, *Colonial Records*, vol. 18, pp. 117–18. Wood argues that "white fire-power and humanitarian treatment" made a strict population quota unnecessary (see Wood, *Slavery in Colonial Georgia*, 117–18).

5. Candler, *Colonial Records*, vol. 18, pp. 112–13, 119–20, 125–29.

6. Ibid., vol. 18, pp. 132–33.

7. Ibid., vol. 18, pp. 682–83.

8. Ibid., vol. 18, pp. 662–63.

9. Ibid., vol. 18, pp. 660–63; Reports of the Jamaican murders appeared in the *Georgia Gazette*, 7 April 1763 (quoted in Wood, *Slavery in Colonial Georgia*, 124–26).

10. Kenneth Coleman, Numan V. Bartley, William F. Holmes, F. N. Boney, Phinizy Spalding, Charles E. Wynes, eds., *A History of Georgia* (Athens: University of Georgia Press, 1977), 229. For a discussion of the legal consequences of defin-

ing slaves as chattel property, see Thomas D. Morris, *Southern Slavery and the Law, 1619-1865* (Chapel Hill: University of North Carolina Press, 1996), 64-65. For discussion of the disallowance of Georgia's slave code, see Wood, *Slavery in Colonial Georgia,* 128-29; M. Eugene Sirmans, "The Legal Status of the Slave in South Carolina, 1670-1740," *Journal of Southern History* 28 (November 1962): 465. South Carolina also experienced legal difficulty in arriving at the proper definition of "slave."

11. Candler, *Colonial Records,* vol. 19, pt. 1, p. 220; Oliver H. Prince, *A Digest of the Laws of the State of Georgia* (Milledgeville, Ga.: Grantland and Orme, 1822), 461; William A. Hotchkiss, *A Codification of the Statute Law of Georgia* (Savannah: John M. Cooper, 1845), 839. For the impact of David Walker's *Appeal* on the South and in Georgia, see Peter P. Hinks, *To Awaken My Afflicted Brethren: David Walker and the Problem of Antebellum Slave Resistance* (University Park: Pennsylvania State University Press, 1997); Elizabeth Cary Howard, "The Georgia Reaction to David Walker's *Appeal*" (M.A. thesis, University of Georgia, Athens, 1967); and Glenn M. McNair, "The Elijah Burritt Affair: David Walker's *Appeal* and Partisan Journalism in Antebellum Milledgeville," *Georgia Historical Quarterly* 83, no. 3 (Fall 1999): 448-78.

12. Candler, *Colonial Records,* vol. 19, pt. 1, pp. 244-45.

13. For discussion of masters' relationship with the law, see Kenneth M. Stampp, *The Peculiar Institution: Slavery in the Antebellum South* (New York: Vintage Books, 1956), 228-29; Ulrich Bonnell Phillips, *American Negro Slavery: A Survey of the Supply, Employment and Control of Negro Labor as Determined by the Plantation Regime,* 2d ed. (Baton Rouge: Louisiana State University Press, 1966), 501; Eugene D. Genovese, *Roll, Jordan, Roll: The World the Slaves Made* (New York: Vintage Books, 1976), 40-41.

14. *Journal of the Senate of the State of Georgia* (Milledgeville, Ga.: S. and F. Grantland, Printers to the State, 1812), 126-27; Erwin C. Surrency, "The First American Criminal Code: The Georgia Code of 1816," *Georgia Historical Quarterly* 63, no. 4 (Winter 1979): 420-34; William B. McCash, *Thomas R. R. Cobb, 1823-1862: The Making of a Southern Nationalist* (Macon, Ga.: Mercer University Press, 1983), 58.

15. Oliver H. Prince, *A Digest of the Laws of the State of Georgia* (Athens, Ga.: Oliver H. Prince, 1837), 804-5; Thomas R. R. Cobb, *A Digest of the Statute Laws of the State of Georgia* (Athens, Ga.: Christy, Kelsea and Burke, 1851), 789, 792; R. H. Clark, Thomas R. R. Cobb, and D. Irwin, *The Code of the State of Georgia* (Atlanta: John H. Seals, 1861), 918.

16. John D. Cushing, comp., *The First Laws of the State of Georgia* (Wilmington, Del.: Michael Glazier, 1981), 1:530. For a discussion of antebellum slave prices in Georgia, see Amy P. Burgess, "Slave Prices 1830 to 1860" (M.A. thesis, Emory

University, Atlanta, 1933). For Towns's address to the Georgia general assembly, see *Journal of the House of Representatives of the State of Georgia . . . 1849 and 1850* (n.p., n.d.), 33–34.

17. Stampp, *The Peculiar Institution,* 206; Phillips, *American Negro Slavery,* 493. For the relevant laws of the other slave states see, John D. Aiken, *A Digest of the Laws of the State of Alabama,* 2d ed. (Tuscaloosa: D. Woodruff, 1836); John D. Ormond, Arthur P. Bagley, and George Goldthwaite, *The Code of Alabama* (Montgomery: Britain and DeWolf, State Printer, 1852); E. H. English, *A Digest of the Statutes of Arkansas* (Little Rock: Reardon and Garritt, 1848); Josiah A. Gould, *A Digest of the Statutes of Arkansas* (Little Rock: Johnson and Yerkes, 1858); John D. Cushing, *The Earliest Printed Laws of Delaware, 1704–1741* (Wilmington, Del.: Michael Glazier, 1978); idem, *First Laws of the State of Delaware* (Wilmington, Del.: Michael Glazier, 1981); *Revised Statutes of the State of Delaware* (Dover, Del.: S. Kimmey, 1852); Leslie Thompson, *A Manual and Digest of the Statute Law of the State of Florida* (Boston: Little, Brown, 1847); William Littell and Jacob Swigert, *A Digest of the Statute Law of Kentucky* (Frankfort: Kendall and Russell, 1822); C. S. Morehead and Mason Brown, *A Digest of the Statute Laws of Kentucky* (Frankfort: A. G. Hodges, 1834); Richard H. Stanton, *The Revised Statutes of Kentucky* (Cincinnati: R. Clark, 1860); Henry Bullard and Thomas Curry, *A New Digest of the Statute Laws of Louisiana* (New Orleans: E. Johns, 1842); *Civil Code of the State of Louisiana* (New Orleans: Published by a Citizen of Louisiana, 1825); *The Laws of the Territory of Louisiana* (St. Louis, Mo.: Joseph Charles, 1808); Levi Pierce, Miles Taylor, and William W. King, *The Consolidation and Revision of the Statutes of the State, of a General Nature* (New Orleans: Bee Office, 1852); U. B. Phillips, *The Revised Statutes of Louisiana* (New Orleans: J. Claiborne, 1856); Wheelock H. Upton and Needler R. Jennings, *The Civil Code of the State of Louisiana, with Annotations* (New Orleans: E. Johns, 1838); John D. Cushing, *Laws of the Province of Maryland* (Wilmington, Del.: Michael Glazier, 1978); William Kilty, Thomas Harris, and John Watkins, *The Laws of Maryland, from the End of the Year 1799* (Annapolis: J. Green, 1819); Virgil Maxcy, *The Laws of Maryland* (Baltimore: Philip H. Nicklin, 1811); Otho Scott and Hiram McCullough, *The Maryland Code* (Baltimore: J. Murphey, 1860); T. J. Fox Alden and J. A. Hoesen, *A Digest of the Laws of Mississippi* (New York: Alexander H. Gould, 1839); A. Hutchinson, *Code of Mississippi, from 1798 to 1848* (Jackson: Price and Hall, 1848); *The Revised Code of the Laws of Mississippi* (Natchez: Francis Baker, 1824); *The Revised Code of the Statute Laws of the State of Mississippi* (Jackson: E. Barksdale, 1857); Charles Hardin, *The Revised Statutes of the State of Missouri* (Columbia: James Lusk, 1856); William C. Jones, *The Revised Statutes of the State of Missouri* (St. Louis: J. W. Dougherty, 1845); John D. Cushing, *The Earliest*

Printed Laws of North Carolina, 1669–1751 (Wilmington, Del.: Michael Glazier, 1977); John A. Haygood, *A Manual of the Laws of North Carolina* (Raleigh: J. Gales and W. Boylan, 1808); Bartholomew F. Moore and Asa Biggs, *Revised Code of North Carolina* (Boston: Little, Brown, 1855); *Revised Code of North Carolina* (Raleigh: n.p., 1854); *Revised Statutes of the State of North Carolina* (Raleigh: Turner and Hughes, 1837); Thomas Cooper and David J. McCord, *Statutes at Large of South Carolina* (Columbia: A. S. Johnston, 1826–41); James L. Petigru, *Portion of the Code of Statute Law of South Carolina* (Charleston: Evans and Cogswell, 1860–62); John Haygood and Robert L. Cobbs, *The Statute Laws of the State of Tennessee* (Knoxville: F. S. Heiskell, 1831); Return J. Meigs and William F. Cooper, *The Code of Tennessee* (Nashville: E. G. Eastman, 1858); Edward Scott, *Laws of the State of Tennessee* (Knoxville: Heiskell and Brown, 1821); Oliver C. Hartley, *A Digest of the Laws of Texas* (Philadelphia: Thomas, Cowperthwait, 1850); Williamson S. Oldham and George W. White, *A Digest of the General Statute Laws of the State of Texas* (Austin: J. Marshall, 1859); *The Code of Virginia* (Richmond: W. F. Ritchie, 1949); William Waller Hening, *The Statutes at Large: Being a Collection of All the Laws of Virginia, from the First Session of the Legislature in the Year 1619* (Richmond: W. Gray Printers, 1819–23); *The Revised Code of the Laws of Virginia* (Richmond: Thomas Ritchie, 1819); *The Statutes at Large of Virginia from 1712 to 1806* (Richmond: Samuel Shepard, 1835).

18. For discussion of the complementary nature of plantation law and state law, see Joseph P. Reidy, *From Slavery to Agrarian Capitalism in the Cotton Plantation South: Central Georgia, 1800–1880* (Chapel Hill: University of North Carolina Press, 1992), 46; and James M. Denham, *"A Rogue's Paradise": Crime and Punishment in Antebellum Florida, 1821–1861* (Tuscaloosa: University of Alabama Press, 1997), 130. I discuss the status of crime victims in chapters 3 and 6.

19. George P. Rawick, ed., *The American Slave: A Composite Autobiography* (Westport, Conn: Greenwood Publishing, 1972), vol. 12, pt. 1, 14–15.

20. Candler, *Colonial Records,* vol. 18, pp. 225–33. For women on slave patrols, see Sally E. Hadden, *Slave Patrols: Law and Violence in Virginia and the Carolinas* (Cambridge, Mass.: Harvard University Press, 2001), 2. Hadden's work is the most thorough study of slave patrols to date.

21. Prince, *Digest of the Laws* (1822), 443.

22. Ibid.

23. Ibid., 441–44; Cobb, *Digest of the Statute Laws,* 1017.

24. For discussion of slave patrols outside Georgia, see Genovese, *Roll, Jordan, Roll,* 618; and Stampp, *The Peculiar Institution,* 214.

25. For a discussion of the inefficiency of slave patrols in Georgia and other slave states, see Stampp, *The Peculiar Institution,* 214; and Ralph Betts Flanders,

Plantation Slavery in Georgia (Chapel Hill: University of North Carolina Press, 1933), 277.

26. Julia Floyd Smith, *Slavery and Rice Culture in Low Country Georgia, 1750–1860* (Knoxville: University of Tennessee Press, 1985), 185; Flanders, *Plantation Slavery* (1933), 278. The quotation of the Georgia planter is from Pugh Plantation Diary, 24 February 1861, Alexander F. Pugh and Family Papers, State Department of Archives and History, Louisiana State University, Baton Rouge, quoted in Genovese, *Roll, Jordan, Roll*, 618. See also Denham, *"A Rogue's Paradise,"* 126. For an excellent discussion of interracial criminal activity in coastal Georgia, see Timothy James Lockley, *Lines in the Sand: Race and Class in Lowcountry Georgia, 1750–1860* (Athens: University of Georgia Press, 2001).

27. John Hope Franklin and Loren Schweninger, *Runaway Slaves: Rebels on the Plantation* (New York: Oxford University Press, 1999), 155; Jonathan M. Bryant, *How Curious a Land: Conflict and Change in Greene County, Georgia, 1850–1885* (Chapel Hill: University of North Carolina Press, 1996), 29.

28. Stampp, *The Peculiar Institution*, 215; Rawick, *American Slave*, vol. 12, pt. 1, pp. 257–58; vol. 13, pt. 3, pp. 147, 158, 167–68.

29. Franklin and Schweninger, *Runaway Slaves*, 156–57.

30. For quotes from ex-slaves, see Rawick, *American Slave*, supp. ser. 1, vol. 4, pt. 2, p. 466; supp. ser. 1, vol. 13, pt. 3, p. 182; William K. Scarborough, *The Overseer: Plantation Management in the Old South* (Baton Rouge: Louisiana State University Press, 1966), 91; and Franklin and Schweninger, *Runaway Slaves*, 156–57, 160–61.

31. *Moran v. Davis*, 18 GA (1855), 722.

32. Ibid., 722–24.

33. Rawick, *American Slave*, vol. 12, pt. 1, p. 86; vol. 12, pt. 2, p. 75; supp. ser. 1, vol. 3, pt. 1, p. 96; supp. ser. 1, vol. 4, pt. 2, pp. 345, 576; Hadden, *Slave Patrols*, 207–20.

34. Rawick, *American Slave*, vol. 13, pt. 3, pp. 79–80; supp. ser. 1, vol. 3, pt. 1, p. 5; Genovese, *Roll, Jordan, Roll*, 618–19.

35. The fictional conversation with Nat Turner is in William Styron, *The Confessions of Nat Turner* (New York: Random House, 1967), 21–22, quoted in Genovese, *Roll, Jordan, Roll*, 28–29. See also *Cleland v. Waters*, 19 GA 41 (1855).

36. *Black's Law Dictionary*, 5th ed., s.v. "Common Law."

37. Philip J. Schwarz, *Twice Condemned: Slaves and the Criminal Laws of Virginia, 1705–1865* (Baton Rouge: Louisiana State University Press, 1988), 13; Thomas R. R. Cobb, *An Inquiry into the Law of Negro Slavery in the United States of America to Which Is Prefixed an Historical Sketch of Slavery* (1858; repr., Athens: University of Georgia Press, 1999), 263. Cobb was a staunch defender of slavery and one of Georgia's foremost legal authorities. He served as reporter of the Georgia supreme

court from 1849 to 1857 and was responsible for the compilation of fifteen volumes of supreme court decisions, as well as two codifications of the state's statute law. His *An Inquiry into the Law of Negro Slavery* was perhaps the most influential treatise on slave law written by a Southerner. Cobb was also the son-in-law of supreme court chief justice Joseph Henry Lumpkin.

38. *State v. Boon,* 1 NC 103 (1801).

39. A. E. Keir Nash, "Fairness and Formalism in the Trials of Blacks in the State Supreme Courts of the Old South," *Virginia Law Review* 56 (1970): 66-76; *State v. Boon,* 1 NC 103 (1801).

40. *Neal v. Farmer,* 9 GA 562 (1851).

41. Ibid., 579.

42. Ibid., 579-80.

43. Smith, *Slavery and Rice Culture,* 194.

44. Ralph Betts Flanders, *Plantation Slavery in Georgia* (Cos Cob, Conn.: John E. Edwards, 1967), 239. Flanders incorrectly stated that the law did not permit slaves to possess firearms.

45. Smith, *Slavery and Rice Culture,* 194; *Cooper and Worsham v. The Mayor and Aldermen of Savannah,* 4 GA 68 (1848). For a discussion of the repression of free blacks, see Ira Berlin, *Slaves without Masters: The Free Negro in the Antebellum South* (New York: New Press, 1974), 182-217.

46. Harold E. Davis, *The Fledgling Province: Social and Cultural Life in Colonial Georgia, 1733-1776* (Chapel Hill: University of North Carolina Press, 1976), 145. Critical race theorists argue that this racist, elitist use of the law continues to the present. The seminal essays in the critical race theory movement may be found in Kimberlé Williams Crenshaw, Neil Gotanda, Gary Peller, and Kendall Thomas, eds., *Critical Race Theory: The Key Writings That Formed the Movement* (New York: New Press, 1995).

3. "NEGROES MIGHT CUT THE THROATS OF OUR PEOPLE"

1. Thomas Jefferson, *Notes on the State of Virginia,* ed. William Peden (Chapel Hill: University of North Carolina Press, 1955), 142. For a discussion of the proper relationship between subjects and law, see Austin T. Turk, *Political Criminality: The Defiance and Defense of Authority* (Beverly Hills, Calif.: Sage Publications, 1982), 30-34.

2. Jefferson, *Notes,* 142; Frederick Douglass, *My Bondage and My Freedom,* ed. William L. Andrews (Urbana: University of Illinois Press, 1987), 118-19.

3. While some slaves were comforted by the "taking-stealing" distinction, others were not, especially those who had adopted Christian notions of morality. For a discussion of diverse slave views on theft, see Eugene D. Genovese, *Roll, Jordan, Roll:*

The World the Slaves Made (New York: Vintage Books, 1976), 607–9; and Edward L. Ayers, *Vengeance and Justice: Crime and Punishment in the 19th-Century American South* (New York: Oxford University Press, 1984), 127–30.

4. Overall distribution of criminal prosecutions from 1755 to 1865: crimes against persons, 289 cases (69.3 percent); crimes against property, 102 cases (24.5 percent); crimes against public order (5.5 percent); unknown type, 3 cases (0.7 percent); total cases, 417. Capital trial records offer a view into the nature and extent of black-on-white felony crimes and the seriousness with which these offenses were taken by the legal system. However, these records must be analyzed with care since they are incomplete, and it is therefore impossible to use them to determine the rates of specific crimes. This evidentiary shortcoming is exacerbated by the fact that numerous crimes went unreported for a host of reasons. This "dark figure" is lower in cases of serious crimes against persons because these offenses were the most detrimental to society; there were usually victims/witnesses; and, in the case of murder, bodies were rarely concealed, so such cases usually came to the attention of authorities. Capital trial records are also skewed toward crimes against persons, especially from the colonial period through the antebellum period, because more crimes against persons were capital crimes than were crimes against property.

5. Jefferson, *Notes,* 162.

6. Thomas D. Morris, *Southern Slavery and the Law, 1619–1865* (Chapel Hill: University of North Carolina Press, 1996), 293–95.

7. Assault with intent to kill accounted for 79 (18.9 percent) of the total 417 cases. (For the sake of clarity and simplicity, assault with intent to kill is described in the tables as attempted murder.) Poisoning accounted for 7 (1.7 percent) of the total number of cases.

8. Seventy-nine defendants were charged with assault with intent to kill. Seventy-three (92.4 percent) were slave men, two (2.5 percent) were slave women, three (3.8 percent) were free men, and one was a free woman (1.3 percent). Slave men accused of assault with intent to kill accounted for 20.7 percent of 194 total defendants.

9. Seven (12.1 percent) of 58 victims were masters, mistresses, or overseers. The relationship between the victim and perpetrator in the remaining 51 cases could not be established.

10. *State v. Elias,* Records of the Superior Court of Macon County, September 14, 1864, drawer 164, box 19, Georgia Department of Archives and History, Atlanta (hereafter, GDAH).

11. *State v. Wade,* Records of the Superior Court of Thomas County, May 25, 1852, drawer 4, box 45, GDAH.

12. Seven of 417 cases between 1755 and 1865 (1.7 percent) were poisoning cases.

Three cases (0.7 percent) were for attempted poisoning. Four of the seven defendants (57.1 percent) charged with poisoning were slave women. Four of six (66.7 percent) poisoning victims were masters, mistresses, or overseers. For the discussion of poisoning in Virginia, see Philip J. Schwarz, *Twice Condemned: Slaves and the Criminal Laws of Virginia, 1705–1865* (Baton Rouge: Louisiana State University Press, 1988), 95.

13. *State v. Sam,* Records of the Superior Court of Cherokee County, March 8, 1864, drawer 12, box 68, GDAH.

14. *State v. Sarah,* Records of the Superior Court of Harris County, October 14, 1858, drawer 165, box 16, GDAH.

15. Manslaughter is defined in Thomas R. R. Cobb, *A Digest of the Statute Laws of the State of Georgia* (Athens, Ga.: Christy, Kelsea and Burke, 1851), 783–84.

16. *Jordan v. State,* 22 GA 548–59 (1857).

17. *Jim v. State,* 15 GA 541–45 (1854).

18. Morris, *Southern Slavery,* 279–84. Here Thomas Morris argues that North Carolina accepted slave provocation because the state lacked protective legislation.

19. *John v. State,* 16 GA 203 (1854).

20. Morris, *Southern Slavery,* 290–92.

21. *State v. Michael Davis,* Records of the Superior Court of Newton County, March 1859, drawer 11, box 3, GDAH.

22. One hundred forty-seven (35.3 percent) of 417 cases between 1755 and 1865 were murder cases. Of the 147 victims in murder cases, 35 (23.8 percent) were slave men, 3 (2 percent) were slave women, 38 (25.9 percent) were white men, 8 (5.4 percent) were white women, 2 (1.4 percent) were free black men, 11 (7.5 percent) were blacks whose sex and status could not be determined, and the identities of 50 (34 percent) are unknown. There were seventy-eight known attempted murder victims, all white; there were ten known poisoning and attempted poisoning victims, all white. All of the known rape and attempted rape victims were white women. All known manslaughter victims were black.

23. Some identifying information is available for victims in eighty-four cases. Thirty-five victims (41.7 percent) were slave acquaintances or kin; two (2.4 percent) were free black acquaintances or kin; twenty-three (27.4 percent) were masters, mistresses, or overseers; and twenty-four (28.6 percent) were whites whose relationship to the defendants could not be determined.

24. Of 147 defendants charged with murder, 125 (85 percent) were slave men; 19 (12.9 percent) were slave women; and 3 (2 percent) were free black men.

25. The weapons used in homicidal assaults could be determined in 118 cases. Hands and/or feet were used in 23 (19.5 percent) cases; knives or axes in 28 cases (23.7 percent); firearms in 20 cases (16.9 percent); clubs in 30 cases

(25.4 percent); poison in 11 cases (9.3 percent); and other means in 6 cases (5.1 percent).

26. For a discussion of black crime in the antebellum North, see Roger Lane, *Murder in America: A History* (Columbus: Ohio State University Press, 1997), 117. For a discussion of similar issues in South Carolina, see Jack Kenny Williams, *Vogues in Villainy: Crime and Retribution in Antebellum South Carolina* (Columbia: University of South Carolina Press, 1959), 35–36.

27. The quoted material from ex-slaves can be found in Norman R. Yetman, *Life under the Peculiar Institution: Selections from the Slave Narrative Collection* (New York: Holt, Rinehart and Winston, 1970), 116–17, 327, quoted in Genovese, *Roll, Jordan, Roll,* 625–27; quoted material regarding the Georgia planter can be found in the Manigault Plantation Records, entry for March 22, 1867, Southern Historical Collection, University of North Carolina, Chapel Hill, quoted in Kenneth M. Stampp, *The Peculiar Institution: Slavery in the Antebellum South* (New York: Vintage Books, 1956), 130. For discussions of "good" and "bad niggers," see Genovese and Stampp on the cited pages, and Lawrence W. Levine, *Black Culture and Black Consciousness: Afro-American Folk Thought from Slavery to Freedom* (New York: Oxford University Press, 1977), 407–20.

28. Genovese, *Roll, Jordan, Roll,* 627.

29. Stampp, *Peculiar Institution,* 131.

30. *State v. Monroe,* Records of the Superior Court of Meriwether County, August 1850, drawer 12, box 59, GDAH. For remaining overseer murders, see Ralph Betts Flanders, *Plantation Slavery in Georgia* (Cos Cob, Conn.: John E. Edwards, 1967), 265. One of the most intriguing overseer murder cases in the history of the Old South, one that presents all of the elements related to violence between slaves and whites in authority, is recounted in Michael Wayne, *Death of an Overseer: Reopening a Murder Investigation from the Plantation South* (New York: Oxford University Press, 2001).

31. *State v. Sarah,* Records of the Superior Court of Meriwether County, February 1858, drawer 12, box 60, GDAH.

32. *State v. Dick, Nelly et al.,* Records of the Superior Court of Laurens County, October 1861, drawer 123, box 60, GDAH.

33. *State v. Aaron,* Records of the Superior Court of Troup County, May 1857, drawer 155, box 20, GDAH.

34. *State v. Burrell,* Records of the Superior Court of Thomas County, May 1852, drawer 4, box 45, GDAH.

35. *State v. Joe,* Records of the Superior Court of Screven County, October 13, 1860, drawer 112, box 4, GDAH. For a discussion of masters and mistresses and

their attitudes toward slave violence and their personal safety, see Genovese, *Roll, Jordan, Roll,* 615–17.

36. *State v. Robin,* Records of the Superior Court of Chatham County, September 1822, drawer 90, box 33, GDAH; *State v. Shadrach,* Records of the Superior Court of Chatham County, September 1822, drawer 90, box 33, GDAH; *State v. John,* Executive Minutes, November 2, 1829–November 4, 1834, drawer 50, box 50, GDAH. The fourth case was *State v. Willis,* Records of the Superior Court of Wilkes County, March 26, 1861, drawer 42, box 72, GDAH. For a discussion of the St. Andrew's Parish Revolt, see Betty Wood, *Slavery in Colonial Georgia, 1730–1775* (Athens: University of Georgia Press, 1984), 191–92.

37. Ulrich Bonnell Phillips, *American Negro Slavery: A Survey of the Supply, Employment and Control of Negro Labor as Determined by the Plantation Regime,* 2d ed. (Baton Rouge: Louisiana State University Press, 1966), 482; Flanders, *Plantation Slavery* (1967), 274–76; Joseph P. Reidy, *From Slavery to Agrarian Capitalism in the Cotton Plantation South: Central Georgia, 1800–1880* (Chapel Hill: University of North Carolina Press, 1992), 28–29.

38. James C. Scott, *Domination and the Arts of Resistance: Hidden Transcripts* (New Haven, Conn.: Yale University Press, 1990), 102. Scott argues that even though few direct confrontations between authorities and subordinates occurred, subalterns resisted their oppression through cultural forms and behaviors—a "hidden transcript" that those in power could not fully comprehend. For a discussion of Cesare Lombroso, see Stephen Shafer, *The Political Criminal: The Problem of Morality and Crime* (New York: Free Press, 1974), 2, 19. For a discussion of the political effects of black criminality, see Schwarz, *Twice Condemned,* 34.

39. Schwarz, *Twice Condemned,* 140–43. It is often a difficult to determine premeditation from the extant evidence. When slaves used farm implements to kill, the act could have been spontaneous or premeditated; when they used knives, guns, or poison to kill, premeditation is more easily inferred because, in many instances, those weapons had to be surreptitiously obtained and concealed.

40. Ibid., 3.

41. Allen D. Candler, ed., *Colonial Records of the State of Georgia* (Atlanta: Franklin Printing and Publishing, 1904), vol. 5, p. 475.

4. "SOME CONVENIENT METHOD AND FORM OF TRYAL"

1. For quotes from ex-slaves, see George P. Rawick, ed., *The American Slave: A Composite Autobiography* (Westport, Conn: Greenwood Publishing, 1972), vol. 12, pp. 1, 3, 5; vol. 12, pt. 1, p. 310; vol. 13, pt. 4, p. 129; supp. ser. 1, vol. 3, pt. 1, p. 64.

2. For the Hammond quote, see William Harper, James Henry Hammond, Wil-

liam Gilmore Simms, and Thomas Roderick Dew, *The Pro-Slavery Argument as Maintained by the Most Distinguished Writers of the Southern States* (Philadelphia: Lippincott, Grambo, 1853), 130–31.

3. Philip J. Schwarz, *Twice Condemned: Slaves and the Criminal Laws of Virginia, 1705–1865* (Baton Rouge: Louisiana State University Press, 1988), 8.

4. "Tattler," an unidentified writer to the *Southern Cultivator*, provided the view of the master as "lawgiver and judge, protector and friend" (see Tattler, "Management of Negroes," *Southern Cultivator*, vol. 8, *November 1850*, 162–64, quoted in James O. Breeden, ed., *Advice among Masters: The Ideal in Slave Management in the Old South* [Westport, Conn.: Greenwood Press, 1980], 41).

5. Christopher Waldrep, *Roots of Disorder: Race and Criminal Justice in the American South, 1817–80* (Urbana: University of Illinois Press, 1998), 10.

6. Georgia Slave Trials, Telamon Cuyler Collection, MS 1170, box 71, folder 12, Hargrett Library, University of Georgia, Athens (hereafter, Georgia Slave Trials). This account of the trial and all direct quotations are from *State v. Will*, found in this source.

7. For the quote of the antebellum jurist, see Warren Grice, *Georgia Bench and Bar: The Development of Georgia's Legal System* (Macon, Ga.: J. W. Burke, 1931), 87, 90. Grice does not identify this source in the text or notes. For conditions of appointment and tenure of justices of the peace, see Constitution of Georgia (1798), art. III, sec. 6.

8. For a discussion of justices of the peace in Baldwin County, see Glenn M. McNair, "The Trials of Slaves in Baldwin County, Georgia, 1812–1838" (M.A. thesis, Georgia College and State University, Millidgeville, 1996), 59–60. Milledgeville, the largest town in Baldwin County, was the state capital. As the seat of state government and home to the largest number of lawyers, Baldwin County might be considered a model of Georgia criminal justice, with less-developed communities lacking a similar level of judicial sophistication. For Justice Blandford's quote on justices of the peace, see *Bendheim v. Baldwin*, 73 GA 594.

9. Grice, *Georgia Bench and Bar*, 87, 238.

10. Ibid., 87; Ulrich Bonnell Phillips, *American Negro Slavery: A Survey of the Supply, Employment and Control of Negro Labor as Determined by the Plantation Regime*, 2d ed. (Baton Rouge: Louisiana State University Press, 1966), 504.

11. For states' lack of confidence in justices of the peace, see Daniel J. Flanigan, *The Criminal Law of Slavery and Freedom* (New York: Garland Publishing, 1987), 89, 110. For the O'Neall quote, see John Belton O'Neall, *The Negro Law of South Carolina* (Columbia: John G. Bowman, 1848), 35.

12. Constitution of Georgia (1798), Art. III, sec. 1.

13. McNair, "Trials of Slaves," 54–55.

14. *Journal of the House of Representatives of the State of Georgia . . . 1849 and 1850* (n.p., n.d.), 33.

15. Oliver Prince, *Digest of the Laws of the State of Georgia* (Milledgeville, Ga.: Grantland and Orme, 1822), 459–60.

16. *Lingo v. Miller,* 23 GA 187 (1857).

17. Thomas R. R. Cobb, *An Inquiry into the Law of Negro Slavery in the United States of America to Which Is Prefixed an Historical Sketch of Slavery* (1858; repr., Athens: University of Georgia Press, 1999), 268. For a discussion of defense counsel for slaves and indigent whites, see Flanigan, *Criminal Law of Slavery,* 118; R. H. Clark, Thomas R. R. Cobb, and D. Irwin, *The Code of the State of Georgia* (Atlanta: John H. Seals, 1861), 917; and Arthur F. Howington, *What Sayeth the Law: The Treatment of Slaves and Free Blacks in the State and Local Courts of Tennessee* (New York: Garland Publishing, 1986), 193–94.

18. Grice, *Georgia Bench and Bar,* 244.

19. Augustin Smith Clayton, *A Compilation of the Laws of the State of Georgia, Passed by the Legislature since the Political Year 1800, to the Year 1810, Inclusive* (Augusta, Ga.: Adams and Duyckinck, 1812), 133; Prince, *Digest of the Laws* (1822), 459–60.

20. *Flint River Steamboat Company v. Foster,* 5 GA 194 (1848).

21. William Blackstone, *Commentaries on the Laws of England* (1769; repr., Buffalo, N.Y.: William S. Hein, 1992), 1:343–44.

22. Massachusetts Constitution (1780), pt. 1, art. 13. For quotes from James Wilson and Patrick Henry, see Jonathan Elliot, ed., *The Debates in the Several State Conventions on the Adoption of the Federal Constitution* (Washington, D.C.: U.S. Congress, 1836), 2:516, 3:578–79.

23. For jury selection procedures, see Prince, *Digest of the Laws* (1822), 460; Thomas R. R. Cobb, *A Digest of the Statute Laws of the State of Georgia* (Athens, Ga.: Christy, Kelsea and Burke, 1851), 546. I believe guardians acted for free blacks during criminal trials not only because they were responsible for filing appeals and pardons, but also because the law required them to aid free blacks in civil law suits. While the law did not address the issue of trial agency for free blacks with the same degree of specificity as it did for slaves, I believe the general principle was for no black to appear in court without some sort of white assistance, supervision, or control (see Cobb, *Digest of the Statute Laws,* 987–88, 998).

24. For a discussion of the slave-ownership requirement for jurors, see Thomas D. Morris, *Southern Slavery and the Law, 1619–1865* (Chapel Hill: University of North Carolina Press, 1996), 218; and Flanigan, *Criminal Law of Slavery,* 111. For the quote from Justice John Taylor, see *State v. Jim,* 12 NC 142 (1826).

25. Morris, *Southern Slavery,* 219.

26. Blackstone, *Commentaries,* 4:344–47.

27. For challenges in Georgia, see Cobb, *Digest of the Statute Laws,* 835; for challenges in other Southern states, see Morris, *Southern Slavery,* 221–23.

28. For discussion of effects of challenges, see Morris, *Southern Slavery,* 222–23; and Flanigan, *Criminal Law of Slavery,* 111–13. See also *State v. Bob,* Records of the Superior Court of Chatham County, June 19, 1856, drawer 68, box 42, GDAH.

29. For discussion of the composition of Baldwin County juries, see McNair, "Trials of Slaves," 65–85. The records of the Baldwin County Inferior Court are housed at the GDAH, drawer 199, box 25. I drew my sample of other juries from the following cases: *State v. Mason,* Records of the Superior Court of Campbell County, August 12, 1861, drawer 107, box 73, GDAH; *State v. Simon,* Records of the Superior Court of Greene County, March term 1853, drawer 33, box 67, GDAH; *State v. Israel,* Records of the Inferior Court of Hancock County, April 18, 1849, drawer 121, box 46, GDAH; *State v. Elias,* Records of the Superior Court of Columbia County, September 8, 1858, drawer 192, box 26, GDAH; and *State v. Adam,* Records of the Inferior Court of Jones County, September 3, 1835, drawer 76, box 72, GDAH.

30. Michael S. Hindus, *Prison and Plantation: Crime, Justice and Authority in Massachusetts and South Carolina, 1767–1878* (Chapel Hill: University of North Carolina Press, 1980), 154–55; Howington, *What Sayeth the Law,* 120–21.

31. Georgia Slave Trials. This account of the trial and all direct quotations are from *State v. Charles,* found in this source.

32. Cobb, *Digest of the Statute Laws,* 1018–19.

33. Grice, *Georgia Bench and Bar,* 294.

34. Blackstone, *Commentaries,* 4:343.

35. Richard D. Younger, *The People's Panel: The Grand Jury in the United States, 1634–1941* (Providence, R.I.: Brown University Press, 1963), 166–78.

36. Walter G. Charleton, "A Judge and a Grand Jury: Report of the Thirty First Annual Session of the Georgia Bar Association, 1914," 1914, Macon, Ga., quoted in Ruth Scarborough, *The Opposition to Slavery in Georgia prior to 1860* (1933; repr., New York: Negro Universities Press, 1968), 243–44.

37. Grice, *Georgia Bench and Bar,* 82–83; *Biographical Cyclopedia of Representative Men of Rhode Island* (Providence, R.I.: National Biographical Publishing, 1881), 1:120–21.

38. *State v. Ailey,* Records of the Superior Court of Jasper County, April 28, 1854, drawer 35, box 61, GDAH. This account of the trial and all direct quotations are from this source.

39. For a discussion of the impact of court-ordered sales on slave families, see

Thomas D. Russell, "Articles Sell Best Singly: The Disruption of Slave Families at Court Sales," *Utah Law Review* 4 (1996): 1161–1209. For a discussion of Baldwin County justices and slave sales, see McNair, "Trials of Slaves," 60–61.

40. Ibid., 55–57.

41. The Superior Court judges I selected for this sample were Henry M. Jackson (Chatham County), John W. H. Underwood (Floyd County), Joel Branham (Putnam County), Augustus R. Wright (Cass County), Francis N. Cone (Greene County), John J. Floyd (Newton County), John McPherson Berrien (Cass County), William Law (Chatham County), Angus M. D. King (Monroe County), Herschel V. Johnson (Baldwin County), Edward Y. Hill (Troup County), Christopher B. Strong (Houston County), Thomas W. Harris (Houston County), Carlton B. Cole (Bibb County), Osborne Lochrane (Bibb County), and Washington Poe (Twiggs County). I determined their status as slaveowners through examination of *Population Schedules of the Seventh Census of the United States, Slave Schedules* (Washington, D.C.: U.S. Census Office, 1850); and *Population Schedules of the Eighth Census of the United States, Slave Schedules* (Washington, D.C.: U.S. Census Office, 1860).

42. I used the following cases in the random sample: *State v. Mason,* Records of the Superior Court of Campbell County, August 12, 1861, drawer 107, box 73, GDAH; *State v. John,* Records of the Superior Court of Fayette County, April 17, 1865, drawer 94, box 11, GDAH; *State v. Simon,* Records of the Superior Court of Greene County, March term 1853, drawer 33, box 67, GDAH; *State v. Becky,* Records of the Superior Court of Greene County, September term 1860, drawer 33, box 70, GDAH; *State v. Frank,* Records of the Inferior Court of Hancock County, October 14, 1843, drawer 121, box 46, GDAH; *State v. Israel,* Records of the Inferior Court of Hancock County, April 18, 1849, drawer 121, box 46, GDAH; *State v. Elias,* Records of the Superior Court of Columbia County, September 8, 1858, drawer 192, box 26, GDAH; *State v. George and John,* Records of the Superior Court of Columbia County, March 7, 1860, drawer 192, box 26, GDAH; *State v. Hardtimes,* Records of the Inferior Court of Chatham County, March 1821, drawer 90, box 33, GDAH; *State v. Thomas,* Records of the Inferior Court of Chatham County, March, 1821, drawer 90, box 33, GDAH; *State v. Harry,* Records of the Inferior Court of Jones County, December 19, 1833, drawer 76, box 72, GDAH; *State v. Adam,* Records of the Inferior Court of Jones County, September 3, 1835, drawer 76, box 72, GDAH; *State v. Jesse,* Records of the Superior Court of Decatur County, April 29, 1856, drawer 130, box 1, GDAH; *State v. John Boon,* Records of the Inferior Court of Putnam County, September 28, 1822, drawer 1, box 17, GDAH; *State v. Jerry,* Records of the Superior Court of Houston County, October 28, 1853, drawer 158, box 38, GDAH; *State v. Edmund,* Records of the Superior Court of Taylor County, April 9, 1856, drawer 164, box 43, GDAH; *State v. Rose,* Records

of the Superior Court of Taliaferro County, February 26, 1861, drawer 109, box 37, GDAH; *State v. George Moss,* Records of the Superior Court of Taliaferro County, November 20, 1861, drawer 109, box 37, GDAH; *State v. Johan,* Records of the Superior Court of Monroe County, September 10, 1857, drawer 2, box 33, GDAH; *State v. Tucker,* Records of the Superior Court of Richmond County, April 14, 1864, drawer 145, box 15, GDAH; *State v. Pressley,* Records of the Superior Court of Oglethorpe County, October term 1855, drawer 46, box 26, GDAH; and *State v. Amos,* Records of the Superior Court of Lincoln County, October 26, 1864, drawer 88, box 55, GDAH. The slaveholding status of each juror may be found in the tax digests of each county for the year in which the trial occurred; these records are housed at the GDAH. The slaveholding status of Baldwin County jurors is discussed in McNair, "Trials of Slaves," 65–85.

43. Georgia Constitution (1798), Art. IV, sec. 1; Cobb, *Digest of the Statue Laws,* 546–47.

44. These figures are found in *Agriculture of the United States in 1860 compiled from the Original Returns of the Eighth Census* (Washington, D.C.: U.S. Government Printing Office, 1864), 226–27, 247.

45. Significant works on class relationships among Southern whites are Eugene D. Genovese, *Roll, Jordan, Roll: The World the Slaves Made* (New York: Vintage Books, 1976); Lacy K. Ford, *The Origins of Southern Radicalism: The South Carolina Upcountry, 1800–1860* (New York: Oxford University Press, 1988); Steven Hahn, *The Roots of Southern Populism: Yeoman Farmers and the Transformation of the Georgia Upcountry, 1850–1890* (New York: Oxford University Press, 1983); Stephanie McCurry, *Masters of Small Worlds: Yeoman Households, Gender Relations, and the Political Culture of the Antebellum South Carolina Lowcountry* (New York: Oxford University Press, 1995); and Michael P. Johnson, *Toward a Patriarchal Republic: The Secession of Georgia* (Baton Rouge: Louisiana State University Press, 1977).

46. A number of recent works discuss the construction of whiteness and the psychological advantages of white supremacy, among them David R. Roediger, *The Wages of Whiteness: Race and the Making of the American Working Class* (New York: Verso, 1991); idem, *Towards the Abolition of Whiteness: Essays on Race, Politics and Working Class History* (London: Verso, 1994); Grace Elizabeth Hale, *Making Whiteness: The Culture of Segregation in the South, 1890–1940* (New York: Pantheon Books, 1998); Ruth Frankenberg, *White Women, Race Matters: The Social Construction of Whiteness* (Minneapolis: University of Minnesota Press, 1993); Matthew Frye Jacobson, *Whiteness of a Different Color: European Immigrants and the Alchemy of Race* (Cambridge, Mass.: Harvard University Press, 1998). For a discussion of honor, see Bertram Wyatt-Brown, *Southern*

Honor: Ethics and Behavior in the Old South (Oxford: Oxford University Press, 1982), 365.

47. Between 1755 and 1865, 298 cases went to trial. There were 224 guilty pleas or verdicts (75.2 percent); 72 not guilty verdicts (24.2 percent); and 2 mistrials (0.7 percent). Between 1755 and 1811, 33 cases went to trial. There were 31 guilty verdicts (93.9 percent) and 2 verdicts of not guilty (6.1 percent). Between 1812 and 1849, courts tried black defendants for the following crimes, with the following results: 22 were charged with murder, and juries convicted 19 (86.4 percent); 17 were charged with attempted murder, and 16 (94.1 percent) were convicted; 3 were tried for rape, and 3 (100 percent) were convicted; 5 were charged with attempted rape, and 4 (80 percent) were convicted; 5 were tried for arson, and 4 (80 percent) were convicted. Two hundred thirteen black defendants were tried for crimes against persons; 173 (81.2 percent) were convicted. Sixty-six defendants were put on trial for crimes against property; 41 (62.1 percent) were convicted. Fifteen defendants were put on trial for crimes against public order, with 7 (43.8 percent) convicted. Three trials for crimes of unknown type resulted in convictions.

48. Two hundred fifty-seven slave men were tried in Georgia's courts; 207 (80.5 percent) were convicted. Twenty-five slave women were put on trial; 11 (44 percent) were convicted.

49. One hundred nine murder cases made it to the trial stage; 89 resulted in guilty pleas or verdicts, a simple conviction rate of 81 percent. Twenty-three arson cases made it to the trial stage; 11 resulted in guilty pleas or verdicts, a simple conviction rate of 47.8 percent. Thirty-eight burglary cases made it to the trial stage; 28 resulted in guilty pleas or verdicts, a simple conviction rate of 73.6 percent. Six poisoning cases made it to the trial stage; 3 resulted in guilty pleas or verdicts, a simple conviction rate of 50 percent. The cases of twenty-five slave women reached the trial stage. The state charged ten of these women with murder, one with attempted murder, and the remaining fourteen with arson, poisoning, and burglary.

50. Fifteen free black men were tried in Georgia's criminal courts; six (40 percent) were convicted.

51. Fifteen black men were tried for crimes. Three were tried for murder, one for attempted murder, one for attempted rape, four for burglary, five for crimes against public order, and one for robbery. The state tried only one free black woman, and that was for a crime against public order.

52. Conviction rates for the period from 1755 to 1811 are discussed in note 47. From 1812 to 1849, there were 89 cases that resulted in 68 convictions, a simple conviction rate of 76.4 percent. Between 1850 and 1865, 176 cases reached the trial stage; 125 (71 percent) resulted in convictions.

53. Hindus, *Prison and Plantation,* 90–92.

54. Courts initiated 228 prosecutions in the period from 1850 to 1865. Forty-nine cases (17 percent) resulted in acquittals; 36 (12.5 percent) did not result in true bills; and nolle prosequis (the prosecutor decides not to pursue the case) were entered in 24 (8.3 percent) cases. There were 2 mistrials (0.7 percent), and the dispositions in 52 cases (18.1 percent) are unknown. One hundred twenty-five cases (43.4 percent) resulted in conviction; this is the effective conviction rate.

55. Hindus, *Prison and Plantation,* 144–45; Douglas J. Greenberg, *Crime and Law Enforcement in the Colony of New York, 1691–1776* (Ithaca, N.Y.: Cornell University Press, 1974), 72–74.

56. Howington, *What Sayeth the Law,* 210–13, 241.

57. David J. Bodenhamer, "The Efficiency of Criminal Justice in the Antebellum South," in *Crime and Justice in American History,* ed. Eric H. Monkkonen (Munich: K. G. Saur, 1992), vol. 11, pt. 1, pp. 5–9.

58. Ibid., vol. 11, pt. 1, pp. 11–12.

59. For a discussion of these realities, see John Hope Franklin and Loren Schweninger, *Runaway Slaves: Rebels on the Plantation* (New York: Oxford University Press, 1999).

5. "THE SLAVE SHOULD LOOK TO HIS MASTER AND THE COURTS TO AVENGE HIS WRONGS"

1. Thomas R. R. Cobb, *An Inquiry into the Law of Negro Slavery in the United States of America to Which Is Prefixed an Historical Sketch of Slavery* (1858; repr., Athens: University of Georgia Press, 1999), 94.

2. R. H. Clark, Thomas R. R. Cobb, and D. Irwin, *The Code of the State of Georgia* (Atlanta: John H. Seals, 1861), 917. This provision does not appear in the criminal code until 1861. Despite this late date, it appears to be a consolidation and codification of colonial and antebellum law and trial practice. There is no evidence in the historical record that slaves and free blacks made legal decisions in their cases.

3. Thomas D. Morris, *Southern Slavery and the Law, 1619–1865* (Chapel Hill: University of North Carolina Press, 1996), 226.

4. Allen D. Candler, ed., *Colonial Records of the State of Georgia* (Atlanta: Franklin Printing and Publishing, 1904), vol. 18, p. 657; vol. 19, pt. 1, p. 218.

5. Rhodom A. Greene and John W. Lumpkin, *The Georgia Justice* (Milledgeville, Ga.: P. L. and B. H. Robinson, 1835), 415; Oliver Prince, *A Digest of the Laws of the State of Georgia* (Milledgeville, Ga.: Grantland and Orme, 1822), 461.

6. Warren Grice, *Georgia Bench and Bar: The Development of Georgia's Legal System* (Macon, Ga.: J. W. Burke, 1931), 97–101, 263–64, 267–68; Mason W. Stephenson and D. Grier Stephenson Jr., "'To Protect and Defend': Joseph Henry Lumpkin and the Supreme Court of Georgia, and Slavery," *Emory Law Journal*

25 (1976): 580–81. Thomas D. Morris erroneously states that the legislature did not establish the Georgia Supreme Court until the 1850s (see Morris, *Southern Slavery*, 226).

7. Thomas R. R. Cobb, *A Digest of the Statute Laws of the State of Georgia* (Athens, Ga.: Christy, Kelsea and Burke, 1851), 447.

8. Grice, *Georgia Bench and Bar*, 267–68.

9. The quoted material is from the Georgia lawyer, governor, and statesman James Jackson and can be found in Grice, *Georgia Bench and Bar*, 268–69. Grice does not provide footnotes in his work, so it is impossible to determine the source or accuracy of the quote. See also Stephenson and Stephenson Jr., "To Protect and Defend," 579n1.

10. The ten justices of the supreme court who served from 1845 to 1865 were Joseph Henry Lumpkin, Eugenius Nisbet, Hiram Warner, Ebenezer Starnes, Iverson L. Harris, Henry L. Benning, Charles J. McDonald, Linton Stephens, Richard F. Lyon, and Charles J. Jenkins. I determined their status as slaveowners through examination of the *Seventh Census, Slave Schedules* and *Eighth Census, Slave Schedules.* Stephen's slave-owning status may be found in James D. Waddell, ed., *Biographical Sketch of Linton Stephens* (Atlanta: Dodson and Scott, 1877), 95. For a discussion of the role of slavery in creating differences between Northern and Southern judges, see Timothy S. Huebner, *The Southern Judicial Tradition: State Judges and Sectional Distinctiveness, 1790–1890* (Athens: University of Georgia Press, 1999), 2–3.

11. Huebner, *Southern Judicial Tradition*, 1, 8–9.

12. George P. Rawick, ed., *The American Slave: A Composite Autobiography* (Westport, Conn: Greenwood Publishing, 1972), vol. 13, pt. 1, 155. Statements of ex-slaves regarding kind treatment by masters and mistresses must always be considered with a degree of caution because Southern whites whom elderly former slaves did not wish to offend often conducted the interviews that produced them. Ex-slaves also thought white interviewers were government officials who might provide them with aid during the Great Depression. John Blassingame identified these problems in an influential article in 1975 (see John Blassingame, "Using the Testimony of Ex-Slaves: Approaches and Problems," *Journal of Southern History* 41 [November 1975]: 473–92). Blassingame used the Works Progress Adminstration slave narratives extensively in his classic work, *The Slave Community: Plantation Life in the Antebellum South* (New York: Oxford University Press, 1979).

13. Huebner, *Southern Judicial Tradition*, 72–75, 86–87.

14. Stephenson and Stephenson Jr. "To Protect and Defend," 583.

15. Grice, *Georgia Bench and Bar*, 274.

16. *Judge v. State*, 8 GA 173 (1850).

17. *Anthony v. State,* 9 GA 264 (1851).

18. William Blackstone, *Commentaries on the Laws of England* (1769; repr., Buffalo, N.Y.: William S. Hein, 1992), 4:301–2.

19. *State v. Stephen,* 11 GA 227–32, 239–40 (1852).

20. *John v. State,* 16 GA 200–03 (1854).

21. Daniel J. Flanigan, *The Criminal Law of Slavery and Freedom* (New York: Garland Publishing, 1987), 107–8.

22. *Anthony v. State,* 9 GA 274 (1851).

23. *Stephen v. State,* 11 GA 241 (1852).

24. *Alfred v. State,* 6 GA 484–86 (1849).

25. Blackstone, *Commentaries,* 4:34–38.

26. *Thornton v. State,* 25 GA 301–05 (1858).

27. *Hill v. State,* 28 GA 604–13 (1859).

28. *Simmons v. State,* 4 GA 465–74 (1848).

29. *Grady v. State,* 11 GA 254–56 (1852).

30. The culpability of masters for certain criminal acts committed by their slaves are discussed in Cobb, *Law of Negro Slavery,* 265; and idem, *Digest of the Statute Laws,* 780. The criminal liability of masters and husbands for acts of their servants and wives, respectively, is discussed in Blackstone, *Commentaries,* 4:28–29. See also *Pannell v. State,* 29 GA 681 (1860).

31. Simon Greenleaf, *A Treatise on the Law of Evidence,* 15th ed. (Little, Brown, 1892), 1:290–92.

32. For a discussion of common law requirements for admissible confessions, see ibid., 296. For confessions of slaves, see Cobb, *Law of Negro Slavery,* 271.

33. Morris, *Southern Slavery,* 239–40.

34. *Stephen v. State,* 11 GA 233–36 (1852).

35. *Jim v. State,* 15 GA 540–41 (1854). For a discussion of slave confessions made to masters, see Cobb, *Law of Negro Slavery,* 272.

36. *Wyatt (a slave) v. State,* 25 Ala. 9, 15 (1854); *Simon (a slave) v. State,* 5 Fla. 285 (1853); *Sam (a slave) v. State,* 33 Miss. 347 (1857), cited in Morris, *Southern Slavery,* 242–44.

37. *Sarah v. State,* 28 GA 576 (1859); *State v. Clarissa,* 11 AL 57 (1847). For another example of a Georgia slave being whipped to obtain a confession, see *Berry v. State,* 10 GA 511 (1851).

38. Stephenson and Stephenson Jr., "To Protect and Defend," 591–92. For a discussion of the dissipation of duress in confessions, see Greenleaf, *Law of Evidence,* 1:300.

39. *Alfred v. State,* 6 GA 484–85 (1849).

40. Clark et al., *Code of the State of Georgia,* 894–95.

41. *Rafe v. State,* 20 GA 60–68 (1856). The act of 1856 expanded and incorporated an act of 1843 that included the first two questions. The 1843 act was the basis for two 1854 appellate decisions against slave defendants who argued that prospective jurors were biased against them. The rationales for these decisions were the same as those articulated in *Rafe v. State* (see *Jim v. State,* 15 GA 535 [1854], and *John v. State,* 16 GA 200 [1854]). I have decided to discuss *Rafe* at length, rather than the two cases that preceded it, because *Rafe* provides the most thorough explication of the impartiality principles. For a discussion of bias in Tennessee, see Arthur F. Howington, *What Sayeth the Law: The Treatment of Slaves and Free Blacks in the State and Local Courts of Tennessee* (New York: Garland Publishing, 1986), 173.

42. *Monday v. State,* 32 GA 672–73, 678–79 (1861). The court also ruled, in *Henry v. State,* that it was entirely appropriate for these questions to be explained at length to a juror under voir dire (questioning) to ensure his understanding of them (see *Henry v. State,* 33 GA 441 [1863]).

43. I based my assessment of black appellate success on cases defendants appealed to county superior courts and the supreme court, reported in *Georgia Decisions* and *Georgia Reports.* I calculated white appellate success rates using appeals to the Georgia Supreme Court filed by defendants convicted of felony crimes comparable to those of which blacks were convicted from the court's first session to the end of the Civil War. Those crimes were arson, burglary, manslaughter, rape, attempted rape, murder, attempted murder, and stabbing. One hundred twelve defendants filed appeals. Of those who filed appeals, appellate courts granted new trials to 49 (43.8 percent) These cases are reported in *Georgia Reports.* For a discussion of white appellate results in Tennessee, see Howington, *What Sayeth the Law,* 165–66. For a discussion of white appellate success in the Deep South generally, see A. E. Keir Nash, "Fairness and Formalism in the Trials of Blacks in State Supreme Courts of the Old South," *Virginia Law Review* 56 (1970): 77. In arriving at these figures, Nash considered only those appeals filed by whites who had injured blacks and not all whites or all whites convicted of felonies.

44. A. E. Keir Nash, "A More Equitable Past? Southern Supreme Courts and the Protection of the Antebellum Negro," *North Carolina Law Review* 48 (1970): 235–40. Nash elaborated on these themes in "The Texas Supreme Court and the Trial Rights of Blacks, 1845–1860," *Journal of American History* 58 (1971): 622–42; and "Reason of Slavery: Understanding the Judicial Role in the Peculiar Institution," *Vanderbilt Law Review* 32 (1979): 7–218. Works that tend to emphasize the fairness of the criminal justice process for slaves, and to support Nash's thesis generally, are Flanigan, *Criminal Law of Slavery;* idem, "Criminal Procedure in Slave Trials in the Antebellum South," *Journal of Southern History* 40 (November 1974): 537–64; Meredith Lang, *Defender of the Faith: The High Court of Mississippi, 1817–1875*

(Jackson: University of Mississippi Press, 1977); and Howington, *What Sayeth the Law*. Works that question the fairness of antebellum courts are Kermit Hall, *The Magic Mirror: Law in American History* (New York: Oxford University Press, 1989); David J. Bodenhamer, *Fair Trial: Rights of the Accused in American History* (New York: Oxford University Press, 1982); Andrew Fede, "Legitimized Violent Slave Abuse in the American South, 1619–1865: A Case Study of Law and Social Change in Six Southern States," *American Journal of Legal History* 29 (April 1985): 93–150; Michael Hindus, "Black Justice under White Law: Criminal Prosecutions of Blacks in Antebellum South Carolina," *Journal of American History* 63 (December 1976): 575–99; and Philip J. Schwarz, *Twice Condemned: Slaves and the Criminal Laws of Virginia, 1705–1865* (Baton Rouge: Louisiana State University Press, 1988).

45. The cases of the successful appellants are: *State v. Jim,* Records of the Superior Court of Columbia County, September 13, 1843, drawer 192, box 25, GDAH; *State v. Jesse,* Records of the Superior Court of Decatur County, April 29, 1856, drawer 130, box 1, GDAH; *State v. Hill,* Records of the Superior Court of Decatur County, April 28, 1859, drawer 130, box 1, GDAH; *State v. George,* Records of the Superior Court of DeKalb County, April 16, 1853, drawer 177, box 9, GDAH; *State v. Henry,* Records of the Superior Court of Dougherty County, June 2, 1863, drawer 149, box 18, GDAH; *State v. Bob a.k.a. Robin,* Records of the Superior Court of Emanuel County, April 15, 1850, drawer 113, box 17, GDAH; *State v. Judge,* Records of the Superior Court of Houston County, July 30, 1849, drawer 158, box 37, GDAH; *State v. Jim,* Records of the Superior Court of Liberty County, December 2, 1851, drawer 30, box 47, GDAH; *State v. Monday,* Records of the Superior Court of Sumter County, April 11, 1861, drawer 133, box 8, GDAH; *State v. Bill a.k.a. William,* Records of the Superior Court of Thomas County, December 22, 1863, drawer 4, box 46, GDAH; *State v. Allen,* Records of the Superior Court of Bibb County, July 15, 1850, drawer 183, box 12, GDAH; *State v. Edwin,* Records of the Superior Court of Chatham County, May, 17, 1862, drawer 68, box 43, GDAH; *State v. Warren,* Records of the Superior Court of Hancock County, October 13, 1849, drawer 121, box 46, GDAH; *State v. George,* Records of the Superior Court of Putnam County, December 30, 1830, drawer 1, box 17, GDAH; *State v. Guy,* Records of the Superior Court of Screven County, October 17, 1844, drawer 37, box 32, GDAH; *State v. Randol,* Records of the Superior Court of Lincoln County, November 13, 1833, drawer 81, box 23, GDAH; *State v. George,* 1 *Ga. Decisions,* 80; *State v. Peter,* 2 *Ga. Decisions,* 46. The Kermit Hall quote is in Hall, *Magic Mirror,* 134.

46. For the actions of the colonial governor's council, see Candler, *Colonial Records,* vol. 10, pp. 246, 631; vol. 11, p. 305. Leon Higginbotham reaches similar conclusions about the governor's council (see A. Leon Higginbotham Jr., *In the Matter*

of Color: Race and the American Legal Process: The Colonial Period [New York: Oxford University Press, 1978], 256).

47. For pardons and clemency for slaves, see Executive Minutes, November 2, 1802–January 1, 1806, drawer 50, roll 45, GDAH; Executive Minutes, September 23, 1806–November 9, 1809, drawer 50, roll 46, GDAH; Executive Minutes, November 9, 1809–April 30, 1814, drawer 50, roll 47, GDAH; Executive Minutes, May 2, 1814–February 28, 1821, drawer 50, roll 48, GDAH; Executive Minutes, 1822–1827, drawer 50, roll 49, GDAH; Executive Minutes, November 2, 1829–November 14, 1834, drawer 50, roll 50, GDAH; "Executive Pardons from February 20, 1836, to August 31, 1843," record group (hereafter, RG) 1-4-16, accession no. 93-1789A, location no. 2761-12, box 1, GDAH; "Pardons 1854–1857," RG 1-4-16, accession no. 93-1789A, location no. 2761-12, box 2, GDAH. For pardon and clemency rates for whites, see Edward L. Ayers, *Vengeance and Justice: Crime and Punishment in the 19th Century American South* (New York: Oxford University Press, 1984), 64–65n2.

48. Howington, *What Sayeth the Law,* 10.

6. "MAY THE LORD HAVE MERCY ON HIS SOUL"

1. George P. Rawick, ed., *The American Slave: A Composite Autobiography* (Westport, Conn: Greenwood Publishing, 1972), vol. 13, pt. 4, pp. 128–29, 304; supp. ser. 1, vol. 3, pt. 1, pp. 4, 63, 71, 114.

2. Ibid., vol. 13, pt. 4, p. 297; supp. ser. 1, vol. 4, pt. 2, p. 435.

3. One hundred ninety-four convicts were punished. The punishments were distributed as follows: lashes, 36 cases (18.6 percent); hanging, 105 cases (54.1 percent); combination punishments, 50 cases (25.8 percent); other punishments, 3 cases (1.5 percent).

4. Catherine M. Huey, James Duke Collection, Georgia Department of Archives and History, Atlanta, quoted in Mills Lane, ed., *Neither More nor Less than Men: Slavery in Georgia* (Savannah: Beehive Press, 1933), 180–82.

5. Rawick, *American Slave,* supp. ser. 1, vol. 3, pt. 1, pp. 49, 145; supp. ser. 1, vol. 4, pt. 2, pp. 367, 488.

6. I refer to slaves during this part of the discussion because no free black was ever executed in Georgia. In the period from 1755 to 1811, 19 cases resulted in punishment: lashes, 4 cases (21.1 percent); hanging, 13 cases (68.4 percent); combination punishments, 2 cases (10.5 percent). From 1812 to 1849, 55 cases resulted in punishment: lashes, 15 cases (27.3 percent); hanging, 30 cases (54.5 percent); combination punishments, 10 cases (18.2 percent). From 1850 to 1865, 120 resulted in punishment: lashes, 17 cases (14.2 percent); hanging, 62 cases (51.7 percent); combination punishments, 38 cases (31.7 percent); other punishments, 3 cases (2.5

percent). For details of the compensation act, see Allen D. Candler, ed., *Colonial Records of the State of Georgia* (Atlanta: Franklin Printing and Publishing, 1904), vol. 19, pt. 1, pp. 223–24; and John P. Cushing, comp., *The First Laws of the State of Georgia* (Wilmington, Del.: Michael Glazier, 1981), 1:530. For slave prices, see Amy P. Burgess, "Slave Prices 1830 to 1860" (M.A. thesis, Emory University, Atlanta, 1933), 77.

7. Philip J. Schwarz, *Twice Condemned: Slaves and the Criminal Laws of Virginia, 1705–1865* (Baton Rouge: Louisiana State University Press, 1988), 20, 53.

8. For a tabular representation and detailed breakdown of these figures, see Glenn M. McNair, "Justice Bound: Aframericans, Crime, and Criminal Justice in Georgia, 1751–1865," Ph.D. diss., Emory University, Atlanta, 2001; *State v. Moses,* Records of the Inferior Court of Jones County, November 30, 1822, drawer 76, box 72, GDAH; *State v. George,* Records of the Superior Court of Emanuel County, September 22, 1856, drawer 113, box 18, GDAH.

9. For discussion and a table on lashes, see McNair, "Justice Bound," 337–40. Between 1812 and 1849, there were 96 prosecutions. Twenty-four of them were for murder (25 percent); 17 were for attempted murder (17.7 percent); and 3 were for rape (3.1 percent). In the period from 1850 to 1865, there were 288 prosecutions. One hundred twelve of them were for murder (38.9 percent); 59 were for attempted murder (20.5 percent); and 14 were for rape (4.9 percent).

10. Daniel J. Flanigan, *The Criminal Law of Slavery and Freedom* (New York: Garland Publishing, 1987), 13–17; Michael S. Hindus, *Prison and Plantation: Crime, Justice and Authority in Massachusetts and South Carolina, 1767–1878* (Chapel Hill: University of North Carolina Press, 1980), 145–46.

11. *State v. Tom,* Records of the Superior Court of Columbia County, March 5, 1861, drawer 192, box 26, GDAH; *State v. King, a Slave,* Records of the Superior Court of Fayette County, March 16, 1850, drawer 94, box 27, GDAH; *State v. Jeff,* Records of the Superior Court of Talbot County, September 18, 1861, drawer 126, box 7, GDAH; *State v. Bill,* Records of the Superior Court of Talbot County, September 18, 1861, drawer 126, box 7, GDAH; *State v. Primus,* Records of the Superior Court of Talbot County, September 18, 1861, drawer 126, box 7, GDAH; Flanigan, *Criminal Law of Slavery,* 14–15. See also Ralph Betts Flanders, *Plantation Slavery in Georgia* (Chapel Hill: University of North Carolina Press, 1933), 263. Flanders's assertion that branding, ear-cropping, and other "mutilations of the body" were abandoned as the antebellum period progressed is not correct (Ralph Betts Flanders, *Plantation Slavery in Georgia* [Cos Cob, Conn.: John E. Edwards, 1967], 261). Physical mutilation remained a part of combination punishments through the end of the Civil War.

12. *State v. Caleb,* Records of the Superior Court of Oglethorpe County, April

18, 1865, drawer 46, box 28, GDAH; *State v. Charlotte,* Records of the Superior Court of Oglethorpe County, April 18, 1865, drawer 46, box 28, GDAH; *State v. Milton,* Records of the Superior Court of Bibb County, November 21, 1863, drawer 183, box 16, GDAH; Flanigan, *Criminal Law of Slavery,* 13, 16; Schwarz, *Twice Condemned,* 22.

13. Thirty-six convicts were sentenced to the lash: crimes against persons, 24 cases (66.7 percent); property crimes, 9 cases (25 percent); crimes against public order, 1 case (2.8 percent); unknown crimes, 2 cases (5.6 percent). One hundred five convicts were hanged: crimes against persons, 93 cases (88.6 percent); property crimes, 11 cases (10.5 percent); unknown crimes, 1 case (1 percent). Fifty convicts were sentenced to combination punishments: crimes against persons, 35 cases (70 percent); property crimes, 12 cases (24 percent); crimes against public order, 3 cases (6 percent). Three convicts were sentenced to other punishments: crimes against persons, 3 cases (100 percent). See also Hindus, *Prison and Plantation,* 157; Schwarz, *Twice Condemned,* 15.

14. Hindus, *Prison and Plantation,* 157. Because these execution figures are based on requests for compensation from the owners of executed slaves, rather than from court records, the actual execution figures may have differed, with some owners not filing for compensation.

15. One hundred ninety-four convicts were punished: 130 for crimes against whites (67 percent); 39 for crimes against blacks (20 percent); and 25 in cases involving victims whose race could not be determined (13 percent). One hundred five convicts were hanged: 47 for crimes against white men (44.8 percent); 25 for crimes against white women (24.8 percent); 7 for crimes against whites whose sex could not be determined (6.7 percent); 12 for crimes against slave men (11.4 percent); 2 for crimes against slave women (1.9 percent); and 11 involving victims whose race could not be determined (10.5 percent). Thirty-six convicts were whipped: 25 for crimes against whites (69.4 percent); 3 for crimes against blacks (8.4 percent); and 8 for crimes against victims whose race could not be determined (22.2 percent). Fifty convicts received combination punishments: 22 for crimes against whites (44 percent); 22 for crimes against blacks (44 percent); with 6 cases involving victims whose race could not be determined (12 percent).

16. Twenty-six of 30 defendants (86.7 percent) convicted for crimes against white women were executed.

17. Burgess, "Slave Prices," 76.

18. Thirty-three convicts were punished for crimes against the master class: 25 were hanged (75.5 percent); 2 were whipped (6.1 percent); and 6 received combination punishments (18.2 percent). Of 158 victims, 96 (60.8 percent) were white

persons whose relationship to the convict could not be determined. See also Schwarz, *Twice Condemned*, 137–42, 232.

19. *Delta Democrat-Times* (Greenville, Miss.), January 18, 1941, quoted in David M. Oshinsky, *Worse than Slavery: Parchman Farm and the Ordeal of Jim Crow Justice* (New York: Free Press Paperbacks, 1996), 133. Twenty-seven slave convicts were punished for committing crimes against other slaves: 14 were hanged (51.9 percent); 2 were whipped (7.4 percent); and 11 received combination punishments (40.7 percent).

20. Twenty-seven blacks were charged with the murder of white men; 26 (96.3 percent) were hanged. Twenty-six blacks were charged with the murder of slave men: 11 (42.3 percent) were hanged; 13 (50 percent) received combination punishments; and 2 (7.7 percent) received lashes.

21. One hundred five convicts were executed; 98 (93.3 percent) of them were slave men. Fifty convicts received combination punishments; 47 (94 percent) were slave men. Thirty-six convicts were whipped; 31 (86.1 percent) were slave men. One hundred seventy-eight slave men were punished: 98 (55.1 percent) were hanged; 47 (26.4 percent) received combination punishments; and 31 (17.4 percent) were whipped. Eleven slave women were punished: 6 (54.5 percent) were hanged; 2 (18.2 percent) received combination punishments; and 2 (18.2 percent) were whipped.

22. Seventy-five slave men were convicted of murder: 53 (70.7 percent) were hanged; 20 (26.7 percent) received combination punishments; and 2 (2.7 percent) were whipped. Five slave women were convicted of murder: 4 (80 percent) were hanged; and 1 (20 percent) was whipped. Five slave men were convicted of arson: 2 (40 percent) were hanged; and 3 (60 percent) received combination punishments. Three slave women were convicted of arson: 1 (33.3 percent) was hanged; and 2 (66.7 percent) received combination punishments. See Hindus, *Prison and Plantation*, 145.

23. Hindus, *Prison and Plantation*, 145.

24. David J. Rothman, *The Discovery of the Asylum: Social Order and Disorder in the New Republic* (Boston: Little, Brown, 1971), 15, 18; Samuel J. Walker, *Popular Justice: A History of American Criminal Justice* (New York: Oxford University Press, 1980), 13; Thomas G. Blomberg and Karol Lucken, *American Penology: A History of Control* (New York: Aldine De Gruyter, 2000), 25–26.

25. Rothman, *Discovery of the Asylum*, 48–50; Bradley Chapin, *Criminal Justice in Colonial America, 1606–1660* (Athens: University of Georgia Press, 1983), 50–55. Blomberg and Lucken, *American Penology*, 29–32. For examples of the stocks, pillory, branding, and exile as punishments in colonial and early national Georgia, see *Georgia Gazette*, April 3, 1783; March 11, 1784; December 2, 1784; October 16, 1788; August 4, 1791; and September 13, 1792. For ear-cropping, see James C. Bonner,

"The Georgia Penitentiary at Milledgeville, 1817–1874," *Georgia Historical Quarterly* 55 no. 3 (Fall 1971): 304.

26. Rothman, *Discovery of the Asylum,* 52–53, 55–56; Chapin, *Criminal Justice in Colonial America,* 52. For examples of official complaints about jails, see Candler, *Colonial Records,* vol. 7, pp. 215; vol. 10, p. 394. For escapes during the colonial period, see *Georgia Gazette,* February 12, 1784; July 28, 1784; October 27, 1785; and June 26, 1794.

27. Rothman, *Discovery of the Asylum,* 18, 51; Michel Foucault, *Discipline and Punish: The Birth of the Prison* (New York: Pantheon Books, 1977), 48–49. For examples of capital punishment in colonial and early national Georgia, see Candler, *Colonial Records,* vol. 10, p. 245; vol. 11, p. 434; vol. 12, pp. 352, 376–78; and *Georgia Gazette,* June 28, 1764; January 14, 1767; November 11, 1769; December 21, 1784; March 15, 1787; March 22, 1787; November 1, 1787; October 16, 1788; October 23, 1788; March 5, 1795; September 17, 1795.

28. Morgan Godwin, *The Negro's and Indian's Advocate, Suing for Their Admission into the Church; or, A Persuasive to the Instructing and Baptizing of Negro's and Indians in Our Plantations* (London: n.p., 1680), quoted in Albert J. Raboteau, *Slave Religion: The "Invisible Institution" in the Antebellum South* (Oxford: Oxford University Press, 1978), 101; Cotton Mather, *The Negro Christianized: An Essay to Excite and Assist the Good Work, the Instruction of Negro Servants in Christianity* (Boston: n.p., 1706), 4–6, quoted in Raboteau, *Slave Religion,* 101; Thomas Jefferson, *Notes on the State of Virginia,* ed. William Peden (Chapel Hill: University of North Carolina Press, 1955), 142.

29. Candler, *Colonial Records,* vol. 1, p. 57; Betty Wood, *Slavery in Colonial Georgia, 1730–1775* (Athens: University of Georgia Press, 1984), 82, 85. In the slave code of 1755, legislators rescinded the provisions of the 1751 slave code that provided for religious instruction because they thought such instruction was likely to undermine the master–slave relationship (see Wood, *Slavery in Colonial Georgia,* 114–15).

30. Betty Wood, "Until He Shall Be Dead, Dead, Dead: The Judicial Treatment of Slaves in Eighteenth Century Georgia," *Georgia Historical Quarterly* 71 no. 3 (Fall 1987): 377–98. For similar punishments in West Africa, see Philip Schwarz, *Slave Laws in Virginia* (Athens: University of Georgia Press, 1996), 26; and Orlando Patterson, *Slavery and Social Death: A Comparative Study* (Cambridge, Mass.: Harvard University Press, 1982), 10–11.

31. Candler, *Colonial Records,* vol. 18, pp. 558–66.

32. For a thorough discussion of Georgia's workhouse, see Betty Wood, "Prisons, Workhouses, and the Control of Slave Labour in Low Country Georgia, 1763–1815," *Slavery and Abolition* 8, no. 3 (1987): 247–71.

33. Wood, *Slavery in Colonial Georgia*, 191–92; idem, "Until He Shall Be Dead," 384; Harold E. Davis, *The Fledgling Province: Social and Cultural Life in Colonial Georgia, 1733–1776* (Chapel Hill: University of North Carolina Press, 1976), 129.

34. The definition of petit treason is from Michael Dalton, *The Countrey Justice, Containing the Practise of the Justices of the Peace out of Their Sessions* (London: Society of Stationers, 1622), 213, quoted in Thomas D. Morris, *Southern Slavery and the Law, 1619–1865* (Chapel Hill: University of North Carolina Press, 1996), 264–65, 276–77. In the Middle Ages, burning, a punishment of complete extermination, was reserved for those who committed crimes that were thought to most anger the gods—witchcraft, incest, sodomy, heresy, and suicide. Postmortem decapitation, a form of quartering, was an ancient practice reserved for those guilty of high treason. It was carried out in this manner: "The traitor is to be taken from the prison and laid upon a sledge or hurdle (in earlier days he was to be dragged along the ground tied to the tail of a horse) and drawn to the gallows or place of execution, and then to be hanged by the neck until he be half dead, and then cut down, and his entrails to be cut out of his body, and burnt by the executioner; then his head is to be cut off, his body to be divided into quarters, and afterwards his head and quarters to be set up in some open place directed" (L. A. Parry, *The History of Torture in England* [1934; repr., Montclair, NJ: Patterson Smith, 1975], 104–8). The punishment for slaves convicted of petit treason, murder, and arson in Maryland was nearly the same as provided for traitors in England. The slave was "to have the right hand cut off, to be hanged in the usual manner, the head severed from the body, the body divided into four quarters, and the head and quarters set up in the most public places of the county were such act was committed" (George M. Stroud, *A Sketch of the Laws Relating to Slavery in the Several States of the United States of America* [1856; repr., New York: Negro Universities Press, 1968], 87). It is clear from the Maryland example that significant acts of violent slave resistance were viewed as acts akin to treason, and punished accordingly. The remaining citations for this note are in Hans Von Hentig, *Punishment: Its Origin, Purpose and Psychology* (Montclair, N.J.: Patterson Smith, 1973), 80, 98; and Harry Elmer Barnes, *The Story of Punishment: A Record of Man's Inhumanity to Man*, rev. 2d ed. (Montclair, N.J.: Patterson Smith, 1972), 233–36.

35. Schwarz, *Slave Laws in Virginia*, 20; J. A. Soulatges, *Traité des crimes* (n.p.: n.p., 1762), 1:169–71, quoted in Foucault, *Discipline and Punish*, 32.

36. If one considers the use of the lash on plantations, the site of most black crime and punishment, it is clear that this was the most common form of punishment. There were four burnings of slaves during the latter half of the eighteenth century. Three occurred in the same year, 1774, each for a serious offense: two for participation in the St. Andrew's Parish Revolt, and one for setting fire to his master's house.

Postmortem decapitations were similarly rare. Betty Wood has identified four such; I have identified one other. These nine incidents represent a little more than a third of the approximately two dozen executions that have been identified for the colonial period. Wood notes that by the 1790s burning was no longer used as a method of execution. For details of the three immolations, three of the postmortem decapitations, and for Wood's conclusions on the declining use of burning, see Wood, "Until He Shall Be Dead," 384, 387, 392, 395, 398. For the remaining decapitation, see the *Georgia Gazette*, June 6, 1765. The rarity of extraordinary punishment is also evident in studies of slave crime in the South. Michael Hindus's study of South Carolina reports that there was not a single incident of such barbaric punishment between 1767 and 1868 (see Hindus, *Prison and Plantation*, 145–46). In his study of Virginia, Philip Schwarz identifies twenty-five incidents in which the heads of slaves were publicly displayed, and seven incidents in which the bodies of executed slaves were quartered postmortem. These thirty-two instances were part of a total of more than five hundred slave executions in Virginia between 1706 and 1809 (see Schwarz, *Twice Condemned*, 15). Daniel J. Flanigan observes that, in 1729, the Maryland legislature passed a law mandating that slaves convicted of murder or arson of a dwelling were to have their right hands cut off before being hanged, after which their bodies were to be beheaded, quartered, and put on public display (Flanigan, *Criminal Law of Slavery*, 12). Maryland law provided for such punishment, but Flanigan provides no examples and thus the extent of these practices cannot be assessed.

37. Foucault, *Discipline and Punish*, 63; Rothman, *Discovery of the Asylum*, 60.

38. Peter Gay, *The Enlightenment: An Interpretation*, vol. 1, *The Rise of Modern Paganism* (New York: Alfred A. Knopf, 1966), 3.

39. Edward L. Ayers, *Vengeance and Justice: Crime and Punishment in the 19th Century American South* (New York: Oxford University Press, 1984), 34–35.

40. Myra C. Glenn, *Campaigns against Corporal Punishment: Prisoners, Sailors, Seamen and Children in Antebellum America* (Albany: State University of New York Press, 1984), 39–41, 54–55, 57–60. The quoted material, on page 60, came from New York State Senate, "Female Prison," *Annual Report of the Inspectors of the Mount Pleasant State Prison*, Senate doc. no. 20, vol. 1, 67th sess., January 12, 1844, 29.

41. Richard Henry Dana Jr., *Two Years before the Mast: A Personal Narrative of Life at Sea* (Boston: Houghton, Osgood, 1879), 116–17; Glenn, *Campaigns against Corporal Punishment*, 135, 146.

42. Glenn, *Campaigns against Corporal Punishment*, 114–15, 125.

43. Bryan Vila and Cynthia Morris, eds., *Capital Punishment in the United States: A Documentary History* (Westport, Conn.: Greenwood Press, 1997),

24–28; Rothman, *Discovery of the Asylum,* 61; Ayers, *Vengeance and Justice,* 43; Mark Costanzo, *Just Revenge: Costs and Consequences of the Death Penalty* (New York: St. Martin's Press, 1997), 8–9; Hugo Adam Bedau, ed., *The Death Penalty in America: Current Controversies* (New York: Oxford University Press, 1997), 4–6; Walker, *Popular Justice,* 76.

44. Daniel Flanigan asserts that statutes in Louisiana, Arkansas, and Maryland provided for imprisonment of slaves. Flanigan notes that by 1856 the imprisonment provision had been removed from Arkansas statute books. Flanigan also observes, in a note, that there is in the secondary literature no evidence that slaves were ever imprisoned in Kentucky, but this is not reported in the main text of his study. The history of Maryland is more interesting. In 1809 the state legislature provided for imprisonment of slaves but repealed that law in 1818. In 1845 a group of slaves was convicted of insurrection and their owners importuned the governor to imprison rather than execute them; the law was changed to allow the imprisonment of blacks. But by 1858 the governor complained that half the prison population was black; the law was revised to permit slave criminals to be sold out of the state (Flanigan, *Criminal Law of Slavery,* 21–24, 419–20). For an overview of the various debates on Africans and their racial characteristics, see Winthrop D. Jordan, *Black Over White: American Attitudes toward the Negro, 1555–1812* (Chapel Hill: University of North Carolina Press, 1968); George M. Fredrickson, *The Black Image in the White Mind: The Debate on Afro-American Character and Destiny, 1817–1914* (New York: Harper and Row, 1971); Carl N. Degler, *In Search of Human Nature: The Decline and Revival of Darwinism in American Social Thought* (New York: Oxford University Press, 1991); and Ayers, *Vengeance and Justice,* 46–49, 61–62.

45. Thomas R. R. Cobb, *An Inquiry into the Law of Negro Slavery in the United States of America to Which Is Prefixed an Historical Sketch of Slavery* (1858; repr., Athens: University of Georgia Press, 1999), 61; William Alexander Percy, *Lanterns on the Levee: Recollections of a Planter's* Son (New York: n.p., 1941), 23, quoted in Oshinsky, *Worse than Slavery,* 83.

46. Cobb, *Law of Negro Slavery,* 266. Cobb's logic applies specifically to slaves; however, in practice, it applied to free blacks as well, because they were subject to the slave codes and punished accordingly. Cobb also notes that other corporal punishments from the colonial period, like cropping of the ears, slitting of the nose, and castration, were gradually abolished by the 1850s. In Georgia, however, blacks were mutilated in these ways through the end of the Civil War. This factual inaccuracy is probably a deliberate attempt to present Southern criminal justice in the best possible light, since these practices were ongoing as Cobb was writing his treatise. As a lawyer and court reporter he would not have been unaware of them.

47. Stroud, *A Sketch of the Laws*, 77–88; Flanigan, *Criminal Law of Slavery*, 13–18; Cobb, *Law of Negro Slavery*, 266.

CONCLUSION

1. *State v. Monday*, Records of the Superior Court of Sumter County, April 11, 1861, drawer 133, box 8, GDAH; *Monday v. State*, 32 GA 672 (1861).

2. Thirty-nine cases involving masters, mistresses, and overseers reached the verdict stage; 34 (87.1 percent) resulted in guilty pleas or verdicts. One hundred sixty-one cases involving whites not in positions of authority over slaves reached the verdict stage; 118 (73.2 percent) resulted in guilty pleas or verdicts.

3. George P. Rawick, ed., *The American Slave: A Composite Autobiography* (Westport, Conn: Greenwood Publishing, 1972), vol. 12, pt. 1, pp. 109, 137, 242; vol. 13, pt. 4, p. 297.

4. Blacks could only testify against other blacks, "free Indians, mulattoes," and "mustizoes" (see Thomas R. R. Cobb, *A Digest of the Statute Laws of the State of Georgia* [Athens, Ga.: Christy, Kelsea and Burke, 1851], 973).

5. Derrick A. Bell, "*Brown v. Board of Education* and the Interest Convergence Dilemma," in *Critical Race Theory: The Key Writings That Formed the Movement*, ed. Kimberlé Williams Crenshaw, Neil Gotanda, Gary Peller, and Kendall Thomas (New York: The New Press, 1995), 22.

6. Edward L. Ayers, *Vengeance and Justice: Crime and Punishment in the 19th Century American South* (New York: Oxford University Press, 1984), 186–87; A. Elizabeth Taylor, "The Origin and Development of the Convict Lease System in Georgia," in *Black Southerners and the Law, 1865–1900*, ed. Donald Nieman (New York: Garland Publishing, 1994), 333–34.

7. Ayers, *Vengeance and Justice*, 197.

8. Taylor, "Convict Lease System," 340–48.

9. The most infamous of these prison-plantations was Parchman Farm in Mississippi, a cotton plantation that covered twenty thousand acres and forty-six square miles. On its grounds were an infirmary, a post office, an administration building where new prisoners were processed, a brickyard, a slaughterhouse, a vegetable canning plant, and, of course, two cotton gins. The farm was divided into fifteen field camps, each surrounded by barbed wire and each at least a half-mile from the next. Each prison had a barracks to house prisoners. A superintendent, who conducted himself like a slave master of the past, ran the camp; he lived in a Victorian mansion and convict servants tended to his needs. Mississippi chose the superintendent not for his expertise in penology but for his skills and experience as a farmer. A sergeant or overseer managed each camp. The sergeant-overseer was responsible for fixing work schedules, disciplining convicts, inspecting crops,

and setting the daily routine. A steam whistle awakened the convicts at dawn, and sergeant-overseers marched them to the fields to pick the required two hundred pounds of cotton (just as during slavery) under the watchful eyes and shotguns of mounted sergeant-overseers. Supporting these white men was a small cadre of black trustee-shooters, armed convicts who were among the most sadistic and feared in the camps. In exchange for their services as the New South equivalent of slave drivers, these trustees received better food and housing and they did not have to work in the fields. And, as in the penitentiary, when prison-farm inmates failed to adhere to the rules of discipline, guards flogged them with a leather strap three feet long and six inches wide called "Black Annie." By 1915, Parchman was, in every particular, a self-contained antebellum plantation of the worst sort. One observer described the Mississippi prison farm as "the closest thing to slavery that survived the Civil War." The story of Parchman is told in David M. Oshinsky, *Worse than Slavery: Parchman Farm and the Ordeal of Jim Crow Justice* (New York: Free Press, 1996). For a discussion of Georgia's prison farm, see James C. Bonner, "The Georgia Penitentiary at Milledgeville, 1817–1874," *Georgia Historical Quarterly* 55 (Fall 1971): 324.

10. For lynching and mob violence in Georgia, see W. Fitzhugh Brundage, *Lynching in the New South: Georgia and Virginia, 1880–1930* (Urbana: University of Illinois Press, 1993).

11. Jerome G. Miller, *Search and Destroy: African-American Males in the Criminal Justice System* (Cambridge: Cambridge University Press, 1996), 4–7.

INDEX

Page numbers in italics refer to tables or figures in the text.